The Theory of Social Democracy

The Theory of Social Democracy

Thomas Meyer
with
Lewis P. Hinchman

polity

This book is an abridged and adapted version of material first published in German as "Theorie der sozialen Demokratie" by Thomas Meyer © VS Verlag für Sozialwissenschaften 2005

First published in 2007 by Polity Press

Polity Press
65 Bridge Street
Cambridge CB2 1UR, UK

Polity Press
350 Main Street
Malden, MA 02148, USA

ISBN-10: 0-7456-4112-1
ISBN-13: 978-07456-4112-6
ISBN-10: 0-7456-4113-X (pb)
ISBN-13: 978-07456-4113-3 (pb)

A catalogue record for this book is available from the British Library.

Typeset in 10 on 11.5pt Utopia
by Servis Filmsetting Ltd, Manchester
Printed and bound in Great Britain by MPG Books Ltd, Bodmin, Cornwall

For further information on Polity, visit our website: www.polity.co.uk

Contents

Introduction

Democratic theory as a framework

The theory of social democracy describes and explains the social conditions that support the legitimacy of modern democracy, showing both their connection to universal basic rights and their significance for democratic efficacy and stability. American researchers such as Lipset and Dahl have confirmed that social democratic policies and practices enhance the functionality and stability of democractic states.[1] Democracy's foundations remain weak and unstable as long as status inequalities contradict formal political equality and citizens disagree about what political justice requires.[2] In the long run democracy will lose ground if it is understood only as a set of institutions, i.e., without taking into account civic participation and accountability as well. Merely *delegative* democracy and "passive citizenship" are manifestations of *defective* democracy, detracting from the legitimacy of democratic commonwealths.[3]

As a theory, social democracy offers an account of the complex interplay among legitimacy, efficacy, and stability. As empirical science, it seeks to explain the functional deficiencies of *libertarian* democracy, which remains wedded to a purely formal, procedural notion of decision-making. Finally, the theory analyzes strategies and models for preserving social democracy in a globalizing world.[4]

Modern society is marked by a tension between two aspects of rights: their *formal validity*, which is implicit in their use as a standard to legitimize democracy (made explicit in the 1966 UN Fundamental Rights Covenants), and their *efficacy*, i.e., the social conditions that allow them to become meaningful in the "real world" and not just on paper. Therefore, the theory proposed here cannot merely interpret the norms that secure democracy's legitimacy and the institutions that embody it.

It must also analyze some of the prerequisites for the complete actualization of rights in practice. It must likewise explore the circumstances affecting democracy's continuity in the modern world, and show how its contemporary forms might live up to their own intrinsic standards.

These are all themes and tasks incumbent upon any rigorous theory of democracy.[5] To achieve its goals, our investigation will proceed along several lines. It first addresses the *normative* dimension, which stresses the demands for legitimation placed on institutions and policies of a democracy. It then turns to the *empirical-analytic* dimension, inquiring how effectively democratic systems manage their social problems. Next, *stability studies* contribute expertise on the conditions that affect the continuity and durability of democracy. Then, *comparative* studies of democracy examine the success of various, country-specific solutions to the challenges facing popular rule. Finally, recent research on *defective* democracy completes the survey.[6]

Since these approaches converge on the same social and political reality, it should come as no surprise that areas which the scholarly division of labor has carefully distinguished turn out to be inextricably interwoven in practice. For example, the legitimacy of democratic systems affects their stability and capacity to solve problems, and vice versa. The characteristic feature of democracy is that its inputs, outputs, legitimation, efficiency, and opportunities for popular participation are never independent of one another.[7]

Two crucial concepts in social democratic theory are the *formal validity* and *real-world efficacy* of universal basic rights. In all subsequent contexts "*formal validity*" will connote both the formal status of the relevant rights under positive law and their status as universal human rights norms transcending positive law. By contrast, "*real-world efficacy*" refers to the enjoyment of the relevant rights in the practice of everyday life. It designates the de facto control a person has over opportunities to make use of his or her rights. The distinction may be illustrated by such differences as the right to a job versus having one actually available; or the right to an education versus the availability of concrete educational opportunities. The theory of social democracy asks what would have to be done to make fundamental rights as universally available in practice as they are qua formal legal principles.

The present theoretical sketch also attempts to conceptualize *social democracy* as one of the key components of political science by imbedding it in a more encompassing theory of democracy. In the latter, the notion of *social* democracy has clear affinities to and contrasts with both *liberal* and *libertarian* democracy. Following well-established intellectual traditions, we shall mean by liberal democracy a pluralistic regime that respects human rights and abides by the rule of law.[8] It is legally and conceptually flexible enough to accommodate both subcategories: libertarian and social democracy. The former restricts the scope of democracy and fundamental rights to the political sphere, and defines the self-regulating market and unregulated private property as the institutional counterparts of democracy in the economic and social sphere. Social democracy, by contrast, insists that democracy and its associated charter of rights must be extended into the social and economic spheres as well. Specifically, the social order must meet higher standards of democracy by allowing for well-regulated participation, a legal claim to social security, a distribution of wealth and income that takes justice into account, and a democratic state, the regulative and distributive policies of which accord with all of these values.[9] One could also distinguish liberal from social democracy by emphasizing the former's commitment to economic liberalism, as ordinary language usage suggests.[10] However, in the present theory the conceptual triad of *liberal*, *libertarian*, and *social* democracy will be employed consistently in line with the previous definitions.

Our argument is not normative in the sense that it depends on norms derived from any specific ethical system. Rather, because the theory makes a claim to universal validity, it seems prudent to base it on a more modest foundation, one that is "weak" in the sense of having very few assumptions. The theory will then be as independent as possible of any particular scientific, cultural, or political strategies of justification. Only in this way can its claim to universal validity be redeemed. The main principles of the theory construct their normative and democratic foundations exclusively on the United Nations Covenants on Human Rights (1966), which are a valid component of international law, having been ratified by 148 countries representing all cultural regions and levels of development. That document links *civil, political, social, cultural*, and *economic* rights, all formulated in culturally neutral terms, and employed so that they expressly acknowledge the different levels of development attained by diverse countries.[11]

The UN Charter of Rights owes its origins to a distinct line of argument that enjoys a universal, culture-transcendent appeal. In terms of the *logic* of its validation, this argument is stronger than the covenants, because it provides solid reasons for the universal validity of fundamental rights. But in terms of the *politics* of validation it is weaker than they are, because it cannot bind dissenters. This line of argument will be pursued in chapter 1. The goal will be twofold: to clarify the content and meaning of rights by placing them in a broader context, and to justify their claim to universal validity through reasoning that does not depend on their status as part of positive law. Apropos of these normative foundations, the theory of social democracy will also try to ascertain the implications universal rights might have for democratic theory and politics as well as social policy. But even here, the core of the project remains empirical. Its most pressing concern is to clarify the prerequisites and consequences of fundamental rights thus anchored in international law for specific areas of social action in the world as we know it or reasonably expect it to become.

Beginning from normative principles, the theory analyzes the set of institutional, cultural, and organizational strategies best suited to give basic rights concrete meaning in everyday life. We approach that task from three starting points. First, we identify the *empirical risks*, rooted in the social structure, that imperil the real-world efficacy of universal rights. Second, we examine the experiences of different regimes in managing such risks, and assess how efficacious their remedies have been. Third, we attempt to determine how rights could be made meaningful and effective under contemporary conditions. Inevitably, the theory will be contingent within certain limits. That is, its findings depend on empirical circumstances that can only partially be foreseen and reconstructed in practice.

In brief, our theory seeks empirically defensible answers to one complex question: *what kinds of institutions, forums, policies, participatory channels, and rights does a democracy have to create, in order to secure the universal fundamental rights of all its citizens against the structural risks inherent in modern economic and social life?*

There are many compelling reasons to ground social democracy on universal basic rights, not least their status as a relatively non-arbitrary set of assumptions. Rather than building on unavoidably controversial theories of society and justice, our approach begins from normative principles that have been almost universally incorporated into positive law and enjoy widespread support in the theory of democracy as well. In this manner the theory takes its bearings from the broadest possible sources of validation and recognition, ones that can claim to be politically and scientifically unassailable.

Social democracy and the social welfare state

A theory of social democracy has to worry about more than just presenting a theory of the social welfare state. It must ask what sorts of contributions social security, justice, and participation might make to improve the quality of democracy in a given society. It should also highlight the structures of societal democratization that operate outside of the official social security system. One decisive criterion for evaluating the political system, and indeed the entire field of social security, is whether the authors of political decisions are the same people who must obey them. Accordingly, the theory of social democracy has to expand its investigation beyond the social welfare state, while still making use of its research results.

Various subsystems of society must be included in the theory of social democracy because they contribute to the full enjoyment of universal rights under real-world conditions. Some of these are:

1 the political system
2 the system of fundamental rights
3 the political public sphere
4 political culture
5 civil society
6 subsystems of societal democratization
7 political economy
8 the educational system
9 transnational coordination.

The consequences of globalization and the problem of contingency

Political society today has become cosmopolitan in the sense that it is imbedded in broader contexts of regional and global influence. In fact, it is tempting to think of the theory of social democracy as a theory of action within the global arena. Unless global influences are taken into account, it is difficult to see how political, social, and economic rights can be guaranteed or how ultimate responsibility for making policy can be assigned. It may turn out that individual countries and regional political systems will have to adapt to conditions of economic and societal globalization that they cannot readily control.[12]

Initially, though, the prevailing conditions of capitalist democracies are assumed; only subsequently will the implications and exigencies of globalization be discussed. Yet the reader should bear in mind that the latter have been included as constitutive elements in the way that each area of theory is conceptualized. Globalization is implicitly "built into" the very analysis of social democracy's problems and prospects.[13]

Part I

Political Theory

1

Social Rights, Risks, and Obligations

1.1 Contradictions in political liberalism

The legacy and aims of political liberalism

Since the Enlightenment the theory of liberal democracy has provided a virtually unchallenged source of legitimation for most regimes, at least in Europe.[1] By the nineteenth century it became apparent that liberalism had the potential to become more democratic both legally and institutionally. Eventually, the only norms capable of legitimizing political authority in modern societies were those derived from liberal political thought: universal human and civil rights; the rule of law; political power checked by constitutions; and popular sovereignty expressed as majority rule.[2] To be sure, these norms have often been ignored in practice. Nevertheless, with the exception of a few fundamentalist ideologies rooted in identity politics, their claim to universal validity is rarely challenged.[3] In the wake of the collapse of its last great historical nemesis,[4] Marxism-Leninism, the doctrine of political legitimacy implicit in liberalism has swept the field. In the post-metaphysical phase of modernity it has proven to be the only durable foundation of political authority and social order capable of mustering universal consent. Consequently, any modern democratic theory that stakes a claim to universal validity has to remain within its confines.

Even in its earliest form, in the writings of John Locke, political liberalism already offered universal justifications for the notions of a pre-political *equal liberty* for all and of *human rights* designed to preserve that freedom. Once the modern state was founded on democratic consent expressed in a social contract, those original notions led to the establishment of *equal civil rights*. The latter apply to all persons and define the meaning, purpose, and limits of the state's authority.[5] The ideas that legitimize the political and social order in the modern world derive from this liberal legacy: the equal dignity and worth of all persons, and the consequent equality of rights they enjoy in all decisions that affect both private and political autonomy.[6] These rights are "absolute" in the sense that they are not to be balanced against other goods in a utilitarian calculus, i.e., not to be treated as relative to other ends. History justifies us in treating both principles – *private* and *political* autonomy, bonded indissolubly together – as the generative ideas of political liberalism. This is the case even though into the twentieth century the chief architects of liberal theory and party policy, hoping to shore up private property rights, struggled to evade the implication that liberalism ought to become more democratic.[7] Restrictions on political participation such as property qualifications, gender, and educational levels gradually yielded to the evolving inner political logic of liberalism. The principle of equality triumphed over all such restrictions in its concrete forms as *equal liberty* for all citizens and the equal dignity of all persons. It is thus no longer possible to legitimize authority except by appealing to the norms of equality and their uniquely compelling claim to validity.

Within liberalism conflict has erupted over two *cardinal issues* that define the theory of social democracy: to what extent does recognition of human and civil rights shape the encompassing structures of society, and what standards must be met to justify the conclusion that these legitimating norms have been actualized in the real world?[8]

The theoretical tradition of political liberalism eventually split into *libertarian* and *social* wings, mainly due to differences over the way that the fundamental rights of personal freedom and private property ought to be ranked and balanced, and how the very notion of freedom should be defined.[9] The answer to the latter question in turn will supply premises for a further argument about the gap between the *formal validity* and the *real-world efficacy* of rights. To emphasize the *formal validity* of such rights implies that one should take legal steps to secure individual freedom by establishing a legal sphere of privacy shielded from the intervention of third parties. By contrast, insisting on their *efficacy in the real world* means trying to add a dimension of freedom: All citizens should have sufficient control over elementary social and private goods to make their formal-legal freedom meaningful. This is the case only if they can reasonably expect to act in light of their own life plans, assuming these have been autonomously conceived.

The first liberal dilemma: freedom and property

Locke links the rights to freedom and property in a way that makes them appear mutually reinforcing; yet in the end their relationship proves to be ambiguous.[10] He does not limit the notion of property merely to ownership of things. Rather, the term property in his theory embraces three distinct relationships that are to some extent constitutive of freedom: control over one's own body or person, which implies the general freedom of action meant by private autonomy; liberty of thought and belief, especially in religion; and the right to dispose of one's own possessions.[11] The first two dimensions of Locke's concept of property involve reflexive relations with only one reference point: the relationship between a single person and him- or herself. Locke rejects the possibility that third parties might have legitimate interests to defend. But the third dimension raises the possibility of multiple reference points. Two or more persons might be involved in a case of legal ownership, since in principle its enjoyment could affect the rights not only of the property-owner, but of others as well.[12] When property is originally acquired prior to the establishment of civil society and government through a social contract, it involves only a binary relationship between the acquiring person and the thing itself, which Locke assumes belongs to no one and is simply "found" in nature, until labor endows it with the status of property. Only later in Locke's exposition does the ownership of things evolve into a multipolar relationship. Once the state is founded by property-owners, it may lay claims to their property through taxation. Moreover, property may be employed as a means of production, for the full utilization of which the labor of third parties is required. The previous two cases, taken together, suggest that a "mature" property relationship eventually includes four reference points: the owner, the things owned, any number of propertyless fellow-laborers, and the state. Individual property rights may conflict with the rights of the last two, thereby raising a variety of legitimation issues.

Although Locke alludes to all of these dimensions in his theory of property, he does not assign them equal weight or explore their connection to the universal right of equal liberty. Locke cites three reasons why people have a legitimate right to property in things.[13] *First*, because individuals own their own bodies, what they acquire is the product of their own free agency. *Second*, property is an expression of *justice* in the dealings of free persons with one another, since each of them has acquired property in a lawful manner. *Third*, once it has been legitimately acquired, property satisfies one condition for the continuing exercise of freedom on the part of persons qua owners. Once one concedes that there was an original condition in which everyone faced an "unowned" nature unmodified by labor, the conclusion seems inescapable that the propertyless misused their freedom of action and so deserved their fate.

Given these premises, the legitimating relationship between freedom and private property is persuasive. For then it really would be a matter of individual choice whether one wished to work for someone else (except in the case of a slave).[14] The question that Locke never systematically poses is: what value does freedom have to someone who must transfer it to another in order to survive? Here it is not a matter of people having forfeited the right to life in an unsuccessful war, as in slavery, but of unmerited want and distress that drive them to desperate choices. In a property-based theory of freedom, voluntary alienation of one's liberty collides with the principle of an inalienable natural right to freedom, raising the question of how conflicts between rights of equal rank, distributed among different persons, ought to be balanced. This dilemma becomes even more acute once the state has been established. For from that time forward (except on the "frontier") everybody lives in an environment in which resources are less available to be converted into private property by personal labor, since most have already been appropriated by others.[15]

In civil society, in contrast to Locke's state of nature, one will find propertyless people who must depend on the property of others (e.g., by renting land or working for wages) to survive. Their freedom of choice will be hollow, because it will be dominated by the property-owners' priorities. As private individuals propertyless people depend on property-owners and are thus unequal to them in that respect. But as citizens of a state they are equal, albeit consigned to a passive civil status by the fiat of early liberal theorists. Thus the use of property entails a threefold relationship. *First*, property-owners have a connection to the things they own. *Second*, a relationship arises between the persons of the owner and the non-owner in the productive employment of these things. *Third*, all parties to the contract collectively manifested their will in defining the relationship between freedom and property and the procedures for adjudicating it.

Locke's theory of property concedes to the state a limited authority of co-disposition over the property of private persons because it acts in the name of all citizens united by the terms of the original contract. It must at least be authorized to tax private persons (with the consent of parliament), for otherwise it would lack the means to protect basic rights and would therefore be unable to carry out the tasks for which it was allegedly created in the first place. Thus, the grant of an absolute property right, which Locke's theory as a whole seems to imply as the state's ultimate end, would conjure up a paradoxical situation. Modern *libertarians* such as Nozick, Hayek, and Gray, who have radicalized Locke's historically ambiguous theory of freedom-as-property while remaining indebted to its principles, manifest this self-contradictory tendency.[16] Their *minimal state* leaves the decisive question unresolved: how minimal is minimal, since that issue must always be decided politically?

Locke, unlike Hobbes, is concerned with more than the sheer physical survival of the citizenry; he wants firm guarantees of their freedom as property-owners. For that reason he cannot resolve the paradox of freedom by conceding to the state a general right over private property as though it were itself a higher-order property-owner entitled to regulate or take property as it saw fit to perform its mandate. Locke's defense of a nearly absolute conception of property rights does not necessarily follow from the links he forges between freedom and property. Rather, his attitude is a function of the specific historical context in which he wrote, especially the defensive posture suggested to him by his experiences of the confrontations among liberalism, absolutism, and feudalism.[17]

The transition to modern libertarianism

Modern libertarians tend to reject Locke's view that people originally acquire property by extending their right of ownership in their own bodies to the objects in which they have invested their labor. Nevertheless, they insist that a theory of property, based on the right of ownership in one's own person, must be the sine qua non of freedom.[18] While libertarians do indeed criticize some of the premises of Locke's conception of freedom, they also uphold his core principles, in spite of the fact that the practice of market capitalism has brought to light the tensions between this understanding of property and a universalistic conception of freedom. The libertarian view seals off Locke's once fluid conception of property against the implications of this experience with the market, thereby hardening it into an ideology. They interpret only one of the property relations discussed earlier as an expression of freedom – namely, the property-owners' use of their own possessions – forgetting that the other relations can also enhance freedom. This move effectively sidesteps the issue of how freedoms are actually experienced in the real world, since it now appears that rights and liberties can be fully assured via institutional guarantees provided by the state, and that nothing further needs to be done.

By limiting the scope of its theory of freedom as property to the formal-legal and institutional planes, political liberalism ends up facing a twofold dilemma. It cannot show how its *fundamental constitutive norms* can be realized in *actual practice* under real-world conditions. Nor can it plausibly explain how the state, which relies on those norms, can fully develop its *integrative capacity*.

The second liberal dilemma: negative and positive liberty

Isaiah Berlin's famous distinction between positive and negative liberty has always been interpreted so as to favor the latter as genuinely liberal, while dismissing the former as social democratic.[19] One could characterize the notion of negative freedom as formal or defensive, and that of positive freedom as enabling or material.[20] But Berlin himself assigned absolute priority to negative liberty, because he believed that the irreducible pluralism of basic value-orientations left no alternative.[21]

Liberals (including Berlin) balk at giving equal weight to both kinds of liberty, even when the "positive" variety might seem indispensable to make negative liberty meaningful. Most do admit that the state has a right to tax its citizens (depriving them of a portion of their property and so freedom of choice) in order to finance public education and thereby the opportunities of less advantaged citizens. But once one has permitted that much intervention, why not allow even more? The state might try to make it easier for the less fortunate to use their freedom in positive ways by redistributing wealth and/or providing subsidies. Liberals see a slippery slope here. "Positive liberty" can be invoked to justify curtailment of negative liberties in two ways: by promoting the opportunities of the less well-off and by depriving others of the resources they previously had, in order to finance its redistributive schemes. In the end – and this is the point of the libertarian critique – expanding the concept of freedom to embrace its "positive" uses would jeopardize its more crucial "negative" meaning. Therefore, we must assign absolute priority to negative liberty to make sure that freedom itself rests on a solid foundation. On closer inspection, however, the claim that these two dimensions of freedom are antithetical, rooted as it is in Berlin's "agonal liberalism,"[22] is difficult to square with the premises of the liberal tradition.

According to the usual interpretations, traditional liberal freedom is a perfect match for negative liberty, since it is actually constituted by the ownership of tangible property with which third parties, particularly the state, are forbidden to interfere. But this is a mistaken reading. The core of the argument linking freedom to private property rests on the unstated assumption that the agents have already met the test for the positive enactment of their projects: namely, having private ownership of the items necessary to carry these plans to fruition. Thus, an essential element in the positive concept of liberty – having sufficient material resources to act – is illicitly imported into this argument as a condition of freedom itself.

What underlies this assumption is the expectation that in the state of nature, where goods are unowned, individuals wishing to follow their own plans will have enough material resources to do so. Under these special circumstances there is indeed a convergence of positive and negative aspects of liberty, since liberty qua freedom from interference by third parties means enjoying the material resources to act as one intends. However, once nature has been reshaped by labor, appropriated, and distributed, and once the property relations that result from these transformations have acquired a fixed legal status through the founding of the state in a contract, the situation changes radically. From now on only property-owners have direct control of the material resources for free action, whereas non-owners are bereft of such resources. An asymmetrical relationship ensues. Under the social contract, the state's pledge not to interfere in the individual's private sphere, i.e., the guarantee of negative liberty, now means radically different things to owners and non-owners, in terms of their opportunities to enjoy the goods afforded by their liberty. For property-owners, enjoying negative liberty is tantamount to having a guarantee that the chief prerequisite for their *positive* liberty, full control over the material resources they need to act as they see fit, has been granted. Whereas when negative liberty alone is given institutional backing, this means for the non-owners that their isolation from such material resources has simply been reinforced; they lack opportunities to enjoy positive liberty.

The de facto inequality that results when both groups are treated in formally equal ways is of only secondary importance here, since it mainly concerns the problem of justice.[23] The previous analysis of the relationship between freedom and property is intended to make a different point. The true, albeit concealed, meaning of the liberal notion of freedom must be sought in its positive dimension; the reason that the state strives to secure negative liberty against risk is to insure that citizens will enjoy positive liberty. Because the material conditions for positive liberty are so critical to their practice, priority must be given to insuring their availability. But in the liberal view this may only be done by giving institutional support to negative liberty.

This interpretation of freedom produces a paradoxical outcome. To safeguard the negative liberty of *all* citizens, liberal theory restricts positive liberty to only *some* of them, the owners of property. Yet it indirectly concedes that negative liberties exist for the sake of their positive enjoyment and use.

It is this characteristic asymmetry in the deeper layers of the liberal conception of freedom that has been rejected by liberals themselves. Critics of Berlin such as Ronald Dworkin now prefer to defend the claim that *both dimensions, positive and negative, ought to be given equal status.*[24] Only an integrative perspective is capable of bringing out the full, mutually reinforcing meanings of the political values of freedom and equality. They might *appear* to be in conflict, but that is only because they have been subjected to an inappropriate interpretation that limits them to particular contexts.[25]

The asymmetry arises because negative liberty has been given priority *in principle*. However, universalistic arguments can support the claim that a *pragmatic* asymmetry also exists between the two. For liberty to have meaning in the real world, both dimensions of freedom must be actualized without compromising their essential parity. But in political applications negative freedom does enjoy a pragmatic and temporal priority, since the fundamental civil and political rights associated with negative liberty insure that free and equal citizens can deliberate about the best ways to institutionalize positive liberties, especially in the form of social and economic rights. The political path out of a state of affairs in which only social and economic rights are achieved, toward one in which civil and political rights are also protected, has proved to be much thornier in practice than the reverse path from formal security of rights toward a regime of supplementary social security. But this *pragmatic, procedural argument* does not cover the case in which attempts are made to question or downgrade the entire principle of legal guarantees for positive liberties.

The inescapable dilemma faced by classical liberalism finds expression in three types of circumstances under which universal rights are violated. First, social and economic inequalities may begin to spawn relations of social and economic dependency. The latter may violate the dignity of the dependent individuals by undermining their *social autonomy*. In other words, the sphere of social action is here treated as neutral ground in which the validity claims of universal fundamental rights are to be suspended. But any systematic exclusion of the social sphere from the applicability of rights appears to violate the understanding of such rights endemic in the liberal tradition itself. Second, the exclusion of the social sphere from coverage by basic rights tends to infringe the *claims to private autonomy* of those who, qua economic agents, have fallen into a state of dependency inconsistent with human dignity, one that puts them at the mercy of third parties in ways that universal rights should not tolerate. Third, social, economic, and educational inequalities of a certain magnitude prevent those affected from making full use of their political or civil rights. The "political exclusion" argument maintains that liberalism, by permitting extreme inequalities, individual deficits in education and personal development, and relations of dependency, ends up *denying equal civil and political rights* to entire social classes, thereby vitiating their *political autonomy*.

In the end liberalism falls into irremediable contradictions between the formal validity claims inherent in its fundamental legitimating rights and the reality of its institutional commitments. This is the case to the extent that it persists in excluding empirical reality, especially the socio-economic sphere, from the range of validity claims implied by its guiding norm of equal rights.

Social democracy as democratic theory

There are two normative premises that unite all versions of social democracy. First, "libertarian particularism," grounded on the primacy of negative liberty, is rejected in favor of a universal conception of liberty that ranks negative and positive freedom at par. Second, the identification of freedom and property is jettisoned in favor of a universal conception of liberty that balances the liberties of all parties against a property relationship as if they were equivalent. The comprehensive theory presented here in outline attempts to do justice to both premises.

1.2 Social citizenship

How citizens reflexively establish a juridical order

Liberal political theory has shown how universal claims to legitimate political authority can be redeemed. The decisive criterion is to be found in the *political* equality of citizens as partners and stakeholders in the social contract, to which all political authority must ultimately be referred. Citizenship can be defined as a civil status that both legitimizes and obligates. It entails the right of every citizen to decide in common with all others about the rules that constitute the political commonwealth and to retain a permanent, equal right to participate in its future deliberations.

In the modern age political authority counts as legitimate when rights and duties are allocated equitably, consistent with the limits set by inalienable human and civil rights. To achieve a proper allocation, certain perennial, meta-political issues must be confronted: how are human and civil rights to be interpreted and balanced in cases of conflict? What should their scope be vis-à-vis the several dimensions of human conduct, such that they will retain their elementary meaning as guarantors of equal liberty in varying situations?[26] The status of citizen has proven to be the *conceptual and juridical focal point* for resolving conflicts between the formal validity and real-world efficacy of citizens' rights. This has been the case both in social-scientific debates and in the evolution of liberal rights and their contradictions in actual practice.

The concept of citizenship

The development of political and social rights has been a story of the growing awareness of the "barriers that separated civil rights from their remedies" and the political will to draw the appropriate conclusions and make those remedies available to all citizens.[27] The implicit universality of rights sets in motion a long-term process to reform social conditions in such a way that rights will be not only formally but also materially valid. In Thomas Marshall's terminology we might say that control over the means of securing fundamental rights has to become just as universal as the validity of the rights themselves.

In his reconstruction of the historical sequence in which civil, political, and social dimensions of citizenship emerged, Marshall shows how certain social experiences moved the entire process forward. The logic of the original, egalitarian standard of legitimation stimulated its evolution toward ever higher stages and degrees of universality.[28] His theory forms a bridge between the original liberal understanding of universal basic rights and currently accepted international law which has enacted these rights – a sophisticated mix of negative and positive liberties – in the 1966 UN Covenants.

What makes Marshall's theory of the three components of the citizen status paradigmatic is neither his historical account of the successive emergence in history of each element, nor the scholarly justifications offered for it. Instead, he establishes an interpretative link between each stage of their historical unfolding and its respective legitimation, a step that combines explanation with justification. Marshall's *social citizenship theory* has had considerable impact on subsequent research for one principal reason. He shows that the aspect of basic rights being advanced in one stage only maintains its legitimating power by being preserved at the next-higher stage.

Behind the process of expansion in stages, then, lurks the universal validity claim implicit in the idea of fundamental rights, which is repeatedly renewed in the face of continued efforts to impede their enjoyment. Marshall's theory of citizenship has succeeded in reconstructing the developmental logic of universalism in basic rights under free market conditions. That logic is driven by the fact that it is the citizens who interpret their fundamental rights in light of new experiences. In this sense Marshall's theory of social rights likewise contains a theory of citizenship.

Under the egalitarian conditions of modern culture, citizenship becomes unavoidably reflexive, as is evident from the way Marshall has reconstructed its self-exegesis since the rise of political liberalism.[29]

How the dimensions of rights develop historically

Marshall's reconstruction suggests that civil rights had to become more egalitarian and comprehensive in the eighteenth century in order to do justice to their own inherent validity claim.[30] To freeze the development of rights as interpreted by the citizens themselves at some arbitrarily chosen point would inevitably threaten their consolidation and weaken their validity claim. In the nineteenth century an equal right to political participation also had to be institutionalized; otherwise the latent universalism of rights would continue to be blocked by unjustifiable political restrictions. Twentieth-century experiences have revealed a further quandary. Neither political nor civil liberties can be fully realized as the rights of equals unless positive liberties are likewise included, which allow them to be actualized regardless of the social and economic status of the person who enjoys them.

Thus, as Marshall understands it, *social citizenship* designates the process by which citizens progressively reinterpret their own rights. They overcome obstacles encountered in their efforts to satisfy the claims of equal citizenship by learning to understand themselves and codify their basic rights in new ways. The superficial equality characteristic of basic rights in their formal sense gradually provokes movements to give them a more positive underpinning. Thus, "the right to freedom of speech has little real substance if, from lack of education, you have nothing to say that is worth saying, and no means of making yourself heard if you say it. But these blatant inequalities are not due to defects in civil rights, but to lack of social rights."[31] It proves necessary to create a new category of rights to meet the requirements of the fundamental principles of equal liberty and dignity, which rights are intended to express. Only by introducing a new category, social rights, can one draw out the potential inherent in the historically evolving categories of civil and political rights, thereby breathing new life into them.

The development of social rights in the twentieth century thus flows from the self-knowledge of citizens themselves. They realize that the legitimating norm of equality, implicit in the principle of fundamental rights, will surely lose its legitimating value under the prevailing conditions of social inequality unless it is reinterpreted and rendered concrete in light of the tacit norm of "equal social worth."[32] Fundamental rights – and here we find the core juridical meaning of Marshall's social citizenship – can be justified in terms of accumulated historical experience only when they include a *basic right to* "remedies" *against their de facto denial.*

Postmodern critiques

Libertarians can of course attack Marshall's argument on the grounds that any codification of rights above and beyond the negative liberties amounts to an infringement on the rights of others, especially the property rights of third parties.[33] But theirs is not the only source of criticism. Postmodern egalitarian liberalism, which shares the notion of social citizenship in principle, has also joined the critical chorus. Keith Faulks fails to find in Marshall's own reasoning the consistency that the latter uncovered in his historical account of rights.[34] The first objection raised from the postmodern and feminist camp decries the "partriarchal orientations" implicit in any notion of social citizenship that does not thematize society's abridgements of fundamental rights for women.[35] His second objection complains that Marshall never seriously challenges the social class structure. His rights project can therefore be dismissed as a compromise among elites that is unreceptive to the egalitarian implications of citizenship and makes unwarranted concessions to a centralized, undemocratic state.[36] To postmodern critics Marshall's theory seems plagued by a twofold contradiction: a masculine paternalism that denies equal civil rights to both sexes and an elitist paternalism that refuses to extend equal rights to socially disenfranchised classes.

The feminist critique of Marshall's version of social rights discloses a weak point of his theory. Because it was the child of its time, that theory

focused almost exclusively on the historic clash between market capitalism and liberal rights. It never offered a general account of the way
in which such rights might be violated in practice. Nevertheless,
nothing in the theoretical structure of Marshall's argument prevents its
being extended to cover such cases. Quite the contrary; Marshall
himself laid the foundations for just such an extension. Whenever risks
traceable to the social structure deprive identifiable groups of the means
to make full use of their formal rights, the right to acquire those means
must also be guaranteed. The structural conflict that grows from patriarchal gender dominance is sparked more by socio-cultural than by
socio-economic factors. Nevertheless, gender conflict too is a product of
an objective social structure that makes it harder for individuals to
practice their rights. That is why patriarchal gender relations, as they
affect the opportunities for self-determination among female citizens,
have the same impact on the shape of rights as socio-economic class
conflict. Every person has a social right to the prerequisites of full
gender equality.

The nineteenth century identified deficits in equality for men and
women; in the twentieth century these were addressed by enhancing
the legal status of women in many areas. However, discrimination
remains a reality in today's society. The gap between women's formal
status and the reality of their diminished rights cannot be attributed
solely to social stratification or economic interests. Therefore, we must
include among the goals of social citizenship gender democracy and
justice, both to be guaranteed by making available the full range of
relevant social and cultural resources. In particular, the political strategy of "gender mainstreaming" must become a central goal of social
democracy. It would insure that the priorities and needs of both men
and women are consulted whenever political decisions are made.
Ultimately, neither political topics nor resources are gender-neutral or
gender-blind.[37]

1.3 Universal fundamental rights

Comprehensiveness and universality of fundamental rights

In the aftermath of the experiences of World War II and the social crises
that preceded them, the UN's Universal Declaration of Human Rights
(1948) integrated the idea of *social* citizenship into its human rights language for the first time. Its authors implied that the promise of universal fundamental rights could not be kept unless the underlying social
context in which those rights were to be exercised were likewise understood to involve issues of rights. It thereby gave expression to a *post-
liberal* conception of rights even before the outbreak of the Cold War

and its tendency to compartmentalize the different categories of rights. Civil and political as well as social and economic rights were proclaimed in *one* single document.

Democratic and moral theories

The two UN Covenants of 1966 transformed universal fundamental rights into established international law embodying a consensus on two principles. *First*, it was acknowledged that human and civil rights should take effect in distinct social spheres or dimensions, *civil, political, cultural, social, and economic*, all of equal importance, although social and economic rights were understood as relative to the economic potential of any given country. The *second* principle expressed the agreement that all classes of fundamental rights ought to remain neutral vis-à-vis culture, religion, and world views. *This principle carries special weight in democratic theory, because it implicitly demonstrates that a consensus about the global validity of human rights may be reached without any accompanying consensus about the reasons for their validity.* That does not necessarily mean that the validity of human rights is independent of *any* sort of universalistic grounding at all, only that conflicts about reasons need not block agreement about the nature and validity of rights.

The independence of universal political validity from any consensus about its rationale does not prove the irrelevance of attempts to justify it. In fact, there are solid arguments in favor of the position that Rawls's principle of overlap applies by analogy to all parties assenting to a political consensus even in the global arena. While their convictions about the validity of a specific set of reasons for rights may not necessarily motivate their political assent rationally, it may do so cognitively.[38] That is why the strategy chosen here, grounding the normative orientation of the theory of social democracy on the de facto validity of universal basic rights, should not be dismissed as a logical mistake in the manner of legal positivism. Agreement about the basic values and rights that ought to guide the construction of society may be regarded as a second-order ethical and political imperative, one that operates below the threshold of philosophically competing claims to ultimate validity. Given profound differences about religion, world views, and cognition, that imperative may be the only way to enable common action and the actualization of the values under consideration.

The notion of social citizenship is now a positive legal norm, justified on universal grounds and solidly anchored in the UN Covenants as well as many constitutions of contemporary nation-states. By now fundamental rights owe their validity to a normative justification that has, in its essential outlines, almost acquired the status of global cultural patrimony. Thus, the normative foundations of that patrimony no longer have to be invoked for political practice. They draw on the traditions of the Enlightenment and the practical philosophy based on it, religious traditions or world views, and the philosophical or cultural contexts that have shaped them. Whatever their sources, rights do support the norms of democracy, the rule of law, and social citizenship. What motivates the persons and collectivities who subscribe to these norms is the fact that they *can* be justified, even though the content of that justification will not be the same for all of them.

When the draft theory of social democracy offered here relies on the rights charters of the United Nations rather than siding with one of the foundationalist theories, this is not done out of allegiance to legal positivism. Rather, the point is to flesh out three postulates that are themselves normatively well established. *First*, a normative basis for social democracy should include the strongest and broadest possible grounds for respect. *Second*, one of the root convictions of political liberalism in John Rawls's sense should apply to the theory of social democracy: political and legal obligations must be supported by the overlapping consensus rather than by substantive justifications or special ethical codes that might motivate specific groups to assent to them. *Third*, a second-order political and moral principle is at stake here: the postulate that we should try to achieve the deepest possible consensus concerning the practical attainment of legitimate political goals.[39]

The equivalent worth of all categories of basic rights

All five sets of rights addressed in the charter are guided by certain supreme principles. These, the meta-norms of human and civic rights, include *a comprehensive notion of positive freedom* and *equality of rights and opportunities* for every citizen in each area to which the norms refer. Thus, there is a claim to universal equality of rights and opportunities applicable throughout the entire social order that has been recognized by international law and incorporated in the norms that define it. The mere fact that many countries have been remiss in putting some aspects of these norms into effect does not detract from their validity.

Since its passage, the Human Rights Covenant has been ratified by 148 (the Social Covenant) and 151 (the Civil Covenant) countries.[40] Considering the divergent political philosophies of the signatory countries, the covenants achieved a remarkably far-reaching codification of positive liberties. What made it possible was a historic compromise made during the era of East–West competition. Many representatives of the West were willing to accept the inclusion of positive freedoms in the charter in exchange for the assent of the East to the negative freedoms they themselves advocated.[41] Shortly after the collapse of the Soviet Union libertarian elements in the West, especially the United States, began to downplay the legitimacy claims of this section of the charter. But their backsliding does not detract from its claim to universal validity, though it may affect the chances that it will be implemented. The Covenant on Economic, Social and Cultural Rights was signed by the United States in 1979, but to this day it has never been ratified. Besides the Americans' ideologically motivated reluctance to recognize social imperatives as rights at all, the longstanding American disinclination to be bound by international agreements and legal norms probably played a part in the United States' refusal to ratify.

Post-liberal universalism

The International Covenant on Economic, Social, and Cultural Rights contains a version of basic social and economic rights that rests on a sophisticated material understanding of freedom. It is an indispensable reference point for the strict notion of equality expressed in the declaration.[42] Compared with national constitutions, these rights agreements describe in detail the normative standards that any social order must meet to do justice to universal human and civic rights in their material meaning. *They represent the core of social democracy's normative justification.*

The overarching vision that informs the various rights is the *ideal of the free human being, liberated from fear and want*, an ideal that ought to be realized in and for every single person. In successive chapters the covenant ranks the following rights most highly:[43]

- equal rights for men and women
- the right to work
- the right to just and favorable conditions of work
- the right to earn one's living by work that has been freely chosen or accepted
- fair wages and equal remuneration for work of equal value
- a decent living for each worker and his or her family
- safe and healthy working conditions
- the right to form trade unions and the right of such unions to function freely
- the right to strike
- social security
- assurance of an adequate living standard
- protection against hunger
- the right to the highest attainable standard of physical and mental health and the medical care necessary to it
- the right to education, training, and upbringing aimed at the complete development of the human personality and heightened respect for human rights and basic freedoms
- compulsory attendance in primary school; secondary and higher education that is accessible according to individual ability
- the right to take part in cultural life.

Political Theory

A vision of base-level social equality

Taken as a whole these rights provide a broad basis of obligation for social democratic policy-making. In several respects they resemble a "pedestal" or base upon which social and economic equality rest:

1 They guarantee access to gainful employment along with the right of each person to earn an adequate living.
2 They call for social security.
3 They require the decommodification of elementary social goods and their transformation into universally accessible public goods in education and health care.
4 They insist on the protection of human dignity even in work.
5 They insist on the right of workers to be represented by trade unions both in the workplace and in the political arena.

In light of modern theories of justice we can characterize the normative vision underlying the Human Rights Covenant as a form of relatively high, universal *base-level equality* that draws on a positive (material) understanding of freedom.[44]

Mid-range principles

The covenant relates these specific rights to social *autonomy* only indirectly, by invoking the equal respect due all citizens in social and economic contexts. But the declaration does emphasize the dimensions of autonomous co-determination in contexts of social and economic action as well as the social democratic commitment to democratize not just politics, but social institutions and relationships as well. The charter does define a legally binding minimal level at which social goods ought to be equally provided, but it ignores all the issues that transcend this framework, such as the fair distribution of the product of social labor and individual opportunity. Except in the cases of fair conditions of work and just wages, the whole notion of justice does not come into play. It is unsurprising that the criteria for defining a just wage are not specified. All of the social and economic rights addressed in the charter are based on the norm that the equal dignity of all human beings ought to be protected. This position acts as a lowest common denominator, a rallying point for universal consensus. But the price paid for such broad agreement is that the covenant exhibits an unsophisticated understanding of social equality.

The understanding of fundamental rights elaborated in the UN charter can support a theory and political practice of social democracy in certain respects. But by bracketing issues of distributive justice, the UN approach makes it difficult to meet one of Hermann Heller's most important criteria of social democracy. He argued that, in democratic politics, a consensus could best be reached by treating basic values as points of reference guiding further discourse. Yet these basic values (e.g., distributive justice) are precisely the ones the charter glosses over because they are so contentious. Political integration is only possible in the long run if the members of society share an understanding of justice. By nature, basic rights represent the institutional form of *mid-range* principles of justice that citizens themselves must apply in practice.[45]

Modes of validity

Although the rights declared by the UN Covenants have become a valid part of international law, the two groups of rights have unfortunately acquired distinctly different modes of validity. The very text of the documents illuminates the differences between them.[46] Whereas the formal rights were supposed to take effect without delay, the material rights could be carried out "progressively," in proportion to the capacities of the individual countries.[47] The civil and political rights impose "obligations of result" on all countries in accord with the then-current understanding of international law, whereas the material rights only justify "obligations of conduct." Consistent with these distinctions, oversight of the enforcement process of formal human rights may involve legal instruments such as public prosecution. By contrast, the only procedure instituted to guarantee material rights is the preparation of an advisory report to be submitted to the UN Committee on Economic, Social, and Cultural Rights, but that body is not bound to follow the report's recommendations.[48] Neither set of rights makes any provision for individual lawsuits against violators.[49]

Still, the covenant on material rights is now a valid part of international law and therefore imposes a duty on every nation-state to try its best to implement and enforce those rights. In this sense the universal basic rights, taken as a whole, are binding, unrestricted, and all of equal importance. The only thing left up to the discretion of individual countries is the timing. They must assess their respective capacities to insure the full and complete enjoyment of these rights. Under international law, however, every national government and international association of states is obligated *increasingly* to realize social, cultural, and economic rights for all its citizens within the limits of the possible.

In short, there is no doubt that material rights are legally valid. But two issues are still unresolved: to what extent available resources allow for the full implementation of those rights, and whether the responsible authorities have the will to use those resources. For all these reasons, we should concern ourselves less with justifying the validity of the norms that guide the material juridical state than with summoning up the political will to put them into practice. These norms are universal, under the meaning of international law, on three levels: the intrasocietal, the international, and the intercultural. They hold for all persons and political actors *within* each society; they hold for *all* societies; and they are valid independently of the cultural, ethnic, or religious allegiances of the persons who invoke them and the political authorities entrusted with enforcing them.

Justice and fundamental rights

Nevertheless, in principle the theory of social democracy does have to be tied more closely to the theory of justice to define its role in the process of social and political integration. Heller's central insight was that one can refer to a shared idea of justice that defines the core of the material juridical state. In that case citizens and their interest groups or political parties would be able to refer to this shared regulative norm as they attempt to resolve their conflicts. But even here justice is never uncontested, nor does it yield a detailed distributive formula. Instead, the strength of the reasoning that supports it must induce the participants in a political discourse to refer their disputes to it.[50] Political justice functions, then, as a regulative idea capable of defusing conflict by submitting it to agreed-upon rules and procedures. What enables this regulative role to succeed is not so much that universalistic claims to justification have been satisfied. To the contrary, even counterfactual claims to universal justification can achieve the same result under some circumstances. This is the case when all of the participants actually assume that agreement can be reached and take their bearings from that conviction when they go on to present arguments and proposals in public discourse. Thus, the really important point, as social democracy understands it, for the social and political integration of society is not simply that social and economic rights should be manifested in positive law. Rather, there must also be public debate about how to ground the conceptions of justice that give us our basic orientation, for that is how we arrive at strategies that work in practical politics.

Rights presuppose duties along two dimensions of action. *First*, there are duties on the part of those actors who are obligated to make sure that rights-bearers can exercise their rights. *Second*, the beneficiaries of rights also have obligations as stakeholders in a law-governed community.[51] The UN Covenants omit the second dimension, even though it is essential to the project of social democracy.

1.4 Social risks and fundamental rights

The theory of social democracy begins with a critique of the so-called *identity fiction*, which presumes that the formal validity and real-world efficacy of fundamental rights coincide, even in societies structured around free market capitalism.[52] The generative idea of this critique is that persons will not all (or always) be able to enjoy their fundamental rights in concrete circumstances unless the *means necessary to practice them* have also been guaranteed in the form of additional rights. This is the only way to satisfy the standards of universal validity implicit in fundamental rights without falling into contradictions. Of course, this argument involves a whole series of assumptions, especially when presented in its strong form, i.e., as a demand for expanded basic rights, rather than in its weak form as a plea for the minimal protection of human dignity. Accordingly, it must be defended by examining the *political character of risks to real-world enjoyment of fundamental rights that flow from the social structure itself*. In other words, the rationale of the social democratic critique must be derived from the claims to legitimation imbedded in the fundamental rights themselves.

The basic thesis of the social democratic approach to risk owes its classical formulation to Thomas Marshall.[53] In his view, the traditional "formal" fundamental rights grant certain legal benefits; yet these cannot always be made meaningful to those who wish to exercise them unless formal entitlements are accompanied by the means necessary to take full advantage of them. Those means are therefore a necessary addendum to the formal legal claims and must be given express institutional support in a democratic constitutional state. Marshall's theory of social civil rights boils down to the argument that society assumes liability vis-à-vis all of its own citizens for certain classes of *risk*. In particular, when through no fault of their own, and without any opportunity for individual redress, they find themselves bereft of the means to exercise fully their fundamental rights, then society has to act. The correct remedy is an appropriate expansion of the definition of fundamental rights to include social rights.

Given its commitment to a broad conception of democratic theory, a general theory of social democracy cannot dispense with a careful analysis of risk. Such an analysis serves several purposes. *First*, it can defuse the libertarians' argument that in a modern-day liberal democracy it is entirely up to the individual's choice to make effective use of fundamental rights. *Second*, it permits a precise theoretical analysis and ethical/legal accounting of just those social risks that justify *social* basic rights and delimit their *scope*. In this way the theory of social democracy clarifies the connection between social risk-abatement and legitimacy in a democratic society. *Third*, it enables us to identify other social risks that share these characteristics and therefore raise the same kinds of legitimation problems and (possibly) analogous responses.

A modern theory of social democracy accordingly must identify all the social risks that resemble the archetypal form of risk – the impact of modern capitalism on the real-world exercise of rights – in their political character and their implications for legitimacy. In short, the theory of social democracy assigns priority to answering questions that touch on the *impediments and prerequisites* to achieving the full measure of fundamental rights for all persons.

Risk and collective decisions

The social-scientific concept of risk is complex and conceals numerous assumptions.[54] Niklas Luhmann and Ulrich Beck designate as *risks* only those potential cases of harm that arise from decisions made by the affected parties.[55] Threats of harm that can be attributed to the external environment, and for which the affected persons are therefore not responsible, can be defined as *dangers*.[56] This distinction resembles the one drawn by Ronald Dworkin between *option bad luck* and *brute bad luck*.[57] Whereas *option bad luck* is the result of a personal decision made in the expectation of some gain, the harm arising out of *brute bad luck* has nothing to do with the decisions or potential influence of the person involved. Following Dworkin we can further distinguish between *optional* and *non-optional* risks. Optional risks are those in which a person is willing to wager a portion of his/her individually available social goods in the hope of increasing them. Investments and games of chance exemplify optional risks. Non-optional risks are those that may happen whether or not a person has made any choices relevant to them. They are either "facts of life" arising from the biological data that condition human existence, or they are connected to social, economic, or political circumstances to which people are susceptible on account of their specific way of life.

In Dworkin's view, this distinction has implications for the level of responsibility that a political community should assume for the respective consequences each type of risk poses. Gains resulting from *option luck* do not in justice involve any obligation to compensate the less fortunate, while of course the losers must bear any losses themselves. By contrast, the harmful outcomes of *brute bad luck* do entail an obligation – incumbent on the entire political community – to offer compensation to its victims. In both cases Dworkin subsumes the potential harm under the rubric of risk.[58] His conceptual distinctions concerning risk will serve as a foundation for the following analysis.

As a general rule, any danger counts as a risk that arises from failure to coordinate action that was both possible and necessary from the standpoint of responsibility ethics. That is, people can sometimes be regarded as having jointly caused the risk by negligence that, from the standpoint of responsibility ethics, must count as equivalent to positive action if it was in their power to affect its course.[59] Ulrich Beck even goes so far as to postulate a *potential collective subject* for global political society. He urges that harms generated by uncoordinated collective action should be considered risks, since some people *could* have organized themselves as a collective subject to forestall those harms. Their failure to act in unison unfairly imposes risks on others.[60]

In democratic societies, then, any dangers that jeopardize the exercise of fundamental rights will be treated as risks provided that (a) they implicitly involve collective action, and (b) alternative courses of action that could have prevented them were available. The citizen body has an obligation, when deliberating, to make sure that the fundamental rights of all affected parties are not violated by whatever risk-related decisions they make. As distinct from the criteria offered in Dworkin's definition, the risks evaluated here are not the outcome of individual options chosen in the hope of gain; instead they are the result of collective decisions made in the name of all affected parties. And they can only be corrected by collective decision-making. These collective choices follow the logic of game theory. They flow from the calculation of how to choose a set of economic and social institutions and policies that will yield an aggregate satisfaction of social interests and rights superior to that yielded by any other available alternative. In consequence, decision-making collectivities incur political and moral obligations vis-à-vis all social groups whose exercise of fundamental rights will be affected by the results of choices they make about how to manage risks.

Types of risk

The theory of social democracy must clarify the nature and scope of the political responsibilities to be assumed for risk. To do that, it is helpful to distinguish four different types, each with its own special features. Since risk, unlike danger, always carries an element of choice, we may initially identify two kinds in which the decision to act is directly implicated.

First, there are risks that involve *private options* undertaken on the basis of some calculation of private advantage, as when people make investments or choose a profession.

Second, another class of risks includes *political* (or *social-structural*) *options*. Here the state makes decisions calculated to promote the common interest, as by authorizing certain economic arrangements or foreign policies.

Third, *social-technological* risks frequently emerge from private or public decisions to deploy technologies without a full assessment of their externalities, their possible (negative) impacts on third parties.[61] In this case, social risks potentially affect everyone, though they may not issue from deliberate actions.

Fourth, *socio-cultural risks* do not necessarily involve any specific act of collective choice; instead they usually reflect persistent *political negligence* in respect to the foreseeable consequences of governmental inaction (as in cases of political or employment discrimination on account of gender, race, or national origin).[62]

The social risks at stake in the theory of social democracy always concern the denial of basic social goods required for the full enjoyment of fundamental rights. We may designate as social-structural risks all those that do not arise as the result of any individual act of choice by the person concerned, do not lie within that person's sphere of direct responsibility, and which could not be overcome through individual or collective self-help. Such risks are collective in a double sense. First, they concern "typical" situations in life that may be experienced by a great many people in similar ways. Second, they tend to elude the control and influence of the persons whom they befall.

Regarding its implications for such social-structural risks, the theory of social democracy may be construed as a reflexive form of the social theory of fundamental rights. Because it understands liberty in a "positive" sense, it is determined to support the legal entitlement of each person to the means necessary for practicing the fundamental rights that otherwise might remain merely formal and abstract. In this way, the theory of social democracy seeks, by well-chosen political adjustments, to compensate for the risk that some people will lack the means actually to enjoy the funda-mental rights to which they are entitled. Whereas past forms of social democracy have focused on the special risks spawned by the functional conditions endemic to one historical form of economic organization, market capitalism, the general theory of social democracy explores social risks per se. But in the final analysis, it is only the political discourse of cit-izens that determines what will count specifically as a structural risk to their fundamental rights and how such risks might be compensated.

Toward a general theory of social democracy

A theory of social democracy can be called general when its statements and conclusions are oriented to all of the politically optional risks that significantly impair the full enjoyment of the fundamental rights of some members of society and are conditional upon politically optional decisions in matters of principle. Furthermore, there is a broader pattern of argument that underlies the original, historical theory of social democracy. It is this pattern that lends plausibility to the historically specific line of argument focused on the risks of capitalism. This deeper layer of argument involves the disparity between the formal grants of universal basic rights, on one hand, and the de facto withholding of the means necessary to put them into practice, on the other. Certain groups of citizens were denied such means on account of the specific positions of risk in which they found themselves.

It was only after the notion of social entitlement had been accepted by social-scientific theory that the general nature of this *discrepancy problem* emerged with full clarity. In the wake of these debates, the issue likewise entered into discussions of normative principles in the familiar guise of a distinction between positive and negative freedom. The discrepancy problem has two interrelated dimensions:

1 the conceptualization and justification of both dimensions of freedom in their reciprocal relationship
2 the empirical-analytic question of what would have to be done so that people could take advantage of their formally guaranteed rights in everyday life.

As soon as the original question is posed in this generalized form, it becomes apparent that a number of other social structures besides market capitalism can create politically defined risks to the full enjoyment of fundamental rights. Moreover, those risks pertain not to a single, permanent social grouping, but to an ever changing variety of groups. All raise the same universal problem of legitimation: how to create the *social prerequisites* for the real enjoyment of fundamental rights, when these are imperiled by *socially operative structures of risk*.

The women's rights movement in the nineteenth century initiated a historical sequence in which other comparable structures of social risk entered the agenda of democratic theory and politics. All exhibited the same discrepancy problem outlined above. For that reason, to follow up the inherent logic of its own "classical" scheme of analysis and argument, a theory of social democracy will have to present a general account of the implications of politically optional risks for democratic policy-making. Such risks, of course, must be identified in contexts other than the one that social democratic theory originally emphasized, namely, market capitalism. Such a generalized theory of democracy still deserves the epithet *social* for two reasons: because it traces the causes of human rights deficits back to the social structure; and because it provides an account of the social conditions that must be met if the universal validity claims of a democracy based on fundamental rights are to be redeemed.

Models of justification

To evaluate the relationship between social-structural risks and fundamental rights in light of the theory of legitimation, we may call on four models of justification.

1 The *natural law* approach reasons that, since fundamental rights are universally valid, the prerequisites for enjoying them should also be furnished.
2 The *contractual* argument derives the state's obligations to intervene from the reciprocity conditions contained in an implicit social contract.

3 A justification rooted in *political discourse* holds that, since the entire commonwealth is responsible for the incidence of risks to the actual exercise of basic rights, the state has a prima facie obligation to grant full compensation to those adversely affected.
4 The issue is also addressed by the theory of an insurance market, as elaborated by Ronald Dworkin.

The natural law argument actually does little more than invoke the validity of universal rights and point out that they are often violated. If one follows this logic of legitimation, one could derive every conceivably justifiable obligation for state intervention from these two premises alone.[63]

The *contract theory* approach justifies political obligations by elucidating the conditions under which the actors who agreed to the original social contract would have given their consent. It derives features of social insurance and the prerequisites of distributive justice from the commitment to reciprocity anchored in any consensus of free and equal individuals.[64]

The theory of an original *insurance market* proposed by Ronald Dworkin occupies a unique position between contract theory and individual utility calculus.[65] His model generates criteria that would justify the state's obligation to insure against certain risks that jeopardize freedom by diminishing or eliminating opportunities. He combines widely accepted criteria for collective security with an assessment of the risks to individual enjoyment of liberty that society imposes.

The justification of the risk–rights nexus as propounded by *political discourse theory* (e.g., the theory of deliberative democracy) stakes its claims to the legitimacy of the political obligation to manage risks solely on de facto political discourse. The latter is supposed to take place in a democratically organized public sphere and gauge the probability that citizens will be able to make full use of their basic rights under prevailing conditions.[66]

We ought to assign a privileged role to such political discourse for two reasons. First, all other lines of argument can always be introduced into public discourse anyway. Second, in a democracy this is the only reliable way to induce political authorities to act.

In its analysis of the impacts produced by socially generated risks, the theory of legitimation emphasizes especially their *political* character. Thus, in contrast to all the other types of justification, it can convincingly anchor the obligation to compensate for risks to the enjoyment of basic rights in the *citizenship status* of the victims of such risks.

Social issues and risks count as political when they meet two conditions.[67] *First*, all social actions are political that pave the way or call for decisions that bind, or at least that concern the entire society and are made with an eye to the general welfare.[68] The definition of a matter as political is appropriate when there is in principle no exit option available to individuals and/or the collectivity. In different terms, political problems can be characterized as societal challenges that can only be met through *collective consumption*, leaving no choices or options to the individual. *Second*, political decision-making or problem-solving will be perceived as legitimate only if it follows agreed-upon procedures that respect human and civil rights. Accordingly, all social problems that have an impact on those rights are instrinsically political.

Freedom does tolerate insecurity within limits. The risks that flow from the metaphysical homelessness of modernity[69] and the uncertainty of knowledge are themselves prerequisites of individual freedom. The risks to health and life that occasion personal insecurity can be reduced, and their impacts mitigated except in the case of death itself. But they can never really be mastered. The democratic juridical state cannot insure against the risks of uncertainty, nor completely guarantee personal security, since both are prerequisites and results of freedom and personal autonomy. But the state can eliminate those risks of social insecurity that, in avoidable ways, limit a person's opportunities to enjoy liberty. For in those cases we are talking about events, rooted causally in the social structure, that deprive people of the means to take full advantage of their basic rights.

This argument raises similar truth claims for all analogous cases of risk. It targets those risks that are generated by the social structure, the consequences of which the individual cannot escape by his or her own actions, i.e., a specific type of *politically optional* risk. Because individuals normally can influence such risks and their outcomes only via cooperation or political intervention, they have a claim upon the form of risk-management that ends up by guaranteeing the real-world efficacy of their fundamental rights.

The structure of risk and the social contract

Julian Nida-Rümelin has shown that no one is morally entitled to take risks that affect third parties, unless the latter have given their express consent to the decision in question.[70] Thus, in choosing among potentially risky strategies, one may not make calculations of aggregate utility that acquiesce in the violation of the rights of some persons. Since the few have an absolute moral worth, it can never be right to sacrifice them on the altar of collective sum-total utility. Thus, as soon as it becomes obvious that risks have occurred because of such a calculation, the affected parties have moral and political claims to the restoration of their prior legal status. That is the idea behind a new social contract designed for the modern risk society. It revises the conditions of the liberal democratic social contract in light of the experience that modern societies systematically generate social risks that may threaten fundamental rights.

It derives its crucial significance for the theory of social democracy from two of its premises: that all risks arising from the political structure have to be included in the calculus of legitimation, and that one may evaluate risks in terms of their potential to undermine the real-world enjoyment of rights.

Varieties of politically optional risk

The theory of social democracy must account for politically optional risks and assign them to their proper categories in the theory of legitimation. The risks in question are those generated by political decisions that may deprive identifiable social collectivities of the opportunity to practice their basic rights. Politically optional risks should not be undertaken unless the legal and political communities are willing to take responsibility for them, while mutually guaranteeing the continued exercise of fundamental rights. This point has important political and legal ramifications for the relationship between citizens and the political community. The latter has the permanent capacity to deprive the former of the means to exercise their rights; furthermore, only a decision of the citizen body can offer compensation to those whose rights have been infringed. Here a preliminary remark concerning the relationship between personal rights and duties is in order. To compensate parties adversely affected by risks rooted in the political structure, resources to cover the costs of collective security have to be gathered, which means that there will be fewer resources available for other citizens to make "positive" uses of their freedom. This fact gives rise to an obligation, incumbent upon the potential victims of risky actions, to rely first and foremost on individual or collective self-help. This duty draws its justification from the same sources as the argument in favor of social rights. But there is a difference: claims to such rights are to be honored only under the conditions that: (a) human dignity is accorded absolute protection, and (b) claimants have fulfilled their prima facie duty of self-reliance.

The notion of politically optional risks supplies the theory of social democracy with one of its strongest counterarguments against the ideas of legitimation offered by libertarianism. The latter relies on the *empirical* premise that, as long as the formal institutions of liberal democracy are operating to protect liberty, nothing further needs to be done to fulfill the equality norm imbedded in the idea of fundamental rights. That premise rests on a further one: since there is no legal impediment in the way of any person's achieving any social status for which he or she is qualified, people deserve whatever social position they end up occupying. The theory of social democracy refutes these claims by deploying the notions of risk developed previously. If there are risks to the exercise of fundamental rights deriving from the structure of the economy and society and the processes they set in motion, and if the affected citizens cannot adequately offset these by private, autonomous actions, then in a democracy there is a collective political responsibility to offer suitable compensation to victimized citizens.

So the argument against *libertarianism* and in favor of a democratic-juridical obligation to practice social democracy runs as follows. By the logic of its own legitimating norms, the democratic state is obliged to offer appropriate security against all risks arising out of the social structure, provided that these are of a political nature, involve serious limitations on fundamental rights, cannot be reliably countered by individual or collective self-help, and can be managed effectively by means of political steering measures available to society.

These are the conditions for a modern social contract sensitive to the problem of risk. The theory of social democracy has to take account of the *entire range of empirical circumstances and risks affecting people's* chances to take advantage of their basic rights. In consequence, it has to weigh the likelihood that structural conditions will generate new risks comparable to the old ones. That observation holds true for all social risks that fit the following criteria:

Violation of rights: Rights may be violated not only by state intervention or the actions of third parties, but also by social institutions and structures that depend on political decisions.[71]

Collective consequences: Although human and civil rights are always the rights of identifiable individuals, rights violations that flow from social structures typically affect collectivities, i.e., persons in similar social situations. Therefore, they can be influenced by general strategies of action oriented to collective life-situations.

Not manageable by self-help alone: According to the subsidiarity principle, the individual is always first and foremost obliged to look out for him- or herself.[72] Individual or collective self-help in the event that one's own or another's basic rights have been infringed is therefore a primary obligation of every citizen. The right to political assistance comes into play only when a reasonable effort at self-help has failed to correct a breach of fundamental rights.

Amenable to political redress: We should only speak of a violation of fundamental rights when an act can be interpreted as intentional, whether of commission or omission. When a lost wayfarer dies of hunger in the desert, he/she is not the victim of a rights violation, whereas a prisoner who has been allowed to starve to death is. So, to the extent that rights violations result from social structures or institutions, the proper remedy is either to change those structures or to counteract the harm they do through compensating or countervailing structures. Structural social risks to the real-world efficacy of basic rights thus call for adequate and effective political redress.

Dimensions of rights violation

A review of the historical genesis of politically optional risks shows that they are cumulative. New layers of risk are added atop older ones that never quite disappear, even though modern social democracies have adopted fairly effective measures for managing or containing them. From social democracy's normative standpoint, questions about each kind of risk can be posed in three different dimensions, which only synergistically guarantee sufficient resources for positive freedom: namely, of private, social, and political autonomy.

This distinction depends on the assumption made by democratic theory that modern democracies under the rule of law should meet at least the following requirements: that they should (1) respect and protect universal human rights; (2) guarantee equal political rights of citizenship; and (3) extend the protections of human dignity and rights to the domain of social cooperation outside the state's territorial limits. Democracies that guarantee the entitlement to equal political rights in a purely formal way, such as by general elections, but not the two other groups of fundamental rights are considered defective by modern democratic theory.[73]

The UN Covenants on Basic Rights oblige every nation-state to guarantee all five categories of modern basic rights without rank-ordering them. And these guarantees must be considered fully binding under international law. Consequently, they call for a form of social democracy in which all persons are assured of the same level of protection for their *private, political, and social autonomy*. In the final analysis it is the state alone that can back up these rights guarantees. Rights to social autonomy are not conceived as broadly or defined as clearly as rights to political autonomy. Yet it is evident that the protection of human dignity and of fundamental liberties must apply in the social sphere as well.[74] Thus, in the strong form presumed here, the theory of social democracy applies only to the *citizens* of a given country. It claims validity for citizens of other lands only in a weaker form derived from the foundational principle of *universal human rights*.

In social democracy the political obligations of the state derive their legitimacy from the link between fundamental rights and the types of social risks that tend to undermine them. These *rights violations* may result from social-structural risks that affect *private, social, or political autonomy*.

The genesis of politically optional risks

In the history of Western juridical democracy the following types of social-structural risks to basic rights have predominated. This list has been prominent both in the political arena and in scholarly debates, although the dates given are only rough approximations, indicating when the issues first became salient. We include:

1 risks arising from the structures of the *capitalist market economy* (1830s)
2 risks associated with the cultural matrix of *gender relations* (1860s)[75]
3 risks growing out of the *cultural heterogeneity* of modern societies (1960s)[76]
4 risks inherent in the processes of industrialism (1970s)[77]
5 risks connected with *accelerated* modernization (1990s)[78]
6 risks emerging from social and economic *globalization* (1990s)[79]
7 *reflexive* risks arising from the structures of risk-management themselves (1990s).[80]

This list is open-ended in two senses. Our ability to understand the particular risks and their consequences has improved; moreover, society itself has become more open to the possibility that political risks of a similar kind may continue to surface and have to be managed.

Risks and the justification of rights

The social contract theory advanced by Julian Nida-Rümelin holds that, when the contracting parties choose strategies of risk-management, they are forbidden to apply calculations of aggregate utility that ignore violations of the rights of some of their members. All persons possess an absolute moral worth, which may not be overridden by considerations of collective utility.[81] If we inquire what sorts of collective choice (or toleration) underlie the politically optional risk structures investigated here, the response would be threefold. First, experience has proven some of them (such as a capitalist market economy, cultural heterogeneity, industrialism, and economic globalization) to be preferable to any other available alternative. Other cases (e.g., gender relations) involve the effects of traditional cultural patterns that the liberal state must strive to overcome. Another category includes second-order risks that arise either from the institutions chosen or from attempts at compensating for the problems generated by those institutions (accelerated modernization, reflexive risks).

The risks that arise from these politically optional arrangements may adversely affect the social, economic, and cultural rights of certain groups. The political community that bears responsibility for these risky choices is then obliged to make suitable offers of compensation or risk-avoidance to each victimized group.

Arguments derived from the "politics of risk" entail three consequences for the theory of legitimation. *First*, they refute the libertarians' claim that the social risks described above are entirely the fault of their victims. *Second*, they provide a contractual justification for the state's obligation to support its citizens' rights to positive freedom. This justification is quite independent of the one that emphasizes the validity of "material" rights under international law. Nevertheless it offers additional support to the argument in favor of the latter's universal applicability. *Third*, they undergird the claim of all citizens beset by one of these politically optional risks to be allowed to maintain for a reasonable time the status they had enjoyed prior to the incidence of risk.

1.5 Self-reliance and civic duties

Fundamental rights and duties

In both law and practice, liberal and social rights have been distinguished according to the kinds of obligations they generate: either *obligations of result* or *obligations of conduct*. It will be argued here that there are analogous distinctions in the relationship between these classes of rights and *social duties*. There have been several attempts to draft a Universal Declaration of Human Duties for the UN General Assembly parallel to the fundamental rights already approved by that body, but all were rejected. There are several reasons for their cool reception. The draft submitted by the InterAction Council consists mainly of moral obligations binding on all persons, not duties specific to political or social citizenship.[82] In contrast to its earlier manifestations, democratic theory that relies for legitimation on political and social rights can no longer ignore the way that democratic social welfare states actually work. The theory of social democracy must now investigate the functional logic of social subsystems as well as the political logic of implementing its schemes in a liberal democracy,[83] otherwise it will not be able to offer empirically informed guidance for political action. Both the functional logic of the social-political system (especially in respect to the financial crisis of the modern social welfare state) and the logic of political legitimation will have to take careful account of social duties in the interpretation and application of fundamental rights guarantees.[84]

The normative problem of coordinating rights with duties in social citizenship also has a historical, dynamic dimension: it emerges ever more clearly as social and political rights are expanded and implemented. It was not until the structural crisis of the modern social welfare state had precipitated comparable problems in all the societies pursuing a social democratic agenda that the need to link rights and duties became obvious. Given what we now know, any theory of social democracy that only justified entitlements, without talking about reciprocal norms of duty, would lack both legitimation and relevance.

How duties may be justified

The crucial normative argument in this context may be borrowed from Ronald Dworkin, who argues that the elementary right to liberty attributed to every person accountable for his or her own actions implies a prima facie duty to lead one's life in a responsible manner.[85] Thus, the right to liberty likewise justifies the obligation of each person to request aid from the community only when self-help falls short. It is therefore appropriate in a generous social welfare state to make rights guarantees contingent upon the fulfillment of complementary duties by the beneficiaries, without thereby imperiling their rights and entitlements. Just as citizens can forfeit their political and civil rights by acting contrary to their country's constitutional order, so too they can forfeit their social rights by continually failing to carry out the correlative duty: i.e., doing their share toward the maintenance of the social security system.[86] It is legitimate for social welfare states to emulate the Danish government in the 1990s, which made the level of some social welfare payments, e.g., unemployment compensation, contingent on proof that the recipients were seriously trying to find work.

The recent practices of advanced social democratic regimes have shown that two levels of social security can legitimately be maintained to shore up the entire system. The higher-level system of social security insures that those who suffer adverse consequences from social-structural risks will not end up worse off than they were before those consequences occurred. The forms of insurance offered at this level should aim mainly to restore recipients' self-reliance, for example by offering them further education and training. Any beneficiaries who persist in refusing to perform their duty of working to restore their own capacity for self-reliance, for example by continually turning down job offers, should expect to have their wage-replacement payments curtailed as a result, and legitimately so. But there are limits to such cuts. They cannot be so deep that they jeopardize the maintenance of a socio-cultural standard of living consistent with human dignity. Overlooking that distinction can lead to a violation of the rules of justice, as well as the rights of those who have made a real effort to become self-supporting, and have suffered a marked decline in their previous status by doing so. The higher level of social security aligns with social rights and/or the right to compensation for social-structural risk, while the elementary level is justified by universal *human rights*, those that can claim unconditional validity for all human beings regardless of their achievements.

Rights and duties

Attempts to clarify the relationship between rights and duties in political philosophy have made one dilemma apparent.[87] It turns out that the

guarantee of political and social rights not only justifies the performance of duties but also presupposes it, whereas rights implicitly claim
unconditional validity. The dilemma arises because rights always imply
correlative duties as a condition of their being respected, but there may
not always be collective actors in a position to fulfill those duties.[88]
Nevertheless, careful reasoning will show that there is a duty in such
cases to create the requisite collective actor through self-organization. In
the initial phase, this duty falls to those who can take the appropriate
initiatives at the least cost to themselves. In the second stage it provides
them with rights to recruit other capable persons to help them fulfill
their obligations under the law.

There are also obligations to take part in the political activities of the
commonwealth, and respect the rules and norms of the democratic
juridical state. Even the fulfillment of private contracts presupposes a
degree of law-abidingness that contractual logic could neither engender
nor guarantee. In its capacity as a guarantor of social rights, the *social
welfare state* presupposes the highest degree of social self-reliance on the
part of its citizens: to wit, their self-restraint in making claims against
it.[89]

Whereas rights can be granted formal recognition in institutions and
backed by sanctions, most of the correlative duties seem to involve
"mere" moral imperatives. To persuade people to obey them, little more
can be said than to stress how important it is that they be obeyed. This
built-in asymmetry poses a dilemma for the practice of modern commonwealths that threatens to undermine their stability. They cannot
live up to their own claims to legitimacy merely by securing their citizens' rights or even by performing reliably their assigned tasks. Social
rights *must* be interpreted in light of the equivalent duties and they *can*
be given institutional recognition within those limits.

Categories of obligation; how far duties bind actors

In order to ascertain which duties are indispensable for social democracy, we need to draw a number of fundamental distinctions.

1 It may be inquired of ethical-political duties both how they are to be
   justified and to what extent and in which forms they can be given
   institutional backing.
2 We may also distinguish the duty to respect *rights* and the duties
   people have to assume *responsibility for themselves.*
3 Finally, duties may be distinguished according to which social
   spheres they govern.

Furthermore, duties may be located at different levels of society or
government. First, we must acknowledge the valid scope of *human and*

civil rights, and of the institutions derived directly from them that are designed to carry out their correlative political duties. Second, a variety of social and economic regulations can be derived from these duties. Third, a number of policy-making strategies suggest themselves in the areas of economic regulation and stabilization of the social welfare state.

The previous three items all involve policy-making options that clearly lie within the sovereign competence of institutional political actors. But there exists a fourth set of duties in the international arena, both to create optimal conditions for political decision-making and to forge cooperation with other actors. These duties also follow from the validity of rights norms. Yet because they require the cooperation of other sovereign decision-makers, their prospects of success are dimmer than in the first three cases. The responsible political actors are certainly obliged to take the necessary political steps, but they cannot be held fully accountable for the success or failure of their efforts. To this extent theirs are obligations of *conduct,* not of result.

Duties as the condition of rights

Dworkin derived the principle of primary self-reliance from the higher-order norm of personal liberty, and assigned it a preferred position vis-à-vis the individual's entitlements against the state or third parties.[90] Jürgen Habermas has attempted to take account of this asymmetry of rights and duties as well. He argues that binding norms of justice, which entail the institutional recognition of rights, have to be supplemented by norms of *solidarity*. The individual person has a moral obligation to society to embrace the latter norm, since otherwise there would be no way to guarantee the system of rights at all.[91] The *solidarity* of each with all others and with the juridical community as a whole appears to be the prerequisite for each individual's being able confidently to invoke his or her rights. The sources that inspire actions taken from motives of solidarity must be sought in collective forms of life governed by ethical considerations. Yet these must not be the sorts of organic communities dreamed of by fundamentalist versions of communitarianism, in which principles are never questioned and individuals are held in a kind of perpetual involuntary membership. Rather, commitment to collective forms of life would be subject to all the usual constraints of a liberal constitution.

Today, some legal codes provide that people may temporarily forfeit their civil rights, including the right to vote and hold office, if they violate civic obligations. Denmark goes even farther, in spite of its generous catalogue of social rights, by making the level of unemployment compensation payments contingent on the recipient's ability to prove that he or she is pursuing continuing education or seriously looking for a job, a policy we review later.

Given that rights and duties complement one another, the theory of social democracy regards the Danish measure as legitimate, provided that it satisfies three conditions. *First,* that rights be curtailed in the proper areas (for example, it would not be permissible to restrict access to basic education or health care); *second,* that the duties to be performed should be as clearly defined as their correlative rights; and *third,* that social services in which human rights are at stake should never fall below the minimum threshold necessary to sustain human dignity.

In evaluating the rules that might be applied to sanction non-compliance with institutionally recognized duties, one notes clear differences among basic human rights, political rights, and social rights. Whereas human rights represent the codification of a universal morality, political rights are based on the rules of reciprocity imbedded in a conditional social contract. The core content of fundamental social and economic rights, finally, also rests on universal moral norms and their implications. However, their specific forms and the politically defined level of entitlements they provide always emerge in the context of contingent ethical decisions made in concrete commonwealths. Hence, they can be more closely aligned with the performance of the obligations to which they give rise than would be tolerated in the case of the norms of a universal morality.

For these reasons the entitlement that all persons have to recognition of their universal political and social rights cannot be treated as totally independent of their willingness to perform the reciprocal duties. In a given situation that entitlement might also be interpreted in light of the political and systemic exigencies faced by the society in question (e.g., its financial plight), which could affect its ability to guarantee any kind of rights at all. That observation especially concerns cases in which a suitable level of social protection cannot be assured for everyone unless there is strict enforcement of the duty to take responsibility for one's own life.

Experience with generous social welfare states in free markets suggests that in most of them we will eventually see a transformation of the social security systems in the direction of greater emphasis on the duty of primary self-reliance. Not only is that trend legitimate in light of the normative link between duties and rights; it may even be morally imperative in order to insure that the rights of all are secure.

1.6 Social democracy and sustainability

Land and labor

Ever since the 1987 Brundtland Report (*Our Common Future*) and the 1992 UN Conference on Environment and Development in Rio de

Janeiro, sustainable development has been high on the agenda of international organizations, NGOs, and many national governments. Everyone except dogmatic neoclassical economists now recognizes that our societies need to become sustainable in the sense that they should not consume the capital stocks, especially of "natural capital," upon which future growth and prosperity depend.[92] The goal of sustainability has frequently been paired with the notion of "development," e.g., in the Brundtland Report. There sustainable development means economic activity conducted to "meet the needs of the present without compromising the ability of future generations to meet their own needs."[93] All definitions of sustainable development acknowledge that we must integrate ecologically sound, long-term resource conservation with the aims of social justice and greater prosperity.[94] Thus, the traditional concerns of social democratic theory – human, civil, and social rights, the partial decommodification of labor, welfare provision, just distribution – have been explicitly incorporated into discussions of environmental conservation. In this chapter we shall inquire into the theoretical foundations of the latter, and explain why its conjunction with social democracy is neither fortuitous nor improbable.

Social democratic theory developed for decades in isolation from the intellectual currents that gave rise to modern environmentalism and its quest for a sustainable economy. Nevertheless, both schools of thought emerged from similar discontents and evolved in parallel ways. Only in the late twentieth century was the point reached where their complementarity could be recognized and their common commitments brought to light. A sustainable society will have to protect labor from the vicissitudes of the market, improve the material welfare of people in the Third World, and encourage the practices of participatory democracy and social justice. Likewise, societies organized around the principles of social democracy will find the transition to environmentally friendly economies both necessary and feasible. After a century of divergence, social democratic and sustainability theories may be on the threshold of reconciliation.

The key figure who connects both forms of thought is Karl Polanyi, who originated the notion of "imbedding." He pointed out that markets and economic rationality, as understood by classical economists and their disciples, had in fact always been imbedded in the more encompassing social system.[95] The practices of "barter and truck," to which Adam Smith had attributed the natural origin of markets, until fairly recently were subordinated to other objectives, especially the maintenance of "social relationships" and status.[96] Hence, the project of liberating the market system from social control and political regulation, allowing the price system to coordinate all human activity, appears a dangerously utopian fantasy. If it were ever fully realized, "such an institution could not exist for any length of time without annihilating the human and natural substance of society."[97] Sensing the destructive potential of unrestricted markets, societies had always limited their scope, at least until the nineteenth century. By then, the teachings of classical economics had made enough headway that certain countries, notably the United States and England, actually reversed the traditional priority, partially disembedding markets from their social matrices. But, Polanyi argued, a fully autonomous market would never emerge, because the members of society would never permit it. They would inevitably seek self-protection in regulation once they grasped the implications of unfettered markets. In effect, the welfare states of the twentieth century, and the social rights and "decommodification" demanded by social democratic theory, are civil society's method of containing the destructive potential of pure market behavior.

The primordial link between environmental sustainability and social democracy emerges when we investigate the transition from pre-market societies to the liberalism of the nineteenth century. The foundations of the former were – and still are – land and labor, understood as elements historically exempted from the logic of market relationships. Labor was nothing but human activity itself; hence, to buy and sell it like any other commodity would mean buying and selling the person "attached" to it. Carried to its logical conclusion, the commodification of labor would annihilate the "protective covering of social institutions," exposing the individual to the vagaries of the labor market. Land designates "another name for nature" or "the natural environment."[98] To transform nature into a commodity would invite environmentally hostile practices, as landowners single-mindedly sought to maximize profit. Polanyi mentions the likelihood that "neighborhoods and landscapes" [might be] defiled, rivers polluted . . . the power to produce food and raw materials destroyed."[99] In both cases, the degradation of labor and devastation of the natural environment, the "commodity fiction" provides the common factor.

Polanyi's analysis suggests how closely allied the movements for social rights and sustainable development *should* have been. Their affinities were not at first recognized, and both proceeded in isolation from one another.[100] But a rapprochement seems finally to be on the horizon. The ecological economics originated by Herman Daly and international charters such as the Brundtland Report and Agenda 21 have demonstrated the links between ecological sustainability and key social democratic principles. Social democracy and sustainable development have essentially the same goal: reimbedding economic activity into a more encompassing matrix that will enable it to satisfy human needs without undermining cultural or natural life-support systems.

These preconditions for economic activity may be characterized as "social capital" and "natural capital," respectively.[101] Social capital refers to networks of trust, cooperation, mutual support, and engagement that allow citizens to accomplish beneficial projects for themselves, rather than by relying on clientelism, patronage, and bureaucracy.[102] Natural capital includes a variety of traditional "natural resources" such as trees, fresh water, topsoil, petroleum, etc.; yet it also includes living systems such as coral reefs, wetlands, even the atmosphere itself.[103] The latter furnish "ecosystem services" either that human beings cannot provide at all (photosynthesis), or that our technologies could only provide more clumsily and expensively than nature does (purifying water, providing nutrients for plant and animal growth).

Social and natural capital have certain obvious resemblances. Both accumulated over long periods without conscious human direction or intervention. Both tend to be stable over time, although they deteriorate if placed under excessive stress. Finally, they tend to be undervalued by the market's price system, since they are regarded as "free" or public goods. In short, both social democratic and sustainability theory want to exempt at least these spheres of life from the logic of the market. Indeed, sustainability theorists argue that unrestrained market behavior eventually tends to degrade *both* natural *and* social capital.[104]

But here the parallels end. Disagreements between social democratic and environmental sustainability theories have involved the scope of permissible market exchanges, the desirability of economic growth, and the very definition of a sustainable society. Social democracy has fought to protect social capital from the corrosive effects of the market, both by institutionalizing social rights and by advocating participatory democracy, "civil society," and other non-hierarchical forms of cooperation. However, its proponents have conceded that a post-industrial economy will be dominated by the market and its price system. Furthermore, postwar social democratic policy-making has been dominated by the Keynesian quest for stable growth.[105] Yet even mainstream advocates of sustainability excoriate the worship of economic growth understood as annual percentage increases in GDP. Indeed, one of the crucial arguments of ecological economics is that "physical growth should cease, while qualitative improvement continues"; that is, we must achieve a "steady state economy."[106] In sum, many theorists of sustainability now seem to advocate a more radical critique of markets, the ideology of growth, and "neoclassical" economic ideas than do the proponents of social democracy.[107] These disagreements are real and serious, but they should not overshadow the many ways in which social democratic and sustainability theories overlap or interlock.

The case for a sustainable economy

What would it mean in practice to decommodify the natural environment? In some instances, it might mean shielding some portions of the earth and seas from economic exploitation by classifying them as national parks, wilderness, biospheres, etc. But we obviously must use and market the earth's resources. The complete decommodification of land – as of labor – will not work. The literature on sustainable development is thus devoted to finding paths toward development that do not jeopardize the planet's long-term carrying capacity.

"Neoclassical" economics treats the economic system as though it operated in a vacuum. Inputs enter the economic system from an unknown source, and exit, in the form of consumption and waste, bound for an unknown destination. Ecological economics aims to remove these blinders by locating the economic system in a specific context: Polanyi's "land," or simply the "global ecosystem."[108] The imbeddedness of the economy in the natural environment implies that the former operates under certain constraints. The earth itself cannot grow, and often it generates new resources at glacially slow rates (e.g., topsoil, aquifer recharge). Worse still, current levels and techniques of exploitation have degraded most of the earth's natural systems and impaired their capacity to provide ecosystem services. For example, forests, aquifers, and the atmosphere have all been compromised.[109] The implications are ominous, since these "sinks" have always been able to absorb and recycle humanity's waste products. We may not be able to count on those "costless" services much longer.

Neoclassical economics has also assumed that only labor creates value, and that the abstract, undifferentiated matter to which value is added has no intrinsic worth.[110] But, contrary to neoclassical dogma, economic activity does not actually create anything. It merely rearranges what nature itself has already arranged into a more highly organized form. Thus, it is unrealistic to assign to nature zero value in the economic process, for we are consuming not just the value humans have added to matter, but also the value nature has bestowed on it by structuring it in certain ways that make it useful in the first place.[111]

For present purposes let us define a sustainable economy as one that follows three rules. First, renewable resources (fish stocks, fresh water, forests) should be exploited at rates of harvest below the natural rate of regeneration. Second, waste flows should be held to a level below the presumed assimilative capacity of the affected systems. Third, nonrenewable resources should be extracted at a rate less than or equal to the rate at which substitutes are found.[112]

Neoclassical economists usually dismiss such restrictions on growth as misguided for three reasons: (a) the price system will send signals, in the form of rising prices, that resources are growing scarce long before we begin to run out of them; (b) human capital (ingenuity, technology) will find substitutes for natural capital – resources or ecosystem services – that become scarce or degraded; (c) most harms to natural ecosystems are "externalities" that can be handled by legal claims for compensation to the injured party or by government regulation.[113]

Ecological economists largely accept the third argument and therefore seek ways to internalize environmental costs in prices.[114] But they offer detailed rebuttals to the first two claims.

First, they argue that the earth and its ecosystem services lack substitutes. Perhaps we can replace specific scarce resources. But we do not know how to "make" another atmosphere and climate suited to human life, nor could we create coral reefs, rainforests, or topsoil. We have discovered that even trying to restore a single endangered species, such as the Pacific salmon, exceeds the expertise of our engineers and biologists.[115] Economists have been seduced by technology's limited success in finding substitutes for certain metals or fuels into believing that human inventiveness can engineer artificial ecosystems. But it cannot, at least not in a way most people would find acceptable or affordable. The earth is our habitation, not an abstract reserve of natural resources. Furthermore, price signals do not necessarily modify behavior in the expected ways. Higher prices for rare animals simply lure more hunters into the market, depleting stocks more quickly.

The transition from neoclassical to ecological economics has been undertaken both in theory and in practice. On the level of theory, some economists have sought to put a monetary value on ecosystem services, so that even their less enlightened colleagues will understand that these services are not "free."[116] Prugh has even attempted to estimate the aggregate services of the *entire* natural ecosystem, finding these to be "worth" $33 trillion a year.[117] Although putting a price on the planet earth appears ludicrous, since what is irreplaceable transcends the commodity form, these calculations do force mainstream economists to recognize that we are freeloading off (usually public) resources and ecosystem services that together exceed the entire yearly global GDP!

Ecological economists are also trying to replace GDP by a better index of economic performance. GDP measures money spent, not the value received; it registers as components of "growth" expenditures that go to clean up toxic waste sites and run the engines of cars stuck in traffic jams.[118] We need an index that would put a negative value on economic activity that adds to GDP merely by liquidating natural capital – for example, a fisherman dynamiting coral reefs to stun and capture fish, destroying the habitat that nurtures them.[119] On the other side of the ledger, there are certainly ways to improve people's lives that escape the nets of GDP but are reflected in other statistics, such as life-expectancy, literacy levels, and social justice. Therefore, proponents of sustainability try to include such non-economic criteria for measuring "development."[120]

On a different front, ecological economists concede that the market does one thing very well: it achieves *allocative* efficiency in distributing scarce resources. But that does not mean it can solve problems such as distributive justice or "scale." That is, the market has no internal signals to indicate when economic activity is approaching or exceeding the carrying capacity of a given ecosystem or even the whole planet. The signals of degradation are often biological, not economic. And even when degradation has obvious economic costs, as in the case of floods, there may be no economically effective way to link those costs to their remote causes, such as deforestation, soil erosion, and the paving of rain-absorbing terrain. To ascertain the proper scale of economic activity is a task for natural science, not economics. If we recognized scale, distributive justice, and allocative efficiency as three distinct problems, we would give up the neoclassical dream that the market can operate free of regulation.

On the level of practice, economists and engineers have sought to improve so-called resource productivity, i.e., obtaining the same amount of utility or work from a product or process while using less material and energy.[121] Sustainability may be attained by perfecting efficiency in design, rather than in the allocation of resources (as per markets); yet this does not mean that sustainable products and processes have to cost more. A well-insulated house may be more expensive to build, but will be cheaper to heat and cool.

Social democracy and sustainability: reciprocal links

Most of the crucial principles of sustainability mesh smoothly with or are even implied by social democratic theory. The pathways from social democracy to sustainable development are much shorter and easier than from or to neoclassical economics or libertarianism. As we have emphasized, the two currents of thought emerged from similar efforts to shelter labor and land from the full impact of commodification.

Let us begin with the time horizon of sustainability. According to the Brundtland Report, sustainable development means that the needs of the present should be met without compromising the ability of *future* generations to meet their needs. In other words, decisions about current resource use imply an intergenerational ethical obligation. Neither classical economics nor libertarian thought offers much support for such obligations. The former assumes that people "discount the future"; that is, they prefer to use resources now rather than in the future, so that the farther off a benefit is, the less it is valued compared with currently available benefits.[122] Markets thus have a built-in "myopia" that discourages any systematic concern for long-term sustainability.[123] Of course, neoclassical economists do not even consider the possibility that current generations might care about future generations.[124] This is not surprising. In liberal societies, as Tocqueville recognized, "the fabric of time is torn at every moment and the trace of generations is effaced."[125] And what is neoclassical economics if not a reflection on the kind of society that gave birth to it?

John Rawls outlines a plausible social democratic position on justice across generations. He notes, first, that "the persons in the original position are not to view themselves as single isolated individuals." To the contrary, "they have ties with certain members of the next generation."[126] For example, the parties in the original position might suppose they will be parents who care about how their descendants fare. As a result, they will pledge to save a certain amount to enhance the prospects of future generations, especially their least favored members. This agreement amounts to "an understanding between the generations to carry their fair share of the burden of realizing and preserving a just society."[127]

Rawls also stresses that we should not think of this capital accumulation process as a never-ending march toward limitless affluence: "it is a mistake to believe that a just and good society must wait upon a high material standard of life. What men want is meaningful work in free association with others. . . . Beyond some point [wealth] is . . . likely to be a positive hindrance, a meaningless distraction at best if not a temptation to indulgence and emptiness."[128] Those lines could easily have been written by the advocates of sustainable development. Rawls is saying that we should strive for a less affluent, steady-state economy "beyond some point." But *what* point? In the end, sustainability is a political issue, one that asks how we can make life worth living for both present and future generations.[129] The revival of the political is a crucial feature of social democratic thinking as well.[130]

The most significant shift of sustainability theory toward social democracy has come from insight into links between poverty and social injustice, underdevelopment, and environmental degradation. Until recently, development was regarded as a technical and economic issue, while sustainability meant protection of endangered species and landscapes with little regard to the needs of local residents.[131] But a recent OECD commission states that "inequality is a critical threat to sustainable development."[132] The Brundtland Report concurs. "Poverty is a major cause and effect of global environmental problems."[133] British environmental economist Edward Barbier concludes: "if poverty alleviation is an ultimate aim of economic development, then efficient and sustainable environmental management is a necessary means for achieving this goal."[134]

People in the developing world are the foremost victims of environmental degradation brought on by unsustainable practices and/or the encroachment of the global market economy on traditional ways of life. According to one study, 57 percent of the rural poor and 75 percent of the urban poor live in areas where ecological destruction and/or severe environmental hazards threaten their well-being.[135] In fact, 40,000 acres of land per day on average worldwide are being converted from grassland into desert.[136] The earth also faces rising demands for and declining supplies of fresh water. The wealthy countries can alleviate the problem by costly water diversions, desalination, and water treatment, but the world's poor cannot.[137] Finally, many of them rely on coral reefs for their livelihood, as these provide food sources, a magnet for tourism, and protection from storm-caused shoreline erosion. But 58 percent of the planet's reefs are threatened, and we may lose them all within a few decades.[138]

For neoclassical economics each nation is responsible for generating and increasing its own "wealth." Ecological economists, by contrast, see the earth as a single ecological whole. Some of its support systems cannot be apportioned to specific countries (the atmosphere, the ozone layer, and the oceans). Thus, if one takes the planetary ecosystem to have an intrinsic value (prior to the value added by labor), then it is rightly the endowment and heritage of all humankind. We need to decide how these resources – and stewardship over them – ought to be shared. And the answer will *not* be that each nation is responsible only for itself.[139] Moreover, ecological economists insist that the long-term wealth of individual nations depends on the viability of their supporting ecosystems, a fact which also has implications for the kind and level of aid that ought to be given by wealthy countries to poor ones.

Moreover, the quest for environmental sustainability has tended to promote participatory capacities and decentralizing tendencies.[140] For example, the Aarhus Convention, which embodies principle 10 of the Rio Declaration, insists that citizens should be participants in reaching decisions about their environment and resources, have full access to justice in such matters, and become partners in implementing decisions. The Brundtland Commission affirms that "effective participation . . . by local communities can help them articulate and effectively enforce their common interest."[141] Finally, Agenda 21, often considered the Magna Carta of sustainability, devotes an entire section to participatory democracy. The Preamble states: "one of the fundamental prerequisites for the achievement of sustainable development is broad public participation in decision-making," especially by women, youth, indigenous peoples, and other frequently ignored elements.

Sustainability, in short, simply cannot be achieved without a far more prominent role for civil society. Accordingly, leading sustainability theorists now embrace the goal of a "strong democracy"[142] along the lines proposed by Benjamin Barber.[143] Moreover, the market tends to undermine the moral foundations on which a sustainable civil society must rest, by chipping away at "social orderliness, human fellow feeling and the sense of community," in other words, social capital.[144]

The only area in which one would expect social democratic theorists to clash with the proponents of sustainability concerns employment and economic growth. Since World War II the dominant formula for prosperity in Western societies has been to stimulate the economy and count on high growth rates to generate rising real wages and nearly full employment. That way, it becomes easier to avoid divisive battles over the distribution of wealth.[145] Welfare state measures, especially forms of social insurance, have furnished the support system that private employers did not or would not provide of their own volition. But the underpinnings of this postwar settlement have been crumbling; adjustments would have been necessary even without a sustainability crisis.

The transition to a sustainable economy may in fact be the new job-creation engine that de-industrializing countries in the global North need. There are many reasons to be optimistic about the outlook. First, "pioneer countries" in the march toward sustainability will have a technological advantage over the laggards. We often imagine that environmental regulation triggers a "race to the bottom" as companies move to places with less regulation to escape the added costs, forcing the regulators to weaken or rescind their rules. But the reverse can occur. Countries or regions with high environmental standards may influence those with less stringent ones to follow their lead (California has often been the bellwether for the United States in this way). In that case, high environmental regulatory standards may help incubate new industries and technologies that will generate jobs.[146] By the same token, low unemployment correlates strongly with environmental improvement, so the two objectives may often reinforce one another.[147]

More broadly, ecological economists point out that the tax codes of most Western nations are often biased against labor and in favor of large-scale capital investments, because they encourage entrepreneurs to externalize costs.[148] For example, agribusinesses are not taxed for the externalities caused by their methods: dying fisheries, climate change, and polluted waterways. If our tax codes built these externalities into the price system, farmers and other entrepreneurs would have reason to operate in more labor-intensive ways that generated less pollution.[149] The result would be more jobs in agriculture, more small farmers staying in business.

The most encouraging scenario envisioned by sustainability advocates forecasts dramatic gains in employment as we improve "resource productivity" in every sector.[150] Many new jobs would be created by retrofitting houses to reduce their heating and cooling costs, reconstructing cities around community, public transportation, and public spaces, replacing leaky water systems, recycling more of our waste. We should not think of these steps as imposing burdensome, unproductive costs ("maintenance"), but as an opportunity to design a more efficient economy that saves us money, provides jobs, and improves the quality of life. Resource productivity may, incidentally, involve *not* meddling with a natural system that is already providing a service, thus wasting money trying to replace it with a human-made substitute. For example, New York City contemplated spending $6 billion on a new water filtration plant. But it decided instead to purchase and preserve land from development in the Catskill Mountains, the city's main watershed, which saved the city $4.5 billion.[151]

Social democratic theorists should also join sustainability advocates in opposing untrammeled free trade, a point discussed later in this volume. It will be difficult for firms to internalize environmental costs without increasing their prices, since prices must reflect the true cost to society of unsustainable practices. But corporations may respond to laws requiring that they internalize costs by moving operations overseas to countries where environmental standards are frequently lax. A system of protective tariffs, scaled to reflect the environmental standards prevailing in the would-be exporting countries, would encourage the latter to move toward sustainability as the price of access to lucrative markets.[152]

The critique of unfettered markets – especially for labor and land – that unites social democracy and sustainability theory reveals a further common element in their approach to ethics and politics. Neoclassical economics abstracts from historical circumstances. Its theories are imagined to possess timeless validity, since they supposedly embody laws analogous to those in the natural sciences. *Homo oeconomicus* is assumed to behave in the same way at all times and in all places. But social democratic and sustainability theory both suggest that even economics is the child of its time. Its formative assumptions were developed in the eighteenth century, when populations and available technologies put incomparably less pressure on global ecosystems.[153] Then, the urgent problems were about overcoming scarcity: how to extract more resources, grow more food, and produce more tons of coal. The earth was still relatively thinly populated, while most people lived in dire poverty. In this rather "empty" world, untrammeled growth was an option, but it no longer is in the world of the twenty-first century.[154]

In our time priorities have changed. Environmental support systems are degraded; "sinks" for waste may be overwhelmed. We simply cannot risk irreversible damage to ecosystems we do not know how to replace.[155] Furthermore, *over*production, not scarcity, has been the bane of advanced capitalist economies in the last century, as evidenced by their recurrent recessions. Meanwhile, (post-)industrial societies are affluent enough that further improvements in the quality of life may best be attained by upgrading public goods, restoring eroded social capital, and reducing the working day rather than stimulating still more private consumption. As historical circumstances change, so too should our economic assumptions. As one advocate of sustainability put it, human beings are social creatures, not atoms; their behavior and customs are flexible. Therefore, "any social system claiming that it alone is legitimate because its roots stem from human nature is self-delusional."[156] Social democratic theorists have made the same point ever since Marx.

Reimbedding markets in both the social and the natural world will entail a triumph of historical insight and empirical investigation over the dogmatism of abstract economic and political thought.

1.7 Justice and political integration

Justice and fundamental rights

In principle, the theory of social democracy need not rely on any special normative grounding, since it can find support for its main objectives in the universal rights approved by the Human Rights Convention of the United Nations in 1966, now valid under international law. Although the agreement imposes "binding duties" on states, the enforcement mechanisms provided for universal rights by the signatory states are rather weak.[157] All of the 148 signatory states committed to supporting economic and social (as well as liberal) rights owe at least some of their legitimacy to their efforts to enforce the convention as valid law. The convention also functions as the normative framework for *social* democracy all over the world. This universal, international-legal foundation for the legitimacy of social democracy is not invoked primarily because its adherents have faith in positive law as a source of legitimacy, but rather for ethical and pragmatic reasons. At first glance the normative framework is reinforced by the simple fact that there *is* a worldwide, normative consensus behind these rights. Yet the consensus presupposes that the signatory states have been motivated by good arguments to give their assent, regardless of what particular ideas might have been offered as justification for the relevant rights. What matters for democratic theory is that there should be well-founded consent. The reasoning offered by the signatories in their respective political and cultural milieus is less important for now.

Fundamental rights are "mid-range principles of justice."[158] They occupy a position midway between principles of justice broadly conceived and political discourses concerned with the application of just policies. A certain understanding of rights underlies the UN Covenants: namely, that of base-level justice expressed as equal rights and duties in the main spheres of societal activity. Especially in their socio-economic aspects, the norms of social security and participation contained in the universal rights of the covenants dovetail with the core structures of social democracy. Thus, because it can count on the rights set forth in the covenants, the theory of social democracy is temporarily relieved of the task of having to offer further justifications for its positions in the way that other special theories of political and social justice must do.

Nevertheless, the theory does need to provide some sort of link to the theory of justice above and beyond its normative grounding in universal basic rights. According to Hermann Heller's sociologically oriented theory of social democracy, what makes the modern state possible is the fact that the adversaries in social and economic conflicts have good reason to expect that they may be able to reach a compromise with one another. This argument, together with recent research, gives solid empirical support to the theory of social democracy. A complex model of rationality illuminates the behavior Heller depicts by providing a more accurate picture of the way citizens actually behave in routine democratic deliberations than does the libertarian model with its calculus of selfish private interests. On closer inspection, the latter model has turned out to be a social scientists' fiction. Heller rightly insists that there must be an internal connection between the sociological approach to democracy and the reasoning drawn from theories of justice. A catalogue of fundamental rights alone is not a solid enough grounding for the theory of social democracy.

The latter thus posits two connections to the theory of justice. The first tries to explain how a widely shared understanding of justice may play a role in the achievement of social democratic goals. The second attempts to clarify the normative foundations of social democracy by identifying the minimal standards of social justice required by social democratic policies.

When participants share a basic value such as justice, this does not mean that they agree on a theory of justice or that there is unanimity from the outset concerning the content of relevant norms. As suggested by Rawls's theory of *political* liberalism, the only thing that has to be assumed is an overlapping consensus that the putative idea of justice can provide rudimentary normative guidance. This notion gives the participants apparently good reasons to suppose that they can come to terms with one another, an assessment that is then sufficiently borne out by the actual practice of seeking a common political ground.[159]

From Kant to Dworkin, justice in this liberal tradition has always been defined as the universalizing norm of freedom, i.e., as the equal liberty or autonomy of all human beings.[160] As a universal political value, liberty is interpreted through the understanding of justice in such a way that being free means no more or less than universalizing the principle of one's own actions.

1 At the level of the *polity*, justice distributes the rights and duties of all citizens equally and backs them up by legally binding institutional recognition.
2 At the *policy* level it offers guidance concerning the just distribution of the opportunities and resources that people need to act freely.
3 At the level of *politics* it guarantees equal opportunities for participation in the political decision-making process and regulates the political culture of conflict-resolution.

The theory of social democracy is based on an *egalitarian theory of human and civil rights* and a moderately egalitarian theory of justice. Both can be justified by universalistic arguments. As for their role in the public sphere, neither depends on any special version of justification for its validity or content.[161] The only proviso is that public discourse must be able to link the moderately egalitarian idea of justice to liberty. As far as the political persuasiveness of the norms of justice is concerned, this pluralism of justifications actually broadens its potential appeal rather than limiting it.

The pluralism of justifications and the overlapping consensus

In order to win majority support for the kind of policy options that social democracy continually requires, there has to be a public consensus about minimal standards of social justice. To some extent that consensus must have already seeped into the political culture of a society. Yet political competition in pluralistic democracies may sometimes call that established consensus into question. It will then need public justification sufficient to rally majority support once again. Thus, part of the project of social democracy must include a willingness to stand behind the normative claims of justice in public discourses. However, the different kinds of reasoning behind such justifications do not have to converge on the meta-political or philosophical planes in order for that project to retain its claim to *political* validity.[162] We encounter a parallel to the argument in favor of an overlapping consensus in Rawls's theory of political liberalism. In public discourses about justice, the parties need only agree about issues that affect political actions. The reasons for their positions certainly ought to be presented and compared, but there is no need to insist on complete unanimity. At the level of political validity it is sufficient that opinions should in fact converge in defining the outlines of a moderately egalitarian conception of justice. Beyond that, the representative actors engaged in public debates should have a clear idea, in *their own minds*, of the validity claims behind their own meta-political convictions, and know how to solicit support for them.

Active neutrality

The theory of social democracy cannot take a position of "passive neutrality" in respect to the strategies for justifying a moderately egalitarian notion of justice. Passive neutrality would assume de facto convergence and dismiss the justification issue itself as superfluous. What motivates the members of a societal collectivity in advancing their respective claims and working toward a consensus of the whole society is the expectation that an exhaustive process of deliberation would eventually gain the assent of all participating actors. That assumption

makes sense only if all actors pursue their respective strategies of justification as far as they can. Those strategies are admittedly not the
direct motive behind political actions, but their indirect significance is
indisputable in cobbling together political majorities. Accordingly, the
theory of social democracy commends an attitude of *active neutrality*,
one which takes a lively interest in the ways that the norms of justice
might be justified, but refuses to take sides with any of the competing
rationales.

Can moderate egalitarianism be justified?

Recent discourses about justice, which emerged in a dialogue with John
Rawls's theory, offer a response to the above challenge.[163] They seek
clarification of three fundamental issues, which must be sharply dif-
ferentiated despite their internal connections. The first question is
whether a universalistic conception of justice can *be justified intersubjectively*. The second inquires whether the *institutions of liberal democracy
and the market economy* can be legitimized universalistically. The third
concerns the social range and depth of a universalistic conception of
justice. What implications does it have for the distribution of resources
and life chances? And what does it tell us about the prospects for
shaping economic and social living conditions as well as the context of
decision-making?

Despite considerable overlap, there are important differences among
the arguments purporting to show how to satisfy the universalistic
claims of social and political justice. Yet in their institutional consequences they exhibit remarkable agreement. Not unexpectedly, differences in their findings and proposals are greatest when they inquire
how resources, participatory opportunities, and rights might be distributed outside the political constitution narrowly defined, i.e., where
broader social and economic arrangements come into play. In these
philosophically sophisticated discourses about justice, there is a
common frame of reference. It includes both a background understanding of the political culture of modernity and a foundation built on
the Enlightenment and political liberalism.[164] All of them share a certain
understanding of equality as it applies to the fundamental rights and
life chances of a human being. The minimal egalitarianism implicit in
the modern idea of justice is the soil on which may be erected the institutional edifice of a liberal democratic constitutional order. We find
broad agreement in recent theories of justice that human and civil rights
must be equal. However, for many of the theorists, notably Robert
Nozick, that is also the last word on the subject.[165] Positions like his, that
want to limit the ambitions of distributive policy – and its associated
conception of justice – to the *system of political institutions* in representative democracy and to a merely *negative* concept of liberty, are the real

founders of *libertarian* democracy. They totally reject the approach implicit in the concept of positive freedom, as well as the egalitarian arguments often linked to it. They affirm instead a weak version of equality of opportunity; yet because they refuse to countenance the inheritance taxes that a real "level playing field" would require, their entire approach proves inconsistent. Conversely, positions that attempt to tie the validity claims of regulative and distributive policy to a concept of positive liberty are the real forerunners of the project of social democracy.

Negative and positive liberty

Isaiah Berlin devised his now famous distinction between negative and positive liberty in order to discredit the latter.[166] In his view, negative liberty just *is* freedom. By warding off interference by state and society, negative liberty creates space for self-determination untrammeled by impediments and interference from without. And that is the sum total of freedom. Berlin's negative concept of liberty privileges the protection of a sphere in which individuals can do or omit what they please, without taking into account the interests of other individuals.[167] It does not have to be imbedded in a universal matrix of equal liberties for other persons, nor is it contingent upon any institutional recognition or sanction. As the simple absence of interference in the individual's private sphere, negative freedom is even possible in an authoritarian political order.

Macpherson has shown that positive freedom as defined by Berlin blurs the lines among three distinct dimensions of meaning:

1 as having a share in the controlling authority
2 as individual self-direction
3 as a metaphysically exaggerated transformation of objectively rational self-direction.[168]

Taking advantage of these confusions, Berlin criticizes the positive concept of liberty for two reasons. First, he points out that the boundary between freedom as individual self-direction and the metaphysically overblown form of objectively rational embodiments of freedom (which at bottom scorn negative liberty) is always poorly defined. In the end, this blurring of boundaries always seems to justify the abolition of liberal freedom in the name of some "higher" liberty, as (supposedly) in Marxist-Leninist historical metaphysics. Furthermore, Berlin recognizes that one must have the means to exercise one's freedom to choose, and that negative liberty is only an enabling condition for doing so; thus these "means" are a necessary element in the full exercise of freedom. But he also wants to conceive liberty in the narrowest and most unequivocal sense, so he treats the means of its realization merely as prerequisites and not as inherent defining features of liberty per se. As Berlin understands it, the concept of liberty ought to be purged of all possibility for misinterpretation by being limited to one idea: the absence of coercion. Macpherson has objected to this reductionist move that "lack of access to the means of life and labour" amounts to an encroachment on the space of liberty that each person is allotted, albeit an indirect one that takes place through socio-economic structures.[169]

The universalistic crux of Macpherson's justified critique of Berlin will look more persuasive if we define the concepts of negative and positive liberty more precisely. *Negative* liberty shall designate the absence of any coercion not sanctioned by general laws to which all alike must submit and in the passage of which all had an equal share. And this definition shall apply regardless of whether acts of coercion emanate from the state or third parties. According to Macpherson, *positive* liberty relates *exclusively* to the question of whether a person has available the material (social) means to act on his or her liberty in accordance with self-generated life plans. The concepts of positive and negative liberty are mutually reinforcing. That is, freedom for all becomes real and not merely verbal, when it is both negatively guaranteed and positively enabled.

Debates in moral philosophy and jurisprudence have identified six specific asymmetries in the relationship between positive and negative liberty, which support the inference that a distinct status ought to be attributed to each of them.

1 Since positive liberties are entitlements to services, they are subject to the scarcity of resources in a way that negative liberties are not.[170]
2 Should specific resources become scarce, citizens may not always be able to claim their positive liberty in full measure, whereas this is never true of negative liberty.
3 Positive freedom depends on services the adequacy of which is often relative to prevailing standards. Consequently, positive freedom depends on both resource availability and cultural criteria, leaving considerable room for discretion. At one end of the continuum one could locate guarantees of sheer survival; at the other, opportunities to live a "nice, easy, pleasant life."[171] The boundaries of positive liberty start to become porous, shading over into aspects of life beyond the strict accounting of justice, where duties of solidarity and philanthropy hold sway.
4 When it comes to underwriting certain positive liberties, as for example in the fields of education and training, reservations arise not only about resource availability but also concerning the personal qualifications of claimants. Therefore, positive liberties as such are

not actionable rights; instead, they are "programmatic demands, for the social implementation of which complex judgments have to be made."[172]

5 Whereas negative liberties only flourish if they are respected by all humankind, the same cannot be said of positive liberties. They may be honored only by a portion of humanity and still remain in effect. And if some decline to provide the services required by positive liberty, others can step into the breach.

6 In some cases involving positive liberties, it is not possible to identify the "natural service providers": that is, those who are partially liable for harm or distress and should therefore take steps to alleviate it. So here, unlike the case with negative liberty, one cannot always establish primary responsibility for interference with liberties.

For all these reasons, positive liberties should be deemed more complex and harder to apply than their negative counterparts. Yet they are not reason enough to abandon the idea of positive liberty itself; rather, they indicate certain conditions, tensions, and risks that a policy of securing positive liberty must always confront. In sum, a dual concept of liberty that gives equal weight to both dimensions while acknowledging their asymmetries is one normative cornerstone of social democracy. It also segues into the related conception of justice as equal liberty, which finds support in recent theories of justice.

Theories of justice

Four "ideal types" can be identified in recent theories of justice, to which nearly all the other relevant positions (except consequentialism)[173] can be assigned.[174] They include John Rawls's contractual theory of justice as fairness; Michael Walzer's communitarian theory of spheres of justice; Ronald Dworkin's theory of resource equality; and Jürgen Habermas's discourse-ethical theory of deliberative democracy. All share key premises: an egalitarian interpretation of justice stemming from the liberal tradition, as well as the conviction that both positive and negative liberties have a place in justice. Finally, all of them eventually grapple with two fundamental issues. How can a theory of justice be given an intersubjectively binding justification? And how can a universalistic concept of political and social justice be accorded substantive meaning?

Enormous differences seem to separate all these approaches. Yet they converge in affirming two points: the fundamental equality of human and civil rights and the centrality of liberal democratic institutions. All tie the concept of positive liberty to the availability of social and economic resources, for without these a person cannot really choose or act freely. Though they approach the problem of justification differently, their disagreements do not necessarily culminate in irreconcilable contradictions of principle.

In the final analysis all these positions presume that everyone under the umbrella of the norms of justice counts as an equal, and thus has an equivalent right to share in deliberation and decision-making. It is, in fact, precisely the practice of this right that serves to justify the norms. This is obvious in discourse ethics and the original position in Rawls. In Dworkin's case, it underlies the model of an original auction, where everyone begins with equal rights and resources. This starting point then legitimizes strategies of differentiation. Communitarianism *à la* Walzer of course always assumes some previously existing context of accepted norms that vary from one community to the next. But in the end he too relies on universalistic contractual arguments capable of being accepted by the members of the community as grounds for agreement.

Ultimately, the difference among these strategies of justification hinges on the choice of the stage at which the equality argument is introduced to advance the process of legitimation. It also hinges on the choice of a procedure through which equal citizens concur on a distribution of rights and resources acceptable to all of them.

There is, however, another area of agreement among these theories that has far-reaching implications for social democracy. All of them extend the norm of equality beyond the sphere of political and civil rights into the domain of social, cultural, and economic resources. The individual, they claim, must have enough of these resources available to realize his or her liberties in the contexts of social action. Once the material dimension of freedom has been brought into the discourse of equality, the differences in their various strategies of justification begin to emerge. Rawls relies particularly on two arguments. First, freedom without the social goods that make it meaningful would be empty. Second, individuals in the original position would take note of the first argument and therefore decide on a distribution of social goods that would allow each of them a reasonable range of choice and opportunity, no matter what their circumstances might turn out to be. Walzer shows that human societies have always taken it for granted that a person's material life prospects are not a matter of indifference. Most societies have assumed that a person ought to have a modicum of social goods and be initiated into the relevant socio-cultural skills and knowledge, in order to have a full share in the life of the community. In both cases, society cannot ignore the material dimension of liberty. Dworkin sees freedom as control of the resources for social action, and deduces from this definition that equal liberty should be interpreted as equality of resources. Aside from his reference to the rights of social citizenship, Habermas does not offer any explicit justification for invoking the material concept of liberty. However, one can be elicited from the logic of discourse theory, above all the empirical circumstances surrounding social conflict over the distribution of resources. These demonstrate that actual discourses about the distribution of resources always presume that the participants in them have a claim to material freedom, whereas in idealized discursive situations only the decision-making procedures are altered, not the underlying sense of what freedom means.

Norms of justice

In contemporary discourse a broad consensus has crystallized around the following points concerning egalitarian justice cum positive liberty.

1 Justice entails equal liberty; hence, all legitimate forms of equality and inequality must be tied to a universalistic understanding of positive freedom.
2 Some account must be given of inequalities of income and wealth.
3 Inequalities are legitimate within limits, as long as they can be defended as consistent with the upholding of others' rights.
4 Justice requires a high base-level of equal life chances.
5 Justice relates not only to the distribution of material and cultural resources, but also to individual and collective chances to participate in decisions made in the state, economy, and society. Especially crucial are those that affect one's opportunity for enjoying private autonomy or the fair distribution of life chances.
6 Justice is reflexive; it relates first and foremost to the procedure through which its criteria and the conditions for applying it in concrete cases are determined.
7 Justice is defined in a twofold manner: by a certain set of criteria and by the procedure through which the parties concerned jointly define and interpret those criteria.

These norms of justice are *institutionalized* in the "mid-range principles" of fundamental rights. They serve as reference points for discourses concerned with their political application, i.e., the regulative and distributive policies of social democracy.

Applying theories of justice in political discourse

There is no single conception of justice that can assume the role of a general normative premise for social democratic theory. The really persuasive idea in Walzer's reasoning is that a theory of justice has to demonstrate its political relevance by elaborating just those arguments that will be recognized in public debates over its application to a concrete society.[175] Walzer's argument does not depend on the specific premises of communitarianism, as the following points demonstrate.

First, in the domain of practical philosophy, the validity of theoretical insights hinges on their ability to anticipate the kinds of arguments that *could* be recognized in the practical discourses of real societies.

Second, as even Rawls recognizes, the divergences of opinion in the "ultimate questions" of faith and knowledge not only do not prevent, but actually facilitate, an overlapping consensus about the reasons for and substance of a shared understanding of justice.

Third, the methodological procedures and thought experiments in Rawls, Dworkin, Habermas, and Walzer can easily be read as arguments that one might present in concrete public debates to formulate good reasons for a possible discourse. Hence, they do not replace public discourse about justice; they contribute to it.

The various approaches thus converge in developing arguments for public discourse about a consensually valid conception of justice. None of them can offer more – or less – than arguments designed to inform public conversations about justice. Different perspectives on justification may be drawn into public debates even though no one expects that they will generate agreement in the foreseeable future.

Pragmatic strategy

Mindful of the problems of European social welfare states, Wolfgang Merkel has suggested that social democracy's political discourse about justice should focus on five factors. He of course recognizes that many countries would show "deficits" in regard to some of them.[176] They are: (1) the poverty rate; (2) expenditures on education; (3) inclusion in the labor market; (4) social welfare expenditures; and (5) income inequality. According to Merkel's argument, a pragmatic approach to applying principles of social justice would require that, when resources were scarce, we ought to prioritize those factors in the order given above as long as good reasons could be adduced for doing so. What good reasons support the original list? In the case of (1), anti-poverty measures should take priority, because poverty constitutes a fundamental violation of human dignity in every field of endeavour. On (2), without education it is difficult to make best use of the possibilities that freedom presents and develop society's full potential.[177] On (3), employment is the prerequisite for obtaining social recognition and a stake in society.[178] In the case of (4), social welfare expenditures may be taken as an indicator of the level of social security. On (5), it is desirable to limit income inequality as long as achievement is also rewarded.

The specified criteria need to be made more concrete. In the area of education it is not only the level of state expenditure that matters, but also the actual equality of opportunity in access to schooling. And in regard to social welfare expenditures, both their amount and their structure affect the outcome. Still, Merkel's approach does show how one can move from the norms of justice through mid-range principles of basic rights to concrete discourses about applications at the policy level. It also shows that, in concrete situations, politically relevant strategies of achieving justice can only emerge from the interplay of norms of justice, fundamental rights, and concrete experiences with empirical shortcomings in actual societies.

2

Regulation, Participation, and Actors

2.1 Political duties

Personal and political duties

Whenever a person's fundamental rights are threatened, the state has an obligation to intervene. That obligation is unconditional and immediate in the case of civil and political rights, but in the case of economic and social rights it must be calibrated to the availability of material resources. It is also unconditional if the affected persons prove unable to furnish their own self-reliant remedies. A political obligation of this kind flows from the idea of basic rights and the social contract implicit in democracy. It is likewise unconditional in respect to *negative* liberties and the defense of *social dignity*; in either case it must be carried out fully and without delay. In terms of the prerequisites for *positive* liberty, it is necessarily constrained by the availability of resources and by rules of balancing vis-à-vis fundamental rights as a whole. This consideration helps explain why the nature of the political obligation changes as the level of social security in a society increases. Before granting assistance, we then have to inquire whether potential recipients of social assistance have fulfilled their own duties to individual and collective self-help.

Even when people assume private risks that turn out badly for them, the state has some responsibility to insure that the standards of human dignity are upheld. But its obligations clearly go farther when certain groups suffer the consequences of politically optional risks. The state must then insure that their post-risk life chances will resemble what they were previously. This must be the policy at least for a reasonable interval, long enough to permit those adversely affected to resume responsibility for their own lives and regain a position in the labor market and society commensurate with their talents and efforts. This goal, closely aligned with basic rights and equality of opportunity, has been defined in recent discussions by the term *social inclusion*.[1] As noted, traditional social democratic theory has been obsessed with entitlements. But given the equivalent ranking of rights and duties, there is no reason why state-sponsored compensation should not legitimately be linked to the willingness of victims of risk to make some efforts of their own, either singly or collectively. Social welfare states simply cannot continue to focus exclusively on social entitlements, since there are no longer enough resources to go around. Moreover, allocating material resources to one set of persons as legal entitlements will inevitably mean denying them to others and so diminishing the scope of their liberty. Thus every inappropriate diversion of resources will appear to some people as an illegitimate deprivation of their liberty.

It is a matter for pragmatic policy-making to decide which political *strategies* should be selected to avoid the harmful consequences that particular risks might entail.[2] However, reasoning from risk theory, we may specify certain marginal conditions that the chosen means must satisfy.

1   Risk-avoidance takes precedence over compensation for the consequences of risks.
2   Risk-avoidance for which individuals can assume responsibility, or which can be achieved by performance of their duties, takes precedence over entitlement claims.
3   Compensatory measures should include provisions for participatory decision-making.
4   In principle, the living standards and capacities of the victims of risk should be no worse after they receive compensation than would have been the case if the risk had never occurred.

Political intervention is usually needed to insure that, when risks may infringe on the fundamental rights of affected groups, they will either be avoided altogether or – failing that – be compensated adequately. When the state assumes ultimate *responsibility to guarantee* compensation, it is free to choose the most efficient strategies as long as the above conditions are met.

The previous arguments should make it obvious why this is so. The state instigates many of the consequences that flow from risks, since it is a collective political agent for the citizens, whether through its active decisions or through its negligence. Thus, as the ultimate decision-maker, it is obliged to take preventive measures or to compensate for whatever risks it helps create.

The state's obligations may be classified according to their type and relevant spheres of applicability. First, in respect to risks associated with violations of human dignity, it may provide legal protection, social or political prevention (as in the areas of gender mainlining and intercultural integration), and social welfare guarantees when risks have adversely affected a person. Second, the state must intervene to secure the social autonomy of all citizens by making social participation a civil right and social security a constitutional responsibility. Third, citizens must be insured against politically optional risks. They should enjoy a socially acceptable minimum standard of living, receive the guarantee of equal opportunities in education and health care, and be assured that their dignity will not be violated in the world of work (labor law). Fourth, the state may intervene to bring about an equitable distribution of the resources that go with citizenship, through regulation of market processes to uphold fundamental rights; guarantees of a functioning public sphere; the granting of equal opportunities to participate in the political process; and (within limits) social democratization.

As this list of the state's obligations suggests, the civil right to an equitable distribution of political resources implies the right to protection of human dignity. This is so because each person possesses an intrinsic worth, but also because the state's efforts in behalf of the dignity of the person bolster the political competence of the person qua citizen.

Spheres of action and their respective goals

The policy-making ambitions of social democracy should also extend into the subsystems of society. For example, one can scarcely expect the state to pursue a policy of social justice if there is no intact deliberative public sphere in the commonwealth. And equality of rights to political participation and opportunity cannot be guaranteed unless a public educational system has been established that seeks to equalize both. Specifically, a social democratic state must assume duties in the following areas.

1 All five categories of rights – including the social and economic – must become obligatory under public law. Moreover, the state must grant institutional recognition to citizenship as a civil right.
2 The political system must insure that everyone has a voice, in order to guarantee to all citizens equal political autonomy.
3 The educational system predetermines everyone's opportunities in life. It likewise decides whether justice can be achieved by compensating for social disadvantages and the unequal quality of productive resources in society. It must operate according to the principles of equality of opportunity and the optimal development of every person.
4 Fundamental political values such as liberty and justice may already be widely accepted by the political culture, but they should also be encouraged in the social institutions that facilitate consensus about the applicability of rights.

5 There must be an intact political public sphere to deliberate about issues of justice and aggregate interests.
6 Civil society is both a crucial expression of political self-determination and an efficacious instrument for enhancing democratic influence on the political system and public sphere.
7 The domains of education, culture, economy, and administration determine how far social autonomy can be actualized and political culture democratized.
8 The social welfare state is the indispensable instrument for guaranteeing social security against risks imbedded in the social structure.
9 Industrial relations delimit the degree of social autonomy enjoyed by dependent employees, while influencing wages and working conditions.
10 Economic governance includes the entire range of instruments designed to balance economic expansion and basic rights.
11 The system of corporate governance determines which interests, social values, and rights will be involved in corporate policy-making.
12 In an open market economy and globalized world, a policy of transnational coordination is a necessary first step in imbedding markets.

On the asymmetry of duties

Given its normative orientation, social democracy must be more than a recipe for statist interventions. Rather, the ideas that define its institutional program are as follows: the greatest possible degree of civil liberty, adequate leeway for the market to develop according to its own inherent dynamic, smoothly operating self- and co-determination in society, and the republican and liberal functions of civil society. Only when self-reliance fails does the state have an obligation to secure positive liberty. And even then the obligation initially devolves upon civil society rather than upon the state; the latter should be brought in only as a back-up guarantor of positive liberties. In principle there exists an institutional asymmetry between the spontaneous, voluntary modes of action characteristic of civil society and the rule-governed routines that typify the state's activity. However, the state has to be a court of last resort, able to assume final responsibility for enforcing guarantees of rights on a permanent basis. It is sometimes urged that the state ought to perform its obligations either by direct administrative fiat, by outsourcing its activities to third parties, or by imposing formal-legal obligations on its citizens. But an often more successful and appropriate alternative is for the state to encourage civil society to provide its own services or supplement efforts already undertaken by active civic bodies.

When a policy of empowering civil society succeeds, many kinds of risk-avoidance and -compensation can be accomplished by social and republican forms of collective self-help. But of course, under the terms of the social democratic model, the state still must intervene when there is any doubt about whether rights will actually be guaranteed. In this sense, social democracy relies on the subsidiarity principle, though it interprets the latter as involving cooperation with civil society. By contrast, both libertarians and communists mistakenly assume that the social welfare *society* must always presuppose a hierarchical social welfare *state* to provide all the services that support citizens' rights.

2.2 Actors, systems, and strategies

Radical constructivism in the tradition

The history of social democratic theory – and still more that of its liberal and socialist predecessors – is marked by the expectation that modern societies can be totally remade on the basis of rationally grounded premises. To carry out this radical reconstruction, a democratic public sphere must have available to it achievable reform blueprints for which majority support can be mobilized. Because of its Enlightenment heritage, the social democratic tradition has usually embraced this political constructivism. The crux of revisionist reformism was the idea that society as a whole could be democratized only if its component subsystems were.[3] This program reinforced the general assumption that all social relations were fundamentally malleable. Voluntarism, visible in the commitment to democratic procedures of consultation and decision-making, was to pervade the reforms of social structures and processes.

The paradigm of *rationalist constructivism* underlying all the various approaches to social democracy differed somewhat from the assumptions of orthodox socialism. The former always attempted to take into account the conditions for social action in highly complex contemporary societies. In principle, this caution set it apart from the *naïve utopianism* characteristic of the theories of action in orthodox socialism.[4] Nevertheless, even the revisionist theories of social democracy adhered to a quite far-reaching and ambitious version of the claim that social reality could be reconstructed almost limitlessly. Thus, the constructivist principle has been the Achilles heel of the theory of social democracy up to the present day, since it left a pronounced normative imbalance in questions of how social change might be carried out.

The theory of actors and the reform of society

An up-to-date theory of social democracy – and the present project aspires to be just that – has to select the actor theory approach as its starting point. That means seeing projects of social transformation from the

viewpoint of the actors charged with carrying them out. It will emphasize the way in which the actors' resources and constraints are determined and limited by the functional logic of societal subsystems and by
the situation of other relevant actors.[5] Radical constructivism would
yield to a case-by-case approach stressing adaptation to systemic preconditions and constellations of actors, on the one hand, complemented
by carefully tailored strategies of social transformation, on the other.[6] As
Giddens has pointed out, a purely systems-theoretical approach can
explain neither how societal subsystems come into being, nor how
system structures are embodied in the interests and motives of the relevant actors. Pure action theories, by contrast, cannot explain the specific
constraints that tie the hands of actors in their respective societal subsystems. The general action-orientations of these societal subsystems
determine the success or failure of the moves of every one of their actors,
although the former also allow a certain leeway for creative reform,
since systems ultimately depend on the actors who embody them.

Societal subsystems such as the economic or educational system are
contexts of social action guided by a higher-order functional purpose.
"The criterion by which they are constituted is a special meaning that
may be identified at the normative level as their peculiar logic or rationality, and at the action level as a particular kind of activity."[7] Schimank
describes three consequences that follow from this and condition the
behavior of actors within the societal subsystems.

First, what the actors *want,* their fundamental interests as participants in their respective subsystems, is shaped by the generalized
meaningful orientations conveyed to them by the contexts of action in
which they normally operate.[8] *Second,* what the actors in these subsystems *ought to do* is defined by institutional arrangements that may act as
rules of the game for concrete decision-making and thereby shape the
normative orientations of the actors. *Third,* what the actors *can* do is
defined by the specific constellation of actors that has taken shape in the
societal subsystem.

Consequently, the constraints on and resources of the actors are relatively indeterminate. The homeostatic equilibrium characteristic of societal subsystems should not be regarded as maintained by some hermetic
code; rather, it is a context of action that plays out through the interests
and orientations of social actors as well as stabilizing institutions.[9]

Social democracy that hopes to meet the standards of social-scientific
knowledge and the de facto conditions that the contemporary world sets
for action must be able to justify and explain all of its normative standards in terms of actor theory. Its normative standards therefore must be:

1 universalistically grounded
2 compatible with the functional logics of the societal subsystems to
   which they relate

3 able to line up majority support so that their projects will be achievable under democratic ground rules.

If even one of these three conditions is not met, the corresponding
section of the theory, or indeed the theory as a whole, will lack a social-
scientific foundation as well as the prerequisites for political success.
Not until the *normative, systemic*, and *political* logics are satisfied can an
achievable program of action be forged from these theoretical projects.[10]
   Traditionally the economic subsystem was at the heart of the theory
of social democracy. The question that social scientists and politicians
passionately debated was how far the political regulation of markets
could go without disrupting their functional logic and conjuring up
socially undesirable consequences that could not be legitimized democratically. For the project of social democracy as seen from the viewpoint
of actor theory, the complex, open-ended dialectic of "coping and
shaping" has been a well-nigh insoluble puzzle.

2.3 Political actors in social democracy

Toward an explanation

There are three approaches to identifying real and potential actors in
social democracy. The first locates them by analyzing the political,
social, and economic *interests* linked to the project of social democracy;
the second offers a *historical* perspective, regarding the relevant actors
as those previously engaged in the struggle to carry out social democracy's agenda; the third approach, from *social theory*, identifies the actors
and their roles in the light of social democracy's contributions to the
processes of social integration.

The analysis of interests

Although the concept of social democracy has to be conceived more
broadly than that of the social welfare state, research on the latter offers
a fruitful starting point. Thomas Blanke has classified the theories
advanced to account for the emergence of the social welfare state. They
provide insight into the diverse interests behind it, and thus into the
identity of the politically relevant actors who represent those interests.[11]
According to Blanke we can distinguish five interpretations of the social
welfare state, each of which highlights a different set of actors as having
been responsible for its emergence.
   The first interpretation, built on the theory of social classes, concen-
trates on the case of Germany, where the key actors included a working-
class culture sustaining strong bonds of solidarity, as well as the major

organizations associated with it: the Social Democratic Party and the labor unions.[12] But since the social welfare state arose as a compromise among competing interests, class theory explanations inevitably identify the chief organizations and social environments of the owners of capital as the – often refractory – partners of the working class. Nevertheless, we must assume that the translation of class antagonisms into definite constellations of political actors and party structures began to break down in the late twentieth century. Hence, it has become more difficult to explain recent trends in the social state as the direct outcome of decisions made by these traditional political actors, none of which now has the undisputed prominence and power that it once possessed.[13]

The second interpretation, a kind of "learning theory," identifies actors only indirectly by describing the processes that have gradually given rise to the social welfare state. According to one influential study, the actors eventually "recognized that the clash between labor and capital is not a zero sum game."[14] Once again, the major organizations of capital and labor dominate the analysis, although with a stronger emphasis on the capital side. Presumably, its actors discovered that the social welfare state can act as a mechanism for damping down social and political crises and thus might operate partially in their own interest. This kind of analysis offers a slightly different perspective on the maneuvers of the actors already described in the class theory approach. Yet the learning theory approach does reveal that the spectrum of potential advocates and actors within social democracy far exceeds what might have been expected. When a crisis arises, many more actors will be mobilized than just the "usual suspects" who could readily be identified on account of their socio-economic interests (i.e., labor unions, business groups, etc.), and even these may take positions that could not be predicted merely by specifying their respective interests.

The third approach draws on the theory of deliberative democracy. It identifies the citizen body itself as the actor most responsible for initiating social democratic reforms. Real-world experiences and their interpretation in public discourse spur an engaged citizenry to fulfill important desiderata of social democracy: that citizens should be capable of political involvement, and not simply be the beneficiaries of the social welfare state but also its authors. This approach sees all citizens as potential actors in social democracy, to the extent that they are willing to accord priority to their political, civic status over their particular social interests. The political culture of a given society and the deliberative quality of its political public sphere both help determine its civic potential.

A fourth interpretation, based on theories of risk, likewise refuses to assign significant causal roles to traditional societal actors such as unions or the owners of capital. Because it regards risk-management as the key task in securing society's "reproduction," this approach assumes that state actors have borne the primary responsibility for establishing the social welfare state. The history of the emergence of such a state in Germany is frequently adduced in support of risk-management theories, since there Bismarck's authoritarian regime brought key elements of the welfare state into being by deploying sovereign power against the active resistance of powerful social and political actors.[15] Experiences or predictions of risk may infuse in state-level political actors a sense of their own legitimacy as they lay the foundations of the social welfare state, or make them believe that, once those structures are in place, they will create their own legitimacy.

A fifth and final interpretation builds on theories of modernization.[16] It presumes that the social welfare state emerges as a professionalized subsystem from the more encompassing social system. This latter, the true "author" of the social welfare state, is subject to pressures for internal differentiation that intensify as modernization proceeds apace.[17]

The social welfare state counts as a dimension of social democracy in tandem with political democracy and social autonomy. Accordingly, if we follow Blanke, we would not consider any actors as co-sponsors of the project of social democracy who were committed primarily to patriarchal or other forms of social insurance that did not seek to institutionalize social rights. Comparing these different approaches reveals that the positional interests anchored in the social structure (those identified by class-theoretical explanations) certainly did play a role. But so too did political, moral or social-strategic, and civic interests. The importance of such motives in explaining the genesis of social democracy underscores that the latter is not merely a party program reflecting specific class interests; it is instead a universalistic model of democracy.

Actor theory also suggests that the *rational choice* approach, which reduces human motivations to rational, egoistic calculation, falls short both as a theoretical explanation of the genesis of the social welfare state and as a paradigm for undertaking historical and comparative investigations. The only account of political actors fully consistent with the rational choice perspective is the class theory approach discussed earlier. But if this approach were strictly true, then not a single European society would ever have become social democratic. Obviously, some have, so the facts themselves speak against rational choice explanations of European history.

Diverse actors, multiple contexts

The project of social democracy can garner support from a range of different economic, political, social, and cultural interests depending on the specific goals it pursues and the rationales furnished for its adoption. Cross-national comparisons reveal the diversity of possible constellations of actors within social democracy, while providing context-specific explanations for their motivations to act. We may distinguish:

1 actors with *economic interests*, such as trade unions, which represent the interests of dependent employees, civil servants, and other occupational branches tied to the social welfare state. They depend directly on the guarantees of social democracy.
2 actors with *political interests* (e.g., parties), either of an economic, positional character, or consisting of citizens cooperating politically. Depending on the traditions of the country in question, these may be: social democratic, left-wing socialist, Christian democratic/welfare state-oriented, populist, or agrarian parties.
3 actors with *moral or cultural interests*: churches, other types of religious communities, intellectuals and academic subcultures, or actors from civil society.

Important elements of the social democratic agenda may be supported even by actors who have no direct socio-economic or political-tactical stake in it. That is, social democracy may be embraced for political and moral reasons, or as a political tactic with other goals in mind. Behind any specific social democratic policy, one may uncover broad coalitions of actors that reach deeply into the ranks of conservative parties and, in individual cases, may even include liberal parties. The number and type of actors supporting social democratic policies thus depend on the specific situation. Economic crises, crises of political confidence, the rise of protest parties and of protest in civil society are all phenomena that may – if only temporarily – heighten the receptivity of party politicians to at least some elements of social democracy.[18] Thus the determination of who will be an actor in social democracy does not take place exclusively or even primarily outside the political system; instead, it depends on fluctuating contexts of the political process itself.

Political parties

In a liberal democracy, parties are responsible for designing programs and institutions that give political and legislative form to the social interests that back social democracy. The latitude such parties enjoy to do this is influenced by two factors: their ties to the interest-articulating structures of the intermediary system of associations and organizations, and an intact, inclusive political public sphere.[19] At any rate this was the historical prerequisite that permitted moral-political interests and social learning experiences to be incorporated into the political program of social democracy in the United States during the 1930s and in Sweden ever since then.

Social democratic parties have always been programmatic; further-more, they have usually been "membership" parties with well-defined bases of support. These characteristics follow from their historical self-image and their reformist aspirations. Elaborate, comprehensive pro-grams were supposed to describe and justify the social changes that the parties hoped to achieve.[20] Their mass memberships embodied the parties' claim to mobilize a majority of society in favor of their reform projects. There was thus an internal connection between the party's organization and role, and the political project of social democracy. In classical party democracy as it emerged from the European workers' movement in the nineteenth century, political parties were to represent socio-economic positional interests or the chief currents of interest in society, aggregating these into political programs designed to gain majority support. Thus, elections could be interpreted as plebiscites about the basic direction of social change.

But the model of party democracy assumed a further condition: a radical pluralism of interests and values in modern society that in prin-ciple could never be superseded.[21] Only a broad array of competing parties could maintain the linkages that direct democracy requires. The spectrum of parties and their programs would mirror the pluralism of values and interests as these exist in society, and actually import the latter into the heart of the decision-making processes at the nation-state level. Thus, elections are not – or should not be – plebiscites about per-sonnel or leadership; they are referenda about *public affairs*, competing programs of action. Confidence that parties in a democracy actually could work that way inspired hopes that social democracy might over-come the resistance of powerful business interests and mobilize public pressure following its electoral successes.[22]

The actual practice of party democracy in Western European coun-tries has in some ways approximated this image of it.[23] But even in its heyday there were always two blemishes on the record of party democ-racy. The party leadership almost always had the upper hand over the base and the party apparatus; consequently, parties rarely acted like dis-cursive communities, communicating society's consensus to the politi-cal system.[24] Still, they were more like associations in Alexis de Tocqueville's sense than like bureaucratic *machines* as understood by Max Weber.[25] Moreover, it was never accurate to talk about the transla-tion of unambiguous programs decided by plebiscite into parliamen-tary and governmental edicts. Programmatic alternatives submitted to the public were always rather vague. And once the parties assumed power, many of the policies they adopted were never submitted to public scrutiny and debate. In addition, in political systems with pro-portional representation, majorities could normally only be achieved by forming coalitions. Social democratic parties, therefore, could not avoid compromising with the interests and views of their coalition partners.

The outcome was a rather opaque politics, in which very few voters found exactly what they had been led to expect, and what they thought they had authorized, in the decisions of the parliaments and governments they had chosen. Nevertheless, votes cast for the parties did on the whole enable voters to choose among the alternative policy directions that the former advocated. And there was a demonstrable relationship between their electoral programs and subsequent government policies.[26] In principle, then, there was a well-established linkage between the internal democracy and discourses of "membership" parties and the actions of their leaders in power.

To be sure, even in the era of maximum party democracy the parties were never the "transmission belts" they have been pictured to be, automatically moving society's interests into the centers of state decision-making with no significant loss of steering capacity. Instead, they were just one element among others in a "parallelogram of forces." Yet they were the *strongest* force in the political field, and their leaders' decisions consistently adhered to the parties' official programs and to the public profiles that the parties advocated and to which their members remained committed. There was simply no other way for them to maintain legitimacy in the public arena and among their own members.

In a classical *party democracy* the parties are the principal agents in a complex of other political actors, all mediating between society and politics. They aggregate, concentrate, and integrate the interests and values of the civic groups, associations, and organizations that they can reach. Likewise, the latter direct their political concerns to the parties, their chief conduits to the centers of power.[27] Such intermediary actors have an important function in a party democracy. They articulate societal interests and values, initiate and shape public discourse about political problems, and propose alternatives in response to such problems. Finally, they help to shape the public sphere, where parties must seek majority support for their own goals, by reaching out to the mass media and other public forums. The whole web of intermediary actors thus has always been more than merely a vehicle for influencing the parties. It has long represented and shaped a *public space*, where practical discourses are conducted, and problem-solving proposals are floated that might eventually garner majority support. This sort of mediation has helped to rationalize, stabilize, and manage conflicting interests over the long term. Cooperation with the trade unions, one of the most powerful actors on the intermediary scene, gave added heft to social democracy in the political arena.

A cross-national comparison, in which key indicators of social democracy were related to political identity and the duration of participation in government by different parties, confirms the conclusions that theory would lead us to expect.[28] Manfred G. Schmidt proved that long periods of government participation by secular conservative or liberal parties correlated unambiguously with weakly developed social democracies.

Political Theory

Conversely, when social democratic parties participated in government for long periods, the indicators of social democracy gained strength. Finally, long tenures in government by Christian democratic or secular center parties corresponded to moderately strong development of social democracy (see table 2.1). These contrasts suggest two interesting findings for actor theory: *First*, as the chief actors in the political system,

Table 2.1 Structures of party democracy in twenty-three countries: participation in government by conservative, liberal, centrist, and leftist parties, 1950–98, and the strength of social democratic indicators[29]

Country	Secular-conservative parties	Liberal parties	Christian-democratic and secular center parties	Social democratic parties	Others	Strength of "social democracy"
Australia	67.5	0	0	32.5	0	Relatively low
Austria	0	1.5	36.3	56.9	5.3	Very high
Belgium	0	16.3	51.8	29.6	2.3	Very high
Canada	32.1	0	67.9	0	0	Medium
Denmark	14.4	26.3	3.7	53.5	2.1	Very high
Finland	9.9	11.9	33.3	29.8	15.1	Very high
France	29.0	18.8	13.6	16.5	22.1	High
Germany, Federal Republic of	0	18.1	55.6	22.7	3.6	Very high
Greece	44.5	10.4	0	26.5	18.6	Medium
Great Britain	70.8	0	0	29.2	0	Relatively low
Iceland	7.9	39.9	28.6	22.6	1.0	Medium
Ireland	65.8	0	20.7	11.2	2.3	Medium
Italy	0	7.5	64.2	21.0	7.3	High
Japan	97.2	0	0	2.0	0.8	Relatively low
Luxembourg	0	20.4	49.2	30.4	0	Very high
Netherlands	0	21.2	56.2	20.6	2.0	Very high
New Zealand	74.0	0	0	25.1	0.9	Relatively low
Norway	12.8	3.5	10.9	72.8	0	Very high
Portugal	0.3	23.8	2.3	10.7	62.9	Relatively low
Spain	4.4	0	11.6	25.1	58.9	Relatively low
Sweden	4.1	7.1	10.3	75.9	2.6	Very high
Switzerland	14.3	31.8	30.0	23.9	0	High
United States	57.1	0	42.9	0	0	Relatively low
Median	26.4	11.2	25.6	27.8	9.0	

parties in government decisively influence the prospects for the full development of social democracy. *Second*, social democratic parties tend to advance the cause of social democracy, but so do Christian democratic and secular center parties, though to a lesser extent.

The transformation of parties

Classical European party democracies are gradually being transformed into "media democracies" of an entirely new type. That shift has fundamentally altered the parties' capacity to act, even those usually regarded as the chief actors in social democracy.[30] In modern media democracies, programmatic parties hoping to open channels of communication between civil society, including trade unions, and the political system have less and less leeway. Structural stresses offer parties and the public sphere as a whole less chance to conduct discourses centered on the standards of justice and basic social values.

Actors in the global arena

For some time now the project of global democratization, at least the aspects of it that matter most to social democracy, has been propelled in several directions by the construction of new institutions, the creation of extra-institutional structures, and their networking.[31] However, many of these developments have been blocked ever since a conservative administration took power in the United States in 2000, and was reelected in 2004. The administration of George W. Bush seems determined to seek a unilateral, hegemonic world order, which it believes is legitimated by its political objectives and which it intends to construct by relying on its military superiority. The economic, strategic, and geopolitical interests behind the Bush administration typically resist the goals of democratic globalization as well as the ecological and social imbedding of transnational markets. Their main objective on an economic level is to enact the *Washington consensus*, which undercuts social democratic values and marks a departure from most postwar US foreign policy, which has usually invoked multilateralist principles. Even though this emerging geopolitical strategy does align with certain traditions in the US political culture, we must not assume that it expresses a stable consensus of American political strategy.[32] The economic motives behind such a novel strategy are obviously very powerful, but they cannot be cited as proof that any "imperialistic determinism" is at work. It is rather the case that one strategic political option supported by a coalition of interests has become temporarily dominant. There are alternatives to it on the American political scene that are quite capable of gaining majority support: namely, the Democratic Party, the American peace movement, and the environmental movement. Still, the example of America's "go it alone" foreign policy underscores a generally valid point: the process of positive globalization depends to an enormous extent on the acquiescence of the big veto-wielding players, and that can never be taken for granted.

We may also imagine that the emergence of counterweights in the arena of world politics, especially the European Union or at least a core group of EU member nations might have a moderating influence on US geopolitical strategy.[33] Thus, the possibility of progress in the politics of global democratization and imbedding the world's economy depends largely on the capacity of the European Union to act geopolitically and to assemble coalitions of competent political actors.

Realistically, there is a limited number of actors whose interests converge on the project of global democratization and who also have power in the global arena. We may briefly enumerate them.

1 Most of transnational civil society, including the constructive wing of the so-called anti-globalization movement and its 4,500 chapters.[34]
2 The great majority of the world's social democratic movements with an interest in democratic globalization, especially its affiliated political parties organized into the Socialist International. The moderate left wing of the American Democrats, which has considerable influence in party councils and perhaps the potential to become its majority faction, should also be included.
3 Regional systems of political cooperation which have emerged, more or less tightly integrated, on every continent, to capitalize on the possibilities of concerted action (the EU, ASEAN, SAARC, and Mercosur).
4 A range of Third World countries and the new democracies just arising in those areas. The People's Republic of China is just starting to make its presence felt as an important actor in promoting some issues on the agenda of positive globalization.[35]
5 The main political currents among member states of the European Union, or at any rate a coalition of influential countries aligned with the axis of France and the Federal Republic of Germany.

As yet these actors have not elaborated a consensus about common strategies. They do share a fundamental interest, however, in replacing both the libertarian form of globalization and American unilateralism by a policy of fair regulation.[36] In short, they agree enough about their fundamental interests and political objectives to cooperate in the medium term. Agreement to coordinate policy and shape events is even more likely if they realize that continuing negative globalization will impose economic, social, and political costs that may increase pressure on recalcitrant actors to toe the line. For many actors, refusal to cooperate would entail the loss of political autonomy.

None of this should obscure the deep dilemma facing social democratic parties in affluent industrial and service societies. On one hand, these parties have overwhelmingly subscribed to the project of extending and deepening democracy via global cooperation in their program discussions and public commitments. And they have vociferously advocated the reimbedding of global markets in socially and ecologically responsible structures. Yet when it comes to their interest in winning elections on the home front, they are much less enthusiastic about drawing practical consequences from their declared commitment to policies of globalization. When they must act, they face two daunting obstacles. The first, the *electoral dilemma*, involves their need to serve the socio-economic interests of their own voters, rather than those that would benefit people in other parts of the world. The second obstacle concerns the obligation they all feel to maintain the most cooperative relationship possible with the administration currently in office in Washington if they wish to accomplish anything noteworthy in a variety of other foreign policy areas. But countervailing pressures from some parts of the parties' rank and file to hold the line on global democratization and a fairer world order may suffice to overcome these obstacles.

Judging by its traditions, potential, and projects, the European Union is the political actor most capable of mobilizing resources for social democracy on a global scale. Of course, it remains to be seen whether the Union will be able to develop this potential fully. Its limited military strength compared to the USA is not really a disadvantage.[37] The European Union can define its proper role and gain the support of a majority of other actors only in its capacity as a civil world power that achieves its goals by cooperation in a participatory world order.[38] Even a conservative US administration will be obliged to cooperate with the European Union over the long term, not least because it could not bear the financial strains of a policy of unilateral worldwide intervention by itself, and because it requires a bare minimum of international legitimacy as a power resource in domestic politics.

The economic, cultural, and political interests of the European Union suggest that it should act as a counterweight to American unilateralism while cooperating in the creation of a democratic global order.[39] The political model that underlies the European Union itself, its transition from the previous political confrontations among the current member states to a new form of sovereignty undertaken for the sake of political cooperation, can itself serve as an example of transnational democratization. In its basic features the EU appears to be a successful solution to the problem of how nation-states can retain much of their sovereignty, while ceding some of it to new forms of transnational and supranational authority. The European Union has found that sovereignty can be divided and apportioned among different levels of authority. It is still an open question whether and when it will manage to elaborate a common foreign and security policy, and thereby become a formidable actor in transnational democratization and social-ecological imbedding of the world economy.

2.4 Political steering and social democracy

State guarantees as obligations

The only constitutional form appropriate to social democracy is representative democracy under the rule of law. The latter's political goals, institutions, and organizational forms are all designed to validate universal human and civil rights. Indeed, all the efforts of social democracy are directed toward securing the formal validity and real-world efficacy of those rights. Given the organizational forms of a complex, pluralistic, and participatory democracy, the theory of social democracy will evince a straightforward preference for the democratic juridical state.[40] This kind of state can guarantee the formal validity of equal universal rights, but by itself it cannot also underwrite their real-world meaningfulness for all citizens. The state has a political obligation to enforce those rights, but can do so only if society itself assumes partial responsibility for attaining its own goals. To encourage society's self-organizing capacity, policy-makers can promulgate pragmatic social reforms especially of redistributive, restructuring, and regulatory policy.

The social structure can be rearranged in several ways consistent with the state's obligation to secure basic rights. Economic governance, the educational system, and social welfare policy all fall within the state's area of competence. Likewise it can experiment with forms of co-determination and try to democratize society's subsystems, provided that it does not undermine their efficiency. Regulatory policy should encourage society to oversee its own activities. This is especially true of the economic subsystem, in which many sectors are capable of considerable self-policing. Redistributive policy should be concerned with achieving justice in the distribution of life chances in society generally, and especially in the areas of education, labor and tax policy, and the organization and provision of social security. In all these spheres of action it is the state that can guarantee the real-world efficacy of rights, because it is the only institution with a mandate to make regulations binding on the entire society. Nevertheless, there is no reason why the state has to monopolize service provision. Instead, in both the regulative and distributive dimensions, it should encourage actors and structures to assume responsibility for organizing the manner of service provision that best blends efficiency with participation.[41]

As Heller argued, social democracy emerges when the material juridical state is extended to include the entire social order, albeit through a process suffused by democracy and the rule of law. Hence, every sphere of society in which rights are at stake is fair game for political reform. All these spheres may be reconstructed by social policy-making, although their processes are governed by political steering. *Political steering* is the sum of all activities by which society – whether in an institutionalized form or not – effectively influences its own structure and development. *Distributive policy* is the sum of the political actions that follow a specific model of the distribution of social opportunities. The *state* is the aggregate of all those political institutions through which society undertakes to regulate itself through binding decisions or obligatory programs of action. Actions and decisions, such as those of civil society, can also be considered political when they intend to lay down binding rules for a collectivity, even though they operate outside of state institutions. Consequently, social democracy is a product of *governance*, which may be defined as the sum total of opportunities for political regulation that include government action, but are not limited to it.

In short, "meta-decisions" must be reached about laying the groundwork for future action in a given sector of society and about the most effective ways for the state to meet its obligation to guarantee rights. In the final analysis those decisions can only be reached in a democratically legitimate way if they are referred to the deliberations of civil society and to the public decision-making and opinion-formation that accompany it. They depend not only on the rights norms themselves, but also on contingent circumstances and collective experiences that are too subtle and heterogeneous to fit neatly into any institutional model of political steering in social democracy.

From monism to pluralism in political steering

In principle modern societies have three modes of political regulation available, which may be combined to yield a whole spectrum of mixed approaches: the state, the market, and civil society.[42] The decision about which of these modes of steering ought to be selected for which politically determined goals, and whether one of them should be used exclusively or primarily, is a *meta-political* issue. Such decisions involve empirical judgments about the kinds of effects each instrument might have, the limits of its effects, and possible unintended consequences. But they also entail value judgments about the suitability of each instrument in light of its possible impact on the autonomy and responsibility of the citizenry. As a type of regulation, civil society is unique in its dependence on the availability of a steering resource, solidarity, which the state can neither generate nor replace, at least in the short run.

If one could write a history of social regulation after the fashion of Karl Polanyi, who did so for the market–state nexus, it would show that all three modes have always played some role in regulation throughout human civilization, although their relative importance has varied dramatically.

It would contradict the principles of an empirically oriented theory to emphasize one of the three modes of steering in isolation from the others, or to enshrine one as *the* pure model or ideal type. That would amount to a monist approach to the steering problem. Instead, empirical reasons lead us to prefer pluralism – the combination of several modes – as the only realistic approach to steering in modern societies.

The traditional debate about steering, which once offered a stark choice between market and state guidance, was always ideologically charged and thoroughly misleading. It stacked the deck from the start against a more complex conceptualization of the steering problem. Current empirical research proves that all three modes of steering have evident advantages, limitations, and drawbacks, and that each needs to be complemented by the others. We have learned to recognize the need for complementary approaches by virtue of theoretically well-founded insights into: (a) functional breakdowns that may occur in every one of the modes – civil society, market, and state – that cause them to fail to attain legitimate political ends; (b) the functional advantages of each mode; and (c) possibilities for combining them in new ways. By learning to work around these functional breakdowns and by optimizing the contributions of all the modes, we can achieve a well-designed coordination of regulatory action, while making it easier to meet politically defined goals.

The theoretical hallmark of *orthodox liberalism* has of course always been its tendency to imagine the market in isolation from the contexts in which it operates – state and civil society – and to attribute to its idealized form a capacity to harmonize most aspects of commodity and service distribution. Having proclaimed the market to be the locus of freedom, liberalism further identified it with the sphere of human and civil rights per se. That move exempted the market from empirical scrutiny concerning its suitability to achieve politically defined goals. Thus, the market qua abstract model was idealized as an instrument of steering and simultaneously immunized against empirical criticism, because it was presumed to be equivalent to freedom itself.

In this respect, the main currents of *orthodox socialism* presented almost a mirror image of liberalism. Until recently, they ritualized and idealized state intervention, which they interpreted as the logical expression of the collective will of society. Likewise, they abstracted state control from its moorings in civil society and market steering. The theoretical blueprints of orthodox socialism thus attributed to the state the role of a supreme executor of the general will, supposed to override the private and particular interests expressed in the market and civil society.

Meanwhile, for many years only the *anarchist* and *anarcho-syndicalist* theories idealized civil society in analogous ways, writing off both the market and the state as instruments of domination intent on suppressing the true general will. Civil society has undergone a renaissance since the end of the age of confrontation between rival ideological systems. Not surprisingly, the kind of thinking that once idealized it has been reinvigorated under a slightly different aegis, even finding adherents among academic theorists. The republican-libertarian project of entrusting the entire political steering of society to the self-governing capacities of civil society is the most recent expression of this tradition.[43]

All three modes of steering have functional drawbacks. Twentieth-century experience suggests that the modern theory of social democracy cannot justify an a priori affinity with or aversion to any one of the instruments of steering: market, state, or civil society. In making its choice to combine them in the most advantageous way, it must always think pragmatically and do what is most likely to solve the problem at hand in accord with its legitimating values.

The effects of globalization

Claus Offe argues that social and economic globalization has precipitated a rapid spread of market logic in both national and transnational societies, coupled with a severe retrenchment in the nation-state's capacity to control events.[44] These trends demand a new design of social and political institutions. The balance of market, state, and society, as well as the steering media available for influencing it (money, power, and solidarity), need to be readjusted to meet the changed situation. Ecological and social experiences in the decades since the onset of the recent wave of economic globalization suggest that a reorganization of cultural and political steering capacities is overdue and will have to confront the growing need for regulation. The internal steering capacity of the modern state has declined for two reasons.[45] First, centralized, bureaucratic interference in complex contemporary societies has in many ways proven to be ineffective and off the mark. Second, a large portion of the younger generation in affluent democracies has shifted the direction of its civic engagement. They are no longer as willing to get involved in the affairs of the major institutions of the political system, toward which most expectations of participation and efforts at political education have until now been aimed. New forms of social and political steering will have to emerge.

Markets need to be reimbedded ecologically, culturally, and socially through political regulations that have been thoroughly aired in public. This is the best way of assigning a higher priority to the norms of an intact life-world and the validity of social rights than to economic logic. Otherwise, democracies could suffer a serious loss of legitimation, while social evolution escapes human control and the impact of accelerating globalization outstrips political accountability. But for now such demands cannot easily be met through the traditional patterns of nationally centered, statist, hierarchical regulation. That dilemma has raised the question of whether an engaged civil society and new forms of cooperation between it and the state might in the future help improve our political capacity to steer social evolution.[46] The *re-regulation* of the economy now on the agenda is not merely a matter of developing transnational institutions; rather, it depends on our ability to regain opportunities for democratic deliberation and participatory decision-making. A vital, transnationally networked civil society can play a powerful role in this process of repoliticization.[47]

The state

The democratic constitutional state, organized as a participatory democracy, is the normative standard for social democracy. In it, citizens would have their rights guaranteed, and they would be given the opportunity to have a say in the decisions that affect their lives. In contemporary politics, participatory democracy means a party-based democracy, supported, checked, and supplemented by a strong intermediary system of societal initiatives, associations, and groups, and an active civil society. As long as the aforementioned normative standards are met, social democracy cannot justify a preference for any particular form of state organization from among the abundant historical possibilities.[48]

The regulatory and redistributive functions of the state in modern societies have been cast into doubt for three reasons:[49]

1 Socio-economic globalization has caused the state to lose sovereignty in external affairs.
2 The state has lost sovereignty in its domestic affairs because of the increasing complexity of societal subsystems.
3 The modern state is overextended. There are limits to its ability to act effectively which show up in various functional "deficits."

Concerning the first point, the more pessimistic theories even claim that sovereign nation-states, and indeed regional systems of political cooperation such as the EU, cannot hope to succeed in their regulatory or distributive policies.[50] Such criticism finds apt expression in an elaborate metaphor that pictures markets as a boundless ocean in which nation-states are only so many islands fighting against a rising tide, with no way to influence ocean currents or sea level.[51]

In open markets the nation-state now allegedly lacks full sovereign control over interest rates, much less enormous investment flows and financial transactions. Moreover, the social-welfare regime, corporate governance, and the system of macro-economic regulation are all exposed to the winds of global competition. In short all these phenomena have slipped through the net of state sovereignty that democratic nation-states once took for granted.[52] Under these circumstances no democratic nation-state can risk making regulations in these critical sectors, since global markets might react to them by initiating capital flight, which in turn would lead to a net decline in social welfare.

The *libertarians* argue that these trends are beneficial, since they insure that the objective rationality manifested in economic logic will trump the fickle decisions of modern mass democracies, thereby serving the aggregate interests of society more efficiently.[53] According to this sort of analysis, the operation of the free market leaves the nation-state few options other than to make itself an attractive location for doing business by adapting its economic and social systems to the exigencies of the world market. If they were right, the state would have little room to shape policy in the ways it once did. As a result, the normative standards so closely associated with the validity claims of social democracy would go unfulfilled on account of new realities that the state cannot master.

There are several twists on the more empirical versions of the thesis that the state is losing its sovereignty over domestic matters on account of the level of internal complexity attained by societal subsystems and their resistance to control from the outside.[54] One "holistic" version observes that state regulatory and distributive policies continue to produce suboptimal welfare results on account of the complexity and interdependencies characteristic of subsystems in the political economy.[55] A second (the pragmatic-functional variant) asserts that a hierarchical, centralized state will not be able to recognize early enough the constraints on action that emerge in the functional systems of society. Hence, it will be in no position to steer those systems in a functionally appropriate, efficient manner.[56] Another variant drawn from systems theory argues that, given the level of complexity attained in the subsystems of modern society and their closed functional codes, the societal subsystem of the state/politics will no longer be able to steer them from the outside.[57]

Clearly, the state faces functional limitations, eroded sovereignty, and problems inherent in its very form of organization.[58] But none of these flaws proves to be insuperable or absolute. The state still retains the capacities and resources to achieve its aims, despite globalization and intensified social and economic complexity.[59]

The thesis about the state's loss of sovereignty in internal and external affairs is empirically tenable only in a modified form. Today state activity is indeed subject to serious limitations; yet it retains considerable latitude to make distributive and regulatory policy calculated to attain social democratic aims. Whether or not the state uses that latitude depends on the ability of state actors to achieve desirable ends in new ways, as for example by developing new forms of cooperation. In discussions about updating social democracy's concept of the state, the notion of the state as facilitator has played an especially prominent part. The facilitative state moves beyond the traditional obsession with attaining objectives through "command and control" measures. Instead it acts as an underwriter or moderator for reaching established goals. In implementing its policies it relies on whatever social, economic, and civil society-based actors seem best suited to attain those aims in the most efficient, economical manner.

This shift in thinking about the fulfillment of state responsibilities actually began as early as the 1970s in some European countries, when local government services started to be privatized. The state continued to guarantee that they would be offered affordably, but no longer assumed direct responsibility for their delivery. Comparable forms of this new division of labor began to emerge in other areas, for example between state and civil society, state and private economy, state and associations, and even state and citizens.[60]

The thesis concerning the essential shortcomings of state steering is empirically well substantiated. Nevertheless, the state's functional deficiencies do not justify the libertarian call to minimize its responsibilities. In fact, the other available modes of societal steering, the market and civil society, exhibit flaws of their own, ones that are if anything more worrisome. Neither of the latter has the legitimacy or capacity to handle the crucial challenge of making regulations regarded as binding society-wide. So, again, we need to adopt a prudent, pluralist approach to steering. It would draw on the market and civil society to provide problem-specific forms of steering in certain cases. Sometimes, these would replace the state, but in other cases they would merely supplement or oversee it.

The market

Twentieth-century experiences have shown that the coordination of micro-economic decisions usually can be accomplished best by the market. But certain qualifications must be appended to this generalization. For one thing, higher political authorities must first have created the framework within which the market's functions are defined. Moreover, market functions have to be subject to rigorous oversight. Finally, the economic decisions that are to be coordinated should have already been established and hedged in by the political decisions of the entire society.[61] Markets, in short, must operate in a symbiotic environment featuring a complex system of politically defined conditions, limits, and steering services. Only then can markets insure the optimal welfare outcome for the entire society in their assigned spheres by following their own functional logic, using prices to make decisions on resource allocation. The (uncontroversial) list of inherent market deficiencies includes the following items.[62]

- Self-regulated markets tend to limit competition, and even eliminate it entirely in extreme cases, due to the emergence of oligopolies and monopolies.
- Self-regulated markets cannot supply the infrastructure services on which they depend, or provide the public goods the availability of which they presuppose.
- The logic of the market only satisfies demand that is backed up by purchasing power; its distributive outcomes are unjust in light of moral criteria.
- On their own, self-regulating markets cannot perform crucial economic tasks such as creating full employment on socially defensible terms, or insuring steady growth and stable prices.
- Self-regulating markets regard natural capital as a free good, and thus tend to destroy the ecological foundations of human civilization.
- Market logic is present-oriented, since it takes its bearings only from current demand and the most likely extrapolations from it.

Markets perform an irreplaceable steering function for society. But they can do this only because the political system has already created a framework for them, and has provided various preparatory and accompanying services that establish the guidelines within which their economic logic may unfold. In his study of the history of the nexus between markets and society, Karl Polanyi demonstrated that markets were always deeply imbedded in the cultural, social, and political contexts of societies that sheltered them except for a brief, catastrophic exception at the beginning of the nineteenth century.[63] There is thus no reason to cling to the counterfactual assumption that markets can function sustainably on their own, or that they would work best if the social contexts of imbedding were dissolved in favor of pure market self-regulation. Ever since the Great Depression all capitalist societies have returned to their previous practices, replacing regulatory monism by a dualism that relies on both markets and the logic of social steering.

After a brief dalliance with radical liberal panaceas meant to get rid of encrusted, state-owned enterprises dating back to the communist era, even post-communist societies have eventually lined up behind a pragmatic policy of imbedding markets. At the dawn of the twenty-first century no profound gulf remains to divide the basic political orientations of modern democracies, even if the old clichés persist in the political arena about the superior logic of either a pure market system or pure state supervision. In short, as far as practical economic policy-making is concerned, there is no longer any alternative to regulatory dualism.

With those caveats, we then conclude that market coordination has proven to be the most effective instrument, in a broad range of private goods, for maximizing general social welfare. But throughout the history of the theoretical discussions about social democracy, this well-established social-scientific insight has had a hard time gaining acceptance even though the lessons of everyday experience have so obviously borne it out. By now it has gradually prevailed in different countries and social democratic factions, especially since the 1980s.

Civil society

The notion of civil society is crucial for the theory of social democracy; however, for a number of reasons civil society cannot be regarded as the successor conception of social democracy in its post-authoritarian phase. Today, we can indeed recognize that statism fails not only on ethical grounds (for not promoting autonomy), but also because, as a mode of steering, it runs up against ever more intractable limitations in complex modern societies and starts to contradict its own normative premises. A later chapter on civil society will describe its immense potential for democratic self-steering and grass-roots influence on the political system. Its activities will turn out to be an increasingly vital resource for political steering in modern societies on all levels. But even civil society is subject to certain characteristic functional drawbacks as a regulatory method. These include:[64]

- the actors' lack of clear, fully articulated mandates
- the fact that the steering resource known as solidarity cannot be counted on; its origins are serendipitous and it is often unsustainable.
- the inchoateness of actors in civil society; they do not develop momentum toward complex, mature forms.
- the "dark side" of civil society; i.e., the tendency for selfish motives to hide behind altruistic-sounding goals.

The inevitability of pluralism in steering

In conclusion, a pragmatic pluralism in steering approaches is the only policy that seems appropriate for the aims of social democracy. None of the available instruments appears to be consistently superior to the others in every respect, but we should adopt some rough guidelines for choosing among them.

First, the most extensive possible coordination via the economic allocative decisions of markets should be preferred as long as they remain politically imbedded. *Second*, self-organization and self-regulation in civil society should be pushed as far as practicable, as long as the state continues to guarantee rights. *Third*, the state should provide unconditional guarantees of rights, but in the most cooperative form possible. Even if the state must act as the ultimate guarantor of citizens' rights, it can fulfill that responsibility better if its decisions are modified and supplemented by the regulatory powers of the market and civil society.

2.5 Democratizing society

Libertarian evasions

There is simply no legitimate place in the theory of libertarian democracy for the project of democratizing society. If one assumes that the meaning of liberty in economy and society is exhausted by the self-regulating market and freedom of contract, then democratic theory will lack the normative concepts even to entertain the idea of democratizing society. From the libertarian viewpoint there are three arguments that speak against that project. *First*, the freedom of property is a crucial element of the concept of negative liberty itself; *second*, society is understood as a private sphere from which the state and politics ought to be excluded; and *third*, societal subsystems will become dysfunctional if the boundaries between private and public are not scrupulously respected. The theory of social democracy takes seriously the risk that universal fundamental rights could be vitiated whenever there is too great an asymmetry in societal cooperation. But the libertarians either disdain that worry or insinuate that it is a pretext for state meddling in society, which by their standards would amount to a rights violation in itself.[65]

Normative and functional conditions

The democratization of society is a crucial issue for the theory of social democracy, because it is precisely in the spheres of non-state activity (except for the private and intimate spheres) that fundamental rights must be made meaningful. Virtually all of the major functional sectors of society – the economy, the educational system, the scientific establishment, the media, public administration, and the social security systems – are characterized by asymmetrical relations of command and subordination. Patterns of authority in these spheres of social cooperation raise two inescapable questions that touch on fundamental rights and democratic theory. First, given that many people are radically dependent on the commands of others, how can their human dignity and autonomy be assured despite their dependency? Second, how might their participation in functional decisions contribute to enabling each subsystem to perform optimally within the larger social ensemble? In short, the problem is how to secure the conditions of social autonomy.

In the tradition of social democratic theory, the prevailing view has been that social democracy should be committed to democratizing all social subsystems, especially the core subsystem, the economy.[66] Proponents believed that radical democratization should ultimately import democracy's *logic of political decision-making* into every functional subsystem of society, so that these would henceforth be governed by deliberation and majority rule. However, in light of more sophisticated political values championed by the present theory of social democracy, that assumption looks untenable for both normative and functional reasons.

Comparative analysis suggests that decisions about society's subsystems should be made at the highest level of a society's democratic institutions. No societal subsystem can claim that its structures, workings, and impact on the broader society ought to be exempt from political legitimation, as long as its actions affect a circle wider than just that of the decision-makers. There are therefore three factors that come into play in decisions concerning the political ordering of society's subsystems.[67]

1 Democratic institutions at the macro-level of society have the ultimate authority to make such decisions.
2 The functional contributions of the respective subsystems to society as a whole must be addressed.
3 The basic rights of the participant in each functional system must be protected.

In a modernized theory of social democracy, the notion of the *democratization of society* may continue to prove useful, albeit in a modified form. However, it could be misleading if it were misinterpreted to mean that subsystem participants ought to follow the logic of simple democratic majority rule in every case.

Functionally appropriate participation

Social democracy ought to favor a form of participatory decision-making in the functional systems of society that would enable both universalistic criteria and functional logics specific to each case to operate simultaneously. Nevertheless, the full democratization of society's functional spheres would contradict the principles and functional conditions of social democracy, paradoxical as that may sound. First, the efficient operation of the various subsystems might be compromised – precisely the factor that determines whether or not a given functional system can provide the benefits that society expects of it. Second, democratization qua majority rule might undermine the state's steering competence over its subsystems. Third, unless legitimacy had been secured via consent, this move could replace democratic, popular sovereignty by group sovereignty.

Consequently, "democratization" as understood by social democracy should not authorize politically guided decision-making to trump system-specific functional logics. What *can* be legitimized normatively and functionally, however, is a form of participatory decision-making that would not disturb functional efficiency. This version of democratization, which would give a say to each subsystem's stakeholders, would seek legitimation in the principles of rights and democratic policy-making. At a minimum it would include the following features.

1 It is imperative to guarantee to employees and other stakeholders sufficient rights of co-determination to secure their social autonomy.
2 The right to co-determination should make it easy to draw on the functional expertise and experience that some individuals can contribute.
3 There should be enough flexibility in co-determination rules to insure that the functional logic of each sector is respected, for example by calling on individual experts with responsibilities in a given area.
4 The functional imperatives of each subsystem should determine the form and decision-making procedures of co-determination.

As long as these criteria are met, co-determination in every social subsystem ought to be mandated; indeed it should actually improve the system's functioning. There are only two caveats: co-determination must not be allowed to upset the balance between functional logic and majority decision, and the decision-making schedules must respect reasonable deadlines. These criteria also allow us to decide what degree and kind of co-determination the affected stakeholders ought to enjoy vis-à-vis management prerogatives.[68] In a business enterprise, for example, investment decisions touch the very core of the functional imperatives that a firm must obey. However, issues such as the organization of the workplace or equal treatment for employees in compensation, qualifications, promotions, etc., concern primarily human dignity, and thus invite more extensive co-determination.

The theory of social democracy defines both upper and lower limits for institutionalizing the requisite strategies of societal democratization and formulates a set of well-founded decision-making criteria for the middle range. It would be a mistake to justify the denial of co-determination by invoking the primacy of a subsystem's functional logic. On the other hand, the full democratization of a functional sector must also be rejected, since it might end up vitiating some of the latter's basic functions that enjoy society-wide legitimacy. In light of the theory of social democracy, the "democratization" of societal subsystems, and especially the term "economic democracy", turns out to be a tradition-laden metaphor that is quite misleading in an operational sense. What really matters is finding ways to *institutionalize participation that respects functional imperatives.*

2.6 Civil society and liberal democracy

The central importance of civil society

The theory and practice of civil society are of vital importance to social democracy. The outlook for civil society should not be judged merely by evaluating the potential for civic engagement or the deficiencies of liberal democratic institutional arrangements. Globalization compels us to rethink the social and institutional division of responsibilities. The question may now be phrased anew: "which spheres of life are to be guided, respectively, by political authority, contractually regulated market exchanges, and self-governing, self-reliant communities and organizations of civil society?"[69] As noted, these are the three patterns, plus hybrids, that modern societies have available to guide their development. Once societies have agreed which current decision and steering problems ought to be handled by which patterns, then the relationships among civil society, the market, and the state will become clearer. The age is long past when policy-making monism prevailed and liberals could plausibly claim to rely on the market alone, socialists on the state, and conservatives on the community. Today the only issue still worth debating is what sort of balance should be struck among the three components of social order to respond to the problems facing present-day societies. To make the right decision about the balance among these components of the social order calls for answers to basic political questions concerning the level of civic competence and the availability of solidarity as a steering resource. In fact, civil society's ability to limit the scope of its own competencies is one of the most important tests of its powers of self-reflection and practice.[70] But it is only in civil society itself that political judgment can be cultivated, which is necessary to assign civil society its proper place in relation to the market and the state. In this sense the processes of consensus-building in civil society become a meta-political forum for reaching decisions.[71]

Civil society as a scheme of political steering matters deeply to social democracy for several reasons:

1 Action in civil society directly fulfills democratic theory's postulate that citizens should share in the self-direction of society.
2 Citizens' interests can be taken into account and representative democratic procedures influenced by the input of civil society in the

democratic decision-making processes at every level of the social system.

3 Civic engagement empowers citizens and allows them to play their role more effectively.

4 As one form of solidarity-inspired civic action, civil society can provide social self-help and aid for third parties, especially those affected by misfortunes. They can do so at a level that both quantitatively and qualitatively exceeds anything that victims could claim as an entitlement or that social welfare agencies could offer. Thus, they prove to be the most critical ad hoc structures for promoting social and civic self-reliance.

Socio-economic potentials

The notion of a *third sector* considers the practices of civil society from a socio-economic viewpoint.[72] While the associations and initiatives of civil society are indeed of interest on account of their contributions to self-legislation and self-government, they also do much to enhance social security, welfare, and living standards. Robert Putnam has shown that civic engagement is irreplaceable as a source of non-material well-being. Its effects extend into areas such as emotional and physical health, the sense that one is recognized and leads a meaningful life, and the whole tenor of one's choices and actions.[73] Yet even in terms of the usual economic indicators of wealth-generation, the third sector, especially its non-profit organizations, contributes inestimably to social welfare. Like other organizations and initiatives in civil society, the third sector shares an orientation toward the common good and preference for voluntary action. But above all it undertakes projects in the areas of social and cultural infrastructure. In Germany the number of non-profit organizations in the year 2000 was estimated at 500,000. In the years 1989 to 1998 alone, their number grew by around 25 percent. It is estimated that at least 17 million people are regularly engaged, and that figure is at the low end of the range. It may be assumed that some 21 million are volunteer members of organizations. These statistics look even more impressive when one considers that the total hours invested in activities serving the common good have been estimated at 2.3 billion. Thus, third-sector activities combine on a grand scale economically measurable contributions to well-being, solidarity-inspired community service, and civic engagement that helps improve the quality of democratic government.[74]

How the state may complement civil society

The democratic state does not have to wait patiently until the activities of civil society appear in the desired forms and degree; it can – and indeed it must – actively encourage them. In fact, it bears much of the responsibility for the emergence of a vibrant civil society. The enabling or facilitating state must do more than merely lay the legal and institutional groundwork by underwriting the negative liberties that sustain the positive uses of freedom in civil society. Beyond that, it can undertake a variety of supportive measures – not least by channeling its own behavior into more cooperative forms – that may help to strengthen civil society.[75] The state that civil society needs is thus not the libertarian minimal state, which recognizes as partners only the autonomous private individual and *homo oeconomicus*. Nor is it the conservatives' strong state that finds expression in hierarchical and authoritarian patterns of action. It is the cooperative state of participatory democracy.

The state can and must create ad hoc structures to promote engagement in civil society. Furthermore, through its own cooperative capacities and invitations, it can itself embody an ad hoc structure that encourages the activities of civil society. Evers, Rauch and Stitz have shown that the state cannot easily get along without civic engagement and should stimulate it by reforming the civil service and combating its anti-civil society bias.[76]

Corporate citizenship

One aspect of civil society's activities neglected by the theory of social democracy is that of corporate responsibility within civil society (corporate citizenship). Business enterprises are always also actors in their surrounding social life-world, for which they are thus partially responsible. In short, they are citizens of civil society and as such they have certain obligations. As the example of the United States shows, companies in this alternative mode can accomplish much, often spending large sums and giving their employees temporary leave from their jobs for public service. As long as citizens' action networks remain intact, they can help prevent a situation in which corporations misinterpret their presence in civil society as a marketing device. In that case, the personal and material resources of corporate citizens can do more even than contribute to the social projects and democratic self-determination of civil society. In certain subsystems their integration into the community can spur them to adjust even their economic behavior to the politically defined goals of civil society and the needs of the surrounding life-world.

Civil society on a regional and global scale

Once they move onto the global stage as NGOs, actors in civil society take on an independent role. Their sector-specific regulatory policies help democratize and improve the efficiency of transnational institutions such as the United Nations. Meanwhile, they create networks that intensify regional political cooperation. For these reasons they play a prominent role in nearly every design for world democracy.[77] There is a real danger, of course, that the "hard" transnational institutions will drive the civil society-related ones into the "softer" margins, so that the latter would play mainly a representational role in global politics. Yet recent experience indicates that the latter may still have significant opportunities to shape events. Their irreplaceable contributions have come in three areas: networking multi-level politics in the transnational context; thematizing important issues in the global and national public spheres; and policing the enforcement of transnational agreements. Observers of current trends predict an "accelerated growth of NGOs."[78] Even though actors of transnational civil society are driving anti-globalization protests, it is the NGOs that play the most constructive roles in the global arena. They have fought tenaciously against the global dominance of markets and to reimbed the latter in a responsible transnational regulatory policy, especially in social, ecological, and macro-economic affairs.

Resources, limits, and boundaries

Critics of civil society sometimes object that it actually deepens inequality and relieves pressure on the political system to deliver necessary structural reform. Empirical studies have unearthed two significant findings on these very points. It is certainly true that the poor and long-term unemployed can't usually be induced to cooperate in altruistic social and political initiatives. However, regions in which social and economic inequality is less pronounced exhibit a noticeably greater enthusiasm for civic engagement than do those with more marked inequalities. One possible explanation for that finding might be that the activities of civil society do not in fact divert citizens from trying to influence the political system. On the contrary, the more active civil society is, the more zealous active citizens will be in setting high standards for the performance of the political system and making sure that its decisions serve the common interest.[79] Hence, an invigorated civil society would not divert attention from necessary structural reforms; it would actually improve their prospects of enactment.

In respect to the normative functional components of social democracy, mature civil society can assume the following responsibilities:

1 democratizing selected sectors of the life-world
2 ramping up the level of input that citizens may have on public opinion-formation and decision-making
3 enhancing collective self-help for reasons of solidarity
4 subjecting administrative actions and political planning to democratic review

5 rectifying the consequences of market systems by including local
   economic actors in the accountability structures of civil society
6 providing ad hoc structures for solidarity-inspired activities; remind-
   ing citizens to do their duties and/or actually performing them.

The dwindling role of "membership" parties in European democracies
in the last quarter of the twentieth century has enhanced the importance
of civil society as a bastion of social democracy. Reinforcing that trend
has been the recognition that many of globalization's effects on the life-
world can properly be addressed only in local and regional political
forums. This would be the case, for example, if a single industrial sector
threatened to shut down across an entire region because of global competition. The project of civil society is indeed an important element in
the model of social democracy; however, it cannot become the single
dominant idea.

Closer analysis of the potential effects of and limitations on civil
society's activities might tempt some to misunderstand its true role.
One could imagine that civil society might become an alternative model
of a democratic order, rather than a corrective to the flaws of current
democratic practices or a supplement to existing steering policy. It is
undoubtedly true that civil society, with its unique potential to stimulate social action, opens up new possibilities for direct social democratization and political self-direction. Nevertheless, civil society cannot be
expected to assume the entire burden of doing necessary social steering
or even guaranteeing fundamental rights, and this for several reasons.
First, the policy-making and -implementing structures of civil society
lack the requisite intrinsic complexity to produce optimal results.
Second, there are limits as to how consistent and predictable its behavior would be. Finally, the source of democratic legitimacy in civil society
is inherently particularistic. Civil society should therefore do the things
that it does best, leaving other responsibilities to the state and/or the
market.

Part II

Political Economy

3

The Social Market Economy

3.1 Fundamental rights and political economy

The social interpretation of liberal rights is rooted in an epoch-making historical experience. In the early capitalist phase of European history it was noticed that, if the institutions of private property in the means of production and the market were operated capriciously and arbitrarily, sweeping violations of the rights and opportunities of large segments of the population in their role as economic citizens would ensue. They would end up suffering a significant infringement of their ability to exercise their civil liberties and the political autonomy that these support. Furthermore, empirical observation shows that certain functional deficiencies in the self-regulating market – from boom-and-bust cycles to self-destructive tendencies in inheritance patterns – tend to accumulate risks that jeopardize citizens' rights, opportunities, and vital goods.

Liberal theory, not to mention its libertarian offspring, tends to identify the institutions of the self-regulating market and the freedom to own property with the universal values of political liberalism: liberty and equality. For that reason neither approach can properly address the failures of those institutions to safeguard essential political goods. Even the Marxist critique equates core liberal values with liberal economic institutions. In the name of true human emancipation it ends up condemning both in favor of utopias devoid of rights guarantees. In the nineteenth century one finds the first stirrings of a democratic, social interpretation of the contradictions within free market capitalism, one that rejects the identification of liberal economic institutions with the fundamental values of political liberalism.[1]

Like their contemporary counterparts, the early critics pointed out that, when gross inequality in the ownership of the means of production and unregulated markets prevail, capricious use of both will conflict with the universalism inherent in fundamental liberal values. Their critique implies that the uses of privately owned means of production, the functional conditions of the market, and the distribution of material opportunities all have to be subordinated to institutional correctives that harmonize them with the principle of equal liberty for all. Thus, in the interest of making them compatible with universal, liberal rights, both private ownership of the means of production and market regulation are demoted to the status of *means* toward higher-order ends. In contrast to the tradition of orthodox socialism, the hallmark of the theory of social democracy has been its refusal to dismiss liberal economic institutions out of hand. Instead, social democracy has insisted that the latter be justified on empirical grounds: namely, whether they could in fact be made compatible with basic liberal values. From the outset, the kind of corrective measures envisaged by this tradition were modest: restrictions on capital under labor law; social welfare responsibilities imposed on business enterprises; and, generally, the imbedding of the economy through regulation. The only way to justify the exact proportions in this multidimensional institutional mix was to show that it would be the best choice to support universal rights. That is the main topic of the political economy component in a theory of social democracy. *Political economy* is dedicated to investigating the relationships among classes, the state, the market, and democracy.[2] As Esping-Andersen has shown, even welfare state regimes must be understood as an instrument of political control over the structures and outcomes of the economic system. Thus, today they represent one of the decisive variables in political economy.[3] The latter's task is to map out the relationships among three variables: the political system, the economic system, and social welfare regimes.

It may prove useful to employ a tripartite theoretical strategy in analyzing the political economy of social democracy. *First*, the normative theory of social democracy sets the terms of the discussion through its derivation of universal rights. In modern democracies every citizen is granted an equal claim to practice those rights. *Second*, another line of reasoning systematically analyzes the historical origins of the problems and risks that socio-economic development poses for the political implementation and validation of fundamental rights. And *third*, empirical-comparative research looks at the strategies chosen to solve those problems in different societies, at least those that have plausibly invoked social democratic goals in doing so. It thus depicts the latitude that political economy in social democracy enjoys as well as the conditions and consequences of its behavior.

Comparative analysis discloses a potentially extensive menu of practices in the political economy of social democracy. Heimann and Polanyi have both shown that markets can work in politically legitimate ways, i.e., in accord with a social contract, only when they are fully imbedded in the social and political systems of society.[4] However, experiences with planned economies offer evidence that the economic system can provide the benefits that the social and political subsystems ask of it – the production and distribution of goods and services – only if it is given sufficient room to operate under its own functional logic in allocating available resources. To this extent the political economy of social democracy must somehow resolve persistent tensions and even contradictions in the premises of its component institutions. It seeks to optimize the interplay of the contradictory elements of the market, the social welfare state, statist regulation, and corporatist actors in order to produce outcomes most favorable to the actualization of universal rights.

In order not to underestimate the full complexity of its subject matter, a realistic economic theory of social democracy must begin with four empirically supported historical and theoretical premises.

First, it should bear in mind Karl Polanyi's thesis that market steering and property relations have at all times been imbedded in functional matrices and social value structures. It is this imbedding that enables the former to fulfill their appointed tasks within historically specific societies.[5] Empirically speaking, the whole project of allowing markets to regulate themselves turns out to be an ideological fiction. The social imbedding of markets always precedes the definition of their functional potential; in fact, the two processes are symbiotically linked in every conceivable real-world case.[6] Thus, in determining the relationship among politics, society, and markets, the preliminary question is always: by what standards and in what form and degree should markets be imbedded?[7]

Second, any model that might be adopted by social democratic regimes would have to compete successfully with alternative economic models as well as survive in the rough-and-tumble of globally integrated markets. If that normative condition is not met, then the model loses both its economic *raison d'être* and its political legitimacy, no matter how impeccable its normative credentials may be.[8]

Third, it is now clear that a realistic, social democratically oriented theory of the economic system will have to take its bearings from the empirically sophisticated *Varieties of Capitalism* approach.[9] But this approach confirms that there is a broad spectrum of functionally workable alternatives for organizing economies and arranging the symbiotic relationships between markets and politics. Thus, social democracy is never forced to choose between a pure Platonic ideal of economic modeling on the one hand, and the status quo on the other. Neither choice can be supported by experience or social science.[10]

Fourth, as noted, there are basically three instruments of political steering that can be applied to the solution of politically defined problems in a democracy: the logic of the market, state action, and the self-organization in civil society. Whether considered separately or in varying hybrid forms, they all exhibit certain performance profiles, each with its own characteristic limitations. Depending on the kind of problem addressed and the task they are called on to handle, these instruments can be characterized in two ways: by reference either to their relative superiority to one of the other steering alternatives or to elements of systematic functional breakdown. None of them should be viewed as a priori morally or functionally superior to any other. The real issue for a theory of political and economic steering in social democracy is therefore a pragmatic one: what is the most appropriate institutional mix for a specific task in a given sector?

How liberal rights may be imperiled

Social critics in the twentieth century gradually developed a scheme for classifying the main threats to rights posed by a capitalist socio-economic order. By its very nature their matrix evolved into a set of guidelines for designing a political economy suited to social democracy. Since it defined threats to rights by reference to historical experiences, it is in principle still open to new experiences that history puts on the agenda. It therefore enables us to identify the ways in which rights might be jeopardized even today.

First, people may fail in their struggle to earn a decent living in the marketplace through no fault of their own. In that case, they may be denied the wherewithal for a dignified human life, or even physical survival itself. That would be equivalent to a blanket denial of all basic rights and a violation of their entitlement to private, social, and political autonomy.

Second, the entitlement to practice even one's negative liberties may be jeopardized by an inadequate income. Market outcomes thus indirectly infringe on people's private and political autonomy.

Third, on account of their penury, people may be forced to accept labor contracts that make it harder for them to maintain a dignified existence. That leads to an infringement of their social autonomy.

Fourth, the unequal distribution of vital goods may prevent some people from seizing positive opportunities, or may disadvantage them in their quest to participate politically. That would in effect imperil their private and political autonomy.

All of these risks increase when markets are treated as self-regulating institutions freed from all the restraints inherent in social and political imbedding.[11]

3.2 Public goods and civil rights

Public goods may be defined as those that can be used and enjoyed by everyone in the natural or political environments in which they are provided. No one who has access to the social or political space where public goods are supplied can or should be excluded from their use. That rule holds true in consequence either of the physical properties of the public goods, the legal regulations governing their enjoyment, or – in certain cases – the legitimate entitlements that some people have to them. Air quality is an example of unrestricted access due to the physical characteristics of public goods, while basic social security exemplifies free use due to legal entitlement. Human rights protection and free public school attendance in many countries are both cases in which legitimate entitlements traceable to basic rights justify the provision of public goods. Even laws and rights can be understood as public goods in this sense. Thus, the two distinctive qualities of public goods are their universality and the unrestricted right to use them. That definition suggests a direct link between a certain understanding of justice and a corresponding conception of how public goods ought to be provided. Suppose that we take justice to mean equal liberty, and specify that liberty in the broadest sense entails that a person's opportunities to act must have material support. Those definitions imply that every individual is entitled to have society provide a system of public goods, in the absence of which the claims of justice could not be met.

As a norm that broadly legitimizes the social order, justice relates to three dimensions of politically responsible social action: the system of social institutions; the array of public benefits and rights; and the distribution of opportunities in society, particularly the way they tie into the contributions of individuals to the sum total of a society's goods and opportunities.

Public goods are to be found in both of the first two dimensions; in fact, strictly speaking they are identical to them. In the first dimension would be included the institutions of government and the court system, which are themselves public goods because every citizen may use them and because their activities benefit everyone. As far as complex modern societies are concerned, the second dimension contains a plethora of services all of which deserve to be considered public goods. This is true, for instance, of air traffic control as well as public schools and public security, not to mention regulation of the quality of foods, local building codes, social security benefits, and the public roads.

Conversely, one could classify certain negative public goods as "public evils." These include externalities generated by private actors that affect everyone in a certain geographic or social space in undesirable, though avoidable, ways. Air pollution and urban decay constitute just two among many well-known examples. But these cases also reveal that, within limits, some negative public goods offer an exit option, one that allows certain groups to exempt themselves from the public, universal character of the negative goods. To be sure, no resident of a run-down city can entirely avoid the negative effects associated with it; but wealthier people can escape more easily than others by moving into "gated communities" with their own services and amenities. The same holds true for certain types of environmental pollution, which the affluent can escape merely by moving to a less polluted place. In the United States, such behavior is sometimes called the "secession of the successful."

Public goods and social security

Individual opportunity, as well as its distribution among specific groups, is partly determined by the ways in which public and private goods may be consumed. The availability of public goods in suitable quantity and quality profoundly affects citizens' opportunities to enjoy their liberties. For instance, public security and infrastructure quality are indispensable even to people whose level of resources otherwise enables them to satisfy most of their wants by purchasing privately produced goods. Others of course may lack the means to obtain from private sources any of the most basic goods without which freedom becomes exceedingly insecure, such as schooling for their children, medical care, and security in their immediate neighborhood. In those cases, it is absolutely essential to provide all the relevant public goods, since otherwise many people's liberties would lack a material foundation, and their allegedly equal opportunity would be a mirage. For that reason the theory of public goods is a crucial component in the theory of social democracy. It is incumbent on the latter to present reasoned arguments concerning several key points: which public goods social democratic policy should make available, what access requirements to them should be imposed, and which public goods ought to be provided in the national, regional, and global domains, respectively. The last issue is especially urgent, because it may not be possible to provide some public goods to certain groups efficiently except at a transnational level. Also, provision at the global level may be the only way fully to satisfy the imperatives of global justice and solidarity.

If the state grants a civil right to income security, this would have to count as a public good as well, even if the individual citizen can only "cash in" the opportunities that the guaranteed income provides through demand for private goods in the market. Put differently, the citizen's purchasing power itself, assuming it reflects a legal entitlement, is created and defined *as* a public good by the political community, regardless of the fact that it may assume the final form of demand for private goods. This point could be expressed in the paradoxical-sounding conclusion that the public good consists in the guaranteed opportunity that some citizens enjoy to be provided with private goods in accord with their own autonomous decisions. Esping-Andersen has described this as the decommodification of the entire status of dependent employment, as opposed to the decommodification only of certain fundamental social goods.[12]

Justice and equality

The mere concept of a public good does not answer all of the questions bound up with the problem of justice. Rather, once answers have been found, public goods are just one of the political and economic ways to put them into practice.[13] The preliminary questions that must be resolved are roughly the following. First, every commonwealth has to clarify just which social goods – and in what quantities – it ought to provide as *public* goods. Second, once public goods are already being supplied, it must be determined whether everyone should receive them free of charge, or whether recipients should have to pay a modest fixed fee that is affordable for everyone, or whether income-adjusted user fees should be levied. Only in the case of public goods in the physical sense would such questions be beside the point. Finally, the commonwealth must clarify the level of contributions or co-payments expected from beneficiaries, and the kind of financing to be adopted for each type of public good. The possibilities here are almost endless. For example, even the universalistic Swedish welfare state, though it is financed predominantly by a highly progressive income tax, still imposes fees on beneficiaries in a number of areas. This is true even when its citizens take advantage of their constitutional guarantee to health care (considered a public good). However, the fee is so low that it never deters anyone from using the health-care system.

Especially in the case of global public goods, two questions have been highly controversial: what financial contribution each country should make to their production and how access to them should be controlled within each country. Two criteria ought to be consulted in answering them. One must first take account of the UN Covenants of 1966 that grant to everyone political, civil, social, economic, and cultural rights, and insist that they be guaranteed on a global scale. They also call for a high base-level of equality and free access to certain public goods. In addition, the covenants require that all the member states of the global community pay their fair share toward financing these public goods, at a level sufficient to insure that they are readily available, but not so as to jeopardize the equal rights of the citizens of the donor countries.

State, market, and civil society

Theoretically and politically, there can be no question that decisions about public goods and guarantees of their production necessarily involve the logic of state action. Indeed, social democrats sometimes imagine that the state has sole responsibility for producing and guaranteeing the availability of public goods. However, what really matters when it comes to guaranteeing public goods is simply *that* they are made available, not *how*. As their underwriter, the state is certainly free to decide on pragmatic or economic grounds how to provide them. It may contract out the delivery of such goods to private producers; it may leave the field to the initiatives of civil society; or it may co-produce public goods together with one or both of those actors, as long as it assumes the role of ultimate guarantor.[14]

There is one argument drawn from the theory of economic rationality in favor of assigning the production of public goods to the sphere of state action on which all theoretical and political positions would agree. In the by-now classic thought experiment of game theory, the prisoner's dilemma, no single rational agent has an interest in sharing any of the production costs of public goods, although each has an interest in using them.[15] Since no one can be prevented from using a public good once it has been produced, all parties speculate that they will have an opportunity to become free-riders on it. So, in case of doubt, they would rather forego the production of the public good entirely than bear a portion of its costs, when it is not clear that all other beneficiaries of it would also have to share in those costs.

This standard line of argument has been used to test economic contract theories of public goods, to see whether they would still hold up if the prospective beneficiaries of a given public good had made their contract in the absence of state sanctions. On the basis of methodological individualism, scholars have concluded that it is only effective state sanctions that can persuade the beneficiaries to share in the costs of the public good. Without those in the background, the good would never get produced at all.[16] The findings of economic theory on this point are also tantamount to a prediction that civil society cannot be expected to produce public goods. Although anticipated public benefits and public procedures might encourage the production of such goods, civil society, by definition and by nature, lacks the coercive sanctions necessary to prevent free-riding.[17]

Incentives for civic engagement

Recent debates suggest that engagement in civil society should be regarded neither as a spontaneous phenomenon, nor as an act of extraordinary moral virtue. A commitment to civil society not only presupposes a good deal of state encouragement; it also requires changes in the structures and forms of state action itself.[18] The state can and must create ad hoc structures to encourage civic engagement; moreover, it must convert itself into just such an ad hoc structure.

Evers, Rauch, and Stitz have presented empirical evidence to support this conclusion in their studies of the way that elements of the state, the market, and civil society mesh in the delivery of social services in schools, senior-citizen care, and the cultural sphere. They show that these new forms of public services have reawakened both social approval of and the need for civic engagement. Moreover, in these same areas new and promising ways to overcome the rigid divisions among the market, state, and civil society have begun to emerge. All three have been combined in creative ways depending on the specific tasks to be managed. These hybrid forms, combining diverse organizational models and problem-solving resources, can boost the effectiveness of service provision and in many instances attune it more successfully to the public interest. This way of joining state mandates and entrepreneurial initiative with the commitment and initiative of the stakeholders themselves promises to take full advantage of the best features of each form of social action, while eliminating their respective deficiencies. In practice these new forms of cooperation tend to render rigid boundaries among the sectors increasingly obsolete.

A plethora of important public goods in contemporary societies can be produced by non-state agents, especially via the initiatives and networks of civil society and the "third sector." These would certainly include public goods that improve and enrich the quality of life, such as efforts to preserve the neighborhood environment. Yet there are some public goods that touch on fundamental human and civil rights. Here the principles of social democracy require that the state itself should assume the ultimate responsibility for underwriting those rights, even when, acting in a pragmatic spirit, it transfers responsibility for providing the services to private or civil society agents best situated to deliver them efficiently. That is, only the form of provision can be left to non-state initiatives. The state has a duty to guarantee both that services are reliably rendered, and that the quality of their delivery remains reasonably high.

3.3 The market–state complex

Defying the historical experience of the previous two centuries, libertarianism continues to draw its normative standards from the assumption that, in a liberal constitutional order, anyone is free to acquire property in the means of production. On that assumption it makes no conceptual sense for the liberal state to try to regulate the circumstances under which property is acquired. Anyone is free to make contracts with whomever he/she pleases. The fact that property in the means of production is unequally distributed – and everything that implies for human dignity and freedom – has no impact on the way libertarians interpret liberal theory and practice.

The logical counterpart to the libertarian theory of property-acquisition is an understanding of the market as a sphere of liberty. On that interpretation, the market could claim the same dignity and sanctity as a bastion of freedom that liberal democratic constitutionalism claims for itself in the political arena. Statist intervention in economic matters would then almost be tantamount to interference with civil liberties. Of course, the state is still obligated to maintain the functional integrity of the market as the primary institutional locus that guarantees and secures the liberty of economic citizens. But, on this libertarian reading of its duties, the state is authorized to limit the scope of market operations only in those few cases of conflict between the functional ends of the state and legitimate market functions.

In this manner the libertarian version of basic liberal values exalts the institutions of economic liberalism to the level of absolute universal values, as if the market were an end in itself. By contrast, the generative idea of the *social* interpretation of basic liberal values is that these institutions should be regarded as means to an absolute end, the suitability of which always has to be evaluated in light of empirical observation.

From the libertarian point of view, the functional deficiencies of existing markets can be caused only by outside interference.[19] Consequently, the identification of the market as a bastion of freedom is a means of immunizing it against critical scrutiny. It becomes obvious that the disagreement between the libertarian and social interpretations of liberal democracy boils down to their differing judgments about the legal status of property in the means of production and the market system. All the other differences in the way they conceptualize democracy and political economy follow from this one.

Experience demonstrates not only that self-regulating markets violate fundamental rights, but also that their economic performance level sometimes falls below expectations. We may distinguish six causal complexes that account for market failure. Their existence suggests that unless markets are subject to economic regulation they will become dysfunctional.[20]

First, when monopolies arise there will be no market at all unless political intervention creates one. Even then, perpetual political supervision is needed to insure that market-like services are delivered.

Second, the functional logic of markets leads them to generate undesirable side effects. Negative externalities crop up whenever market participants shift costs and burdens onto third parties who were not involved in the market transactions. These displacements then give rise to social costs such as pollution and unemployment that have to be indemnified by the political community as a whole. Besides these and other local risks, global markets also provoke transnational financial crises, which in some economies may lead to capital destruction, lower growth, and mass unemployment.

Third, there is a need for regulation of both price and quality in sectors inherently characterized by asymmetrical information between providers and consumers of goods and services.[21] This information gap tends to produce a new type of risk. To take an example, toxic substances that consumers themselves may not recognize as such often pose risks to their lives and health, forcing them to rely on expert opinion to evaluate the level of risk in specific cases.[22]

Fourth, left to their own devices, markets tend to drift toward monopolization and/or the accumulation of market power via oligopoly. In that sense they undermine their own functional logic.

Fifth, markets respond only to the effective demand of current market participants. Consequently, they can neither supply public goods nor implement collectively approved future projects.

Sixth, the logic of the market follows the rhythm of the boom-and-bust cycle, including its recurrent economic recessions. During the crisis phases of the business cycle, markets cause bankruptcies, unemployment, and the loss of anticipated tax revenues.

In spite of their functional deficiencies, markets are far superior to any known alternative method of coordinating economic decision-making, i.e., as institutions for the productive allocation of resources, the satisfaction of private consumer preferences, and the stimulation of technical and scientific innovation. Therefore, the only sensible way to limit their risks is through imbedding and regulation that preserve their core functions. Unless subjected to well-designed regulations and macro-economic coordination, markets will not display their functional advantages, without their flaws simultaneously doing unacceptable harm to common interests and basic rights. Either economic regulatory policy should seek to avoid such externalities entirely, as in the case of environmental deterioration, or it should compel those responsible for the externalities to foot the bill for them, so that society will not have to pay it, as is the case with rules concerning job protection.

Because externalities and their causes are so multi-faceted, the most promising remedies chosen by economic regulatory policy-makers will be equally diverse. But they will include some of the following:

1 the establishment of a framework of laws
2 oversight measures and reporting requirements
3 structures of corporatist co-regulation
4 a macro-economic policy on the demand side
5 micro-economic policies to improve the supply structure
6 a well-conceived intervention in the economic process.

Asymmetrical information in markets poses two distinct challenges, each of which requires a different type of regulation. One case involves the demand for full disclosure about the true properties of certain products, for example the composition of foodstuffs, the toxic content of industrial agents, or information about the actual interest rate to be paid on loans or credit cards that are advertised in misleading ways. In the other case, the problem is how to evaluate the kind and quantitative level of risks to which the consumers of some potentially harmful products are exposed. Thus, for example, citizens must ultimately almost take on faith what experts tell them about the minute threshold levels of ambient radiation that may pose a risk to their health and lives. In such cases it is incumbent on regulators to clarify and publicize expert opinions. Above all regulatory bodies have an obligation to intervene early so as to prevent unacceptable risks from ever occurring in the first place.

Macro-economic regulation, corporatist co-regulation, and micro-economic supply-side policy are jointly responsible for achieving three main targets: growth, full employment, and incomes. In short, the market inherently generates different types of risks and thus always requires both preliminary and after-the-fact regulation. To this extent, the ritualized confrontation of market and state proves misleading.

On account of their inherent flaws, markets cannot be interpreted as the economic and institutional equivalents of juridical democracy. Their scope and limits have to be decided politically with an eye to securing fundamental rights and common interests in several areas: productivity, the provision of goods, attention to need-based demand, the extent of economic freedom of action, and full employment. Market arrangements should be viewed as political decisions that must be legitimated on the basis of the sovereign rights of political and social citizenship.

The superiority of market logic

The experiences of twentieth-century theory and practice suggest that markets usually work effectively and with few undesirable side effects to achieve the coordination of micro-economic decisions, at least whenever they are imbedded in a higher-order political framework. In this way the full development of market logic is constrained by an oversight authority equipped with sanctions, while political decisions identify the sectors to be coordinated by markets. However, the market cannot accomplish the steering function entrusted to it all by itself. The political system must have done its part to establish a framework, fulfill certain preconditions, and provide support services that *complement* the economic logic of the market and allow it to unfold only *within these boundaries*. The Great Depression of the late 1920s and the 1930s proved the folly of the idea that markets could function sustainably if they were detached from the social context of their imbedding and abandoned to a self-regulation immune to external influences. In practice, every capitalistically organized economy since then has opted for a political economy that replaced the monism of the market by a regulatory pluralism that emphasized social steering. After short-lived experiments with libertarian panaceas against the encrusted state-run economic systems inherited from the communist era, even the societies of Central and Eastern Europe have adopted the program of *pragmatic imbedding* of markets.[23] Today quarrels between libertarians and social democrats concern mainly the legitimation and goals involved in steering and imbedding economic processes, as well as their extent and the choice of instruments to attain them.

3.4 Imbedding the economy

The superiority of (imbedded) markets has gradually been accepted by social democracy almost everywhere. But, as the history of theoretical discussions in social democratic circles shows, its victory has not come easily, in spite of the intuitive practical lessons that have consistently upheld it. The tempo of its acceptance varied from one country to another, but it has become part of social democracy's generally accepted stock of ideas only since the 1980s. Three key figures were especially responsible for this volte-face.

First, Eduard Bernstein argued that old-fashioned orthodox socialism had mistakenly rejected market steering. Its advocates followed Marx in predicting that the process of industrial concentration would inevitably keep on simplifying macro-economic structures until the final stage of capitalist development was reached, when control of the economy would fall into the hands of a few monopolistic and oligopolistic firms.[24] To the orthodox socialists, taking over the few remaining command centers of an internally monopolized economy seemed like a simple matter. Socialist planners would be able to redirect the economy toward different ends, now legitimized at the level of the entire society. Bernstein, who understood the internal complexity of capitalist economies, demanded that the social democrats of his day abandon the goals of economic planning and socialization.

He insisted that increasing macro-economic complexity forces us to recognize the market as the only institution capable of coordinating the staggering variety of information and interests without incurring indefensible losses of labor productivity, societal resources, consumer sovereignty, and opportunities to influence economic outcomes. As the Soviet communist alternative of state planning based on across-the-board nationalization of industry matured, and its economic, political, and social costs became obvious, arguments like Bernstein's began to gain ground even in hard-line social democratic circles.[25]

Second, during the 1920s the economist Eduard Heimann supplemented the complexity argument by insisting that monopoly-free markets could themselves sometimes be regarded as the best instruments to promote the socialization of production decisions.[26] They can do so because they put so many citizens – in the extreme case all of them – in charge of supply-side decisions through their role as consumers, i.e., more citizens than even the supervisory boards of planned economies

do. When economic steering is dominated by all-embracing bureaucra-
tization, social control is in fact defeated. The vision of *economic democracy* propounded around that time was based on the idea that markets
would be self-regulating in key economic sectors. But proponents also
wanted to revise constitutional law and institutional practice to insure
that trade unions and other political representatives of society would
have a say in establishing the framework for economic intervention and
strategic investment decisions.[27]

Third, once pro-market arguments had won the day, attention soon
turned to schemes for replacing private property by various forms of
communal property to be organized and operated macro-economically
through free markets. Eventually, the theories of functional socialism
advanced by Gunnar Adler-Karlsson as well as theoretical explanations
for the shortcomings of Yugoslavian socialism precipitated a paradigm
shift that would become definitive for the modern theory of social
democracy. They concluded that the coordinating role played by
markets could not be effective unless a capital function based on private
property in the means of production were at work in them.[28]

These three historic stages in the debate culminate in the modern paradigm of political economy and thus establish the only terms on which
social democracy today can still formulate its solutions. Its boundary
lines are demarcated by three principles: the indispensability of the economic core function of market steering; the productive function of
private property; and the need to imbed markets socially and politically.
Hence, when social democracy is forced to confront the fundamental
questions of political economy, the pragmatic response is to devise
mixed forms of state–market partnership tailored to specific situations.
There can no longer be any "either/or" decision between the two forms
of steering.

Every political steering project is pervaded by the conflicting interests of participating actors in an opaque situation. The political
economy of social democracy is defined by tensions and trade-offs:
between productivity and growth on one hand, social justice and security on the other; flexibility and innovation on one side, the protection
of dependent employment and comprehensive social security on the
other; an acceptable level of freedom to own property and make contracts on one hand, social integration and regulation on the other;
autonomous entrepreneurship here, and there, social autonomy and
political guidance and coordination. The most successful method of
handling these tensions and trade-offs calls for empirical practices that
combine several regulatory principles. When a regulatory mix in social
democracy's political economy works well, it seems to embody certain
principles.

First, given that all citizens have an equal right to the greatest possible private autonomy, the economic order should allow maximum

individual freedom of action and contract. There must be as much market as possible.

Second, concerning the norm of positive liberty and the availability of individual and social goods implied by it, economic policy should strive to maximize labor productivity, that is, the optimal sustainable utilization of available resources in the production of goods and services. This norm also implies an economic policy committed to optimizing resource productivity. Finally, it entails a policy dedicated to achieving a just distribution of social goods above and beyond the market outcome.

Third, in corporate governance, workplace organization, and state intervention, the dignity and liberty of all stakeholders ought to be respected.

3.5 *Varieties of Capitalism*

An empirical theory of social democracy has to adjust its normative aspirations to fit the institutional contexts that comparative research has brought to light. In fact, investigators have identified a range of different types of political economy and explained why they have developed in distinctive ways. It is undeniable that industrial and service economies in Western societies differ markedly in their institutional arrangements and their methods of imbedding production and welfare state regimes. The preferred pattern of interactions among the political, economic, and social welfare systems has to be economically efficient enough to guarantee that its social welfare targets will be met. Yet at the same time the norms of social democracy should prevail throughout the political economy. They must not be sacrificed to a narrow emphasis on growth and productivity. Empirical research on typologies of welfare state democracy must therefore figure out how economic efficiency might be blended with social democratic norms in a free market environment.

The micro-economic approach

David Soskice and Peter Hall prefer a micro-economic perspective in designing their comparative studies of developed market economies.[29] Their work differs from earlier investigations in focusing on the multiple configurations of market economies, and especially the ways in which their internal dimensions reciprocally influence one another. It attempts to account for the unique characteristics of each of the respective systems in its totality. What particularly sets their approach apart from previous comparative studies is their focus on the organization of capital rather than labor as the decisive variable in explaining how different types of capitalism work.

Political economy is to be understood as a social and economic arena in which each actor tries "to pursue his or her interests through rational strategic interaction with the others."[30] Business enterprises are identified as the actors that define the economic structure. As technological change accelerates and international competition intensifies, they become the actors whose activities determine the potential economic performance of each country. They do so in an institutional context where they establish both external contacts and relationships (with suppliers, customers, partners, unions, interest groups, and governments) and internal ones (with their own employees). To prosper, firms must master different aspects of the political economy. In addition to winning the competition for customers, they must also seek financing, regulate wages and working conditions, make sure their workforces have the requisite skills and abilities, and secure access to resources and the latest technologies.[31]

In short, businesses find themselves caught in a multidimensional web of relationships, and their success depends on their ability to coordinate a range of diverse actors. Differences in institutional frameworks of political economies generate systematic variations in entrepreneurial strategies. The typical patterns of coordination among business enterprises offer useful insights into the ways different kinds of market economies work and the outcomes they produce. Their perspective offers answers to the most crucial question of political economy: which structural environment is most likely to enhance the prospects of individual firms and thus also the potential economic performance of the market economy as a whole? What should governments do about unanticipated challenges, and which macro-economic steering policies look most promising? Are certain strategies of economic and social policy-making transferable from one political and economic context to another, or does every political economy necessarily have to work out its own context-specific solutions? Further questions arise concerning institutional stability and the tendency of technological innovation and competitive pressures to induce change in political economies. Finally, the Hall and Soskice approach helps answer a central question of political economy: whether globalization causes country-specific advantages in economic coordination to dwindle into insignificance, such that we could expect an eventual convergence of different models.[32] Because business increasingly has to operate in a transnational environment, questions about that setting become urgent. Can global markets be integrated formally into the political sphere without disturbing their long-term competitiveness?

Coordinated and uncoordinated market economies

Soskice and Hall initially distinguish between coordinated and "liberal"[33] or uncoordinated market economies (abbreviated as CMEs and LMEs).[34] Their distinction is based on an analysis of the possible ways in which business enterprises may coordinate their activities. One way involves competition and market relationships, the other features strategic interaction among firms. Whether a firm coordinates its activities via the market or through strategic interaction depends largely on the institutional context in which it operates. Their typology rests on the observation that certain types of business coordination predominate in some economies while barely affecting others.

The political economies of individual countries may be arranged on a scale between the two ideal-typical poles, in accord with the coordination strategies that their firms employ. LMEs (uncoordinated market economies) are at one end of the scale. Here ties among business enterprises and other actors are routed mainly through competitive relationships. They are characterized by exchanges of goods and services, i.e., purely business relationships in the context of competition and formal contracts. At the opposite end of the spectrum are CMEs, coordinated market economies, in which firms more frequently enter into strategic relationships with unions, creditors, and other actors. This non-market form of coordination entails an array of external business relationships as well as communications networks based on exchanges of personal information that build the trust which sustains other forms of collaboration.

Because the transitions from one ideal type to the other are fluid, market and strategic coordination are separated only by degrees. Yet beyond a certain threshold, these gradual transitions give way to qualitative differences in the modalities and consequences of real-world patterns. Soskice and Hall identify five spheres of political economy in which corporations confront crucial coordination problems that they solve in distinctive ways.

1 *Industrial relations* Corporations have to decide how and with whom to negotiate about working conditions for their employees. In industrial relations, the main issues center on wages and productivity rates, which obviously affect the firm's eventual success. But employment and inflation rates are also indirectly involved, and these help determine the economy's overall performance. The level and extent of wage coordination here are crucially important. For example, are wage negotiations carried on at the national level, or in the individual firm or plant, or somewhere in between? Also, to what degree are wage negotiations centralized in the hands of union officials and management?

2 *Vocational training and continuing education* Corporations must insure that their employees get suitable job training. From the employees' viewpoint the question looks slightly different. How much time, money, and energy should they invest, and for what type of training?

Solving this coordination problem is not just a vital concern for the firm and the individual employee; it also affects the competitiveness of the entire economy. In comparing market economies, one must inquire whether some corporatist arrangement exists among the state, employees, and unions to offer vocational training.

3 *Corporate governance* Even in matters that concern corporate hierarchies and control, important coordination problems come to light. The main interest of business enterprises is to insure access to finance capital, while that of the investors is to maximize the security of and returns on their investments. Cross-national comparisons allow us to evaluate the structure of corporate governance by focusing on several key factors. Among these are, for example, the size of securities markets and the relative power of shareholders, which affect the legal protection and probable influence of small stockholders vis-à-vis the power of management and the larger stockholders. Corporate governance also touches on control structures; i.e., how corporations are networked with other corporations, especially banks.

4 *Relations among firms* Another important coordination problem involves intercorporate relationships, especially those with suppliers and customers, as firms seek to secure stable demand for their products. In these relationships firms may find solutions to an array of special problems such as industrial standards, technology transfers, and cooperation in research and development.

5 *Labor relations* Companies confront the problem of ensuring that their employees have the necessary training and skills and can cooperate to advance the firm's goals.

If one compares the institutional patterns of interaction in these five areas, two clusters of countries within the OECD group stand out. In one, there are the uncoordinated market economies such as the United States, Britain, Canada, and Ireland. Included in the second cluster of coordinated market economies would be Austria, Germany, Norway, Japan, Belgium, Finland, Denmark, Sweden, and Switzerland.[35] Finally, there is a third cluster that cannot be unequivocally identified with either of the first two, including France, Italy, Spain, Portugal, Greece, and Turkey. The last group tends to resemble the coordinated economies, but with some characteristic twists. Because the countries in this group exhibit institutional similarities, they may be classified as *Mediterranean* market economies. Their hallmarks are a large agricultural sector and extensive state intervention. They represent a certain kind of non-market coordination in the financial sphere, but with liberal arrangements in labor relations.[36]

The United States offers an example of an uncoordinated market economy, while Germany typifies the coordinated variety.

The United States as a typical uncoordinated market economy

Securities markets provide most of the financing for American firms. Those markets usually display a high level of transparency and draw in a variety of heterogeneous actors. This fact accounts for two trends: first, that business enterprises are not tightly integrated with one another, and, second, that the stockholders' interest in achieving the highest possible return deeply influences corporate strategies. Access to outside capital depends on the company's current worth and on freely available information about its recent earnings and market value. For that reason, and because government has lately been tolerant of mergers and hostile takeovers, US managers are under constant pressure to produce higher short-term profits. Unimpressive earnings figures can quickly be punished by bankruptcy or hostile takeover bids.

Associations of capital and labor in the United States tend to be lobbying organizations rather than institutions for self-governance. Trade unions are also weak compared to those in coordinated economies, while employers' associations are neither highly coordinated nor capable of effective cooperation except in lobbying Congress. Finally there is very little legal job protection in the United States, at least in the private sector. As a result, labor relations are often marked by short-term employment contracts and wage negotiations carried on at the level of the individual firm. A flexible labor market is complemented by a system of education that provides mainly general knowledge and skills that can be used in many different firms and sectors. In the United States, management typically enjoys almost unlimited control over the company, including the freedom to hire and fire employees on short notice as business conditions dictate. That control allows corporations to react flexibly to market developments, but increases the pressure on them to adapt to short-term changes. Hence, the American system of labor relations is less successful at developing costly, elaborate production strategies that require stable employment over the long haul. Instead, it favors a model based on standardized mass production as well as low wage and skill levels.

Given that the labor market is so unregulated, and the likelihood of losing one's job is relatively high, American workers tend to invest in rather unspecialized kinds of training that they can continue to use in their next job. And because employers' associations are able to coordinate with each other only to a small extent, they have never succeeded in developing cooperative, industry-specific training programs. That is another reason why American workers tend to prefer training that imparts general knowledge, which is especially well suited to the service sector, where employment is highly sensitive to business cycles. Many companies and sectors therefore face a shortage of highly skilled employees.

The idea of economic freedom has prevailed in the United States since the early days of the Republic. It encourages the belief that the state should intervene in the market only to keep it functioning properly, e.g., by blocking the formation of cartels. This tendency shows up in the fact that the American state has never devised effective instruments for steering and regulation, and that it usually hampers efforts by industry to organize itself. Instead, control over markets is left to a "legalistic regulatory culture, in which independent regulatory commissions see to it that consumers and investors are well enough informed that they can make their own consumer and investment decisions."[37] Furthermore, the American state offers little social compensation for market outcomes. It is not a social welfare state in the European sense, and assumes no responsibility to insure that universal rights become effective in the real world.

Germany as a typical coordinated market economy

In a coordinated market economy like that of Germany, corporations find other ways to gain access to financing than by relying on capital markets. Management's performance is evaluated and overseen not only by the market but also by informal networks, in which banks, employees, state actors, and other firms are represented. Here opportunities arise for personal exchanges of information and the building of trust. Business enterprises usually obtain financing through bank credits, which are gained through their reputations rather than via publicly accessible corporate data and short-term earnings figures. For their part, investors acquire information about a firm's reputation and operations through a dense network of relationships that they cultivate. Such access to "patient capital" allows firms to invest in long-term projects and retain a well-trained workforce even during recessions. Accordingly, German management has less need to react sensitively to prospects for immediate profit or to the fluctuating market value of its own stocks. Tax codes, laws, and broadly integrative networks of firms tend to discourage attempts at hostile takeovers. Top management in German companies rarely has the opportunity to make important decisions unilaterally. Instead, it must seek the approval of boards of directors and networks, in which – besides banks – other companies, employees, and state actors are represented. Consequently, it is not so much the stockholders' short-term interest in higher returns that drives the firm's decisions, but rather the interests of a multitude of stakeholders in society.

German companies frequently adopt production strategies that presuppose a highly trained workforce. Indeed, one of the problems that employers in quality-oriented production regimes face is their dependence on the technical know-how of these highly trained workers. To protect themselves from exorbitant demands on the part of their employees, as well as to prevent the "poaching" of skilled workers by other firms, German corporations have evolved a unique system of industrial relations featuring coordinated wage negotiations between employers and employees in individual industrial sectors. This eventually results in a flattening of wage levels for comparable skills across the entire sector, which makes it more difficult for one firm to lure away another's workers. It also convinces employees that they will receive the same wage in the same sector, regardless of which firm employs them. For this reason, as well as because of its stronger unions, works councils, and high level of legal job protection, Germany has a much less flexible, open labor market than the United States.

The state's role in the postwar German political economy could best be described as enabling. Its opportunities to intervene directly in economic processes have been limited by the country's federal structure as well as the presence of independent institutions such as the Federal Bank and the Federal Cartel Office. Yet the state does encourage the self-organization of societal groupings or semi-official corporatist actors, and equips them with the requisite, quasi-constitutional means to regulate and administer sectors of the political economy themselves, which in other countries would be left to the market or directly regulated by the state. The European Central Bank, with its independent monetary policy-making, and the European Competition Commissioners follow the same political-economic principles as the Federal Bank; hence there is no discontinuity in approach between the German and European levels. Moreover, the state spends a considerable portion of GDP on its social insurance scheme and follows the constitutional imperative to insure "equal living conditions" in all of the German states, for which purpose it has developed a regional system of redistribution.[38]

Implications for the economic order of social democracy

We should be able to extract some strategic guidelines from the *Varieties of Capitalism* approach concerning the economic order and policies of social democracy. *First*, on account of the powerful affinities between relevant political-economic institutions, package solutions may be the best achievable outcome. That is, one may have to combine desirable with less desirable components to optimize social democratic aims. *Second*, regulations anchored in labor law and co-determination rights are needed to protect the health and dignity of dependent employees. These should be institutionalized at the level of industrial relations and company rules and be distinguished sharply from considerations of efficiency.

Complementary institutions

Political economy proves to be a system of tightly integrated spheres, such that practices in one of them depend very much on the character of institutions in the others. The institutions of political economy are historically grounded; they form and develop out of social processes and historical experience. They predetermine the possible patterns of action available to the actors, including especially states.

> Institutions central to the operations of the political economy should not be seen as entities that are created at one point in time and can then be assumed to operate effectively afterwards. To remain viable, the shared understandings associated with them must be reaffirmed periodically by appropriate historical experience.[39]

The sheer inertia of complementary institutions leads to a perpetual replication of the differences between uncoordinated and coordinated economies in every sphere of the political economy. There are three cases of institutional reciprocity that make particularly clear the ways that subsystems in a given market economy relate to each other. Whereas free market conditions in LMEs limit state actors to establishing rather weak regulatory frameworks, those in CMEs can assume the further role of actors in the integrative structure of political-economic institutions. In both cases the radius of their actions is limited by their reluctance to disturb ongoing institutional interactions.

1 *Labor relations and corporate governance* In those spheres of corporate governance where corporate integration, interlocking directorates, and access to finance capital regardless of short-term earnings are the rule, institutional strategies usually rely on practices marked by a higher degree of job security and centralized wage negotiations. Firms that do not have to worry about maximizing short-term profits can offer employees solid assurances concerning wages and job security. By contrast, companies that must seek financing principally in capital markets need to satisfy the immediate interests of their stockholders ("shareholder value") and frequently risk becoming targets of hostile takeover bids. For those reasons they are usually intent on securing the highest degree of autonomy, practically a carte blanche, for management. That sort of corporate governance system matches up well with a flexible labor market and individual wage settlements between employer and employee, allowing firms to react swiftly to changing market conditions. In addition it is inimical to any robust form of co-determination.

2 *Labor relations and job training* In market economies where labor relations are characterized by frequent turnover and wage settlements at the level of the individual firm, it makes sense for both the firm and

its employees to develop vocational training systems that teach mainly general skills and know-how. On the other hand, for companies involved in labor relations with strong unions and coordinated wage negotiations, it appears more efficient to cooperate in setting up joint training programs that offer industry-specific knowledge. By the same token, high, contractually guaranteed wages as well as relatively secure jobs encourage employees to acquire know-how that does not easily transfer to other branches.

3 *Corporate governance and cooperation* In economies where multiple institutions of corporate supervision reduce pressures to maximize short-term profits, it is easier for firms to cooperate with one another in research, product development, and technology transfer. By contrast, where mobile, variegated capital markets ease investment shifts from one firm to another, it is more important for firms to have exclusive control of new technologies. For that reason companies in the latter situation prefer to acquire new technologies by buying up other firms or poaching their personnel rather than engaging in long-term cooperation.

3.6 Types of capitalism compared

According to Soskice and Hall, arrangements of complementary institutions form the solid internal structure of every political economy. Having evolved historically, these continue to act as *filters* for the processing of system-external challenges even in global competition. They put a premium on system-immanent responses as opposed to transformation of the system's structure. None of these types of political economy is superior to the others in every respect. Each is capable in its own way of maintaining a high level of economic performance even under the pressure of globalization.

The production systems of coordinated market economies prove well suited to carry out "diversified strategies of high-quality production," but ill-designed to devise short-term strategies for the product market.[40] Additionally, coordinated economic orders seem to enjoy a comparative advantage in stimulating incremental innovation, but disadvantages in nurturing innovations in basic research. Compared to firms in uncoordinated market economies which profit from flexible labor markets, Japanese companies seem less able to launch radical innovations. Nor can they benefit much from the technology transfers made possible by cooperation. A political economy that is based primarily on *keiretsu*-style corporate groupings encourages firms to develop strategies that reap advantages from the potential for trans-sectoral technology transfers and the rapid reorganization of labor forces. Compared to German or American firms, Japanese corporations have an institutional advantage in mass producing reasonably priced consumer goods, and in exploiting existing electronic technologies to broaden their range of products.

Differences in the institutional frameworks of political economies also underlie systematic distinctions in entrepreneurial strategies. This becomes evident in the way that Great Britain, an uncoordinated economy, and Germany, a coordinated one, react differently to the same challenges. Confronted by exchange-rate swings that make the export of their own products to foreign markets more costly, British firms pass on the higher costs to their customers to maintain profitability. In much the same situation, German firms tend to hold prices steady and accept lower profits while hanging on to market share.[41]

The *Varieties of Capitalism* approach provides an analytical framework capable of explaining those different reactions. British firms must maintain their profit rates in an uncoordinated economy, since they depend on a capital market that rewards the distribution of short-term profits. But they can compensate for the loss of market share by laying off workers in the short term. By contrast, German companies can work through a temporary decline in their profits, because the financial system in a coordinated market economy enables them to get access to capital regardless of short-term profits. When the two types are judged qualitatively, in line with social democratic standards, the structures of uncoordinated economies designed to maximize shareholder value display some significant weaknesses.

First, entrepreneurial strategies geared to maximizing short-term profits exacerbate ecological and social problems by making it harder to include long-term consequences in the factors guiding entrepreneurial decisions. *Second*, various social groups, above all employees, are shut out of important economic decisions by a form of corporate governance that bestows unchecked power on management. *Third*, the commitment of uncoordinated market economies to highly flexible, unregulated labor markets with a "generalist" labor force intensifies the economic and psychological dependence of employees in ways that could be avoided. *Fourth*, the weakness of trade unions and lack of centralized wage negotiations in uncoordinated market economies reinforce their system of labor relations.

Social democratic norms and economic performance

The political economy of social democracy has to broaden the analytical framework of the *Varieties of Capitalism* approach by considering several neglected dimensions of economic performance: *democratization, state-provided social security*, and *social participation*. It is to these areas that positive liberties are particularly relevant, including equality of opportunity, social security, autonomy, and protection from socio-economic risks.

Other concerns of social democracy involved here include the effort to insure human dignity in the workplace, a just distribution of income, and a suitable scheme for representing interests within each firm as well as at the macro-economic level. Nevertheless, these dimensions of economic performance cannot ignore criteria of macro-economic efficiency either, such as unemployment, inflation, and growth.

One of the crucial categories of positive liberty is gainful employment. Not only do people derive income from their wages and salaries, and hence the social goods they need to lead a self-directed life; work is also the foundation for social and cultural recognition and self-esteem. Consequently, access to the labor market is an essential measure of performance for the political economy of social democracy. Since the mid-1980s uncoordinated market economies seem to have enjoyed greater success in some of the most important measures of economic performance such as inflation and unemployment. This is evidently due to a combination of factors already mentioned: their more flexible labor markets, management's greater autonomy and decision-making latitude in adapting rapidly to changing market conditions, and their ability to launch radical innovations by raising large sums quickly in capital markets. Meanwhile, many coordinated market economies have suffered from high structural unemployment. Libertarian authors conclude from these successes that coordinated economies are incapable of adjusting their labor markets to post-Fordist shifts in production methods and global competition. But any such simplistic contrast of coordinated and uncoordinated economies in respect to unemployment rates is misleading. For example, if we compare the unemployment rate in the United States, the prototypical uncoordinated economy, with rates prevailing in coordinated economies over the last twenty years, we find that it is sometimes higher and sometimes lower, varying with overall macro-economic conditions. In the period 1983 to 1988, Sweden, Norway, Switzerland, and Austria all had unemployment rates lower than that of the United States, indeed so low they almost approached Japanese levels of less than 3 percent. Their equally coordinated neighbors Denmark, France, the Netherlands, and Belgium, however, had higher unemployment rates, ranging from 9 to 12 percent. In 1992 the unemployment figures for Sweden, the Netherlands, Norway, Switzerland, and Austria were lower than in the US (7.5 percent). Even in America's boom year of 1998, the unemployment rate there of 4.6 percent was still higher than in the Netherlands, Norway, and Switzerland. In Britain, another uncoordinated economy, the unemployment rate between 1990 and 1998 was above the OECD average in four out of eight years.[42]

As these comparisons reveal, high unemployment in some coordinated economies has a variety of explanations that cannot be reduced to the institutional variables of the *Varieties of Capitalism* approach.

Uncoordinated market economies seem able to respond to market shifts more nimbly and to reduce unemployment during expansionary phases more quickly. But even their institutional structures, especially a flexible, deregulated labor market (rapid turnover, few restraints on firms), cannot prevent high unemployment rates. Moreover, the additional costs that a flexible labor market imposes on the rest of society have to be included in the comparison. Not only the quantity but also the quality of jobs has to be considered. Low-wage jobs, for example, that often match the low skills of their incumbents, can easily push the latter into the trap of the working poor. A labor market that is too flexible and deregulated restricts the full exercise of a person's right to define his or her own life plan, especially at the lower end of the skill and income scale. Additionally, market economies with uncoordinated, decentralized wage-setting processes tend to generate large wage disparities. And where economic inequality exceeds fair and productive levels, as in the United States and Britain, poverty and social exclusion are more widespread than in coordinated economies. The "social inheritance" of positions in life and thus the unjust distribution of opportunity are much more strongly marked in uncoordinated economies.[43]

On the other hand, the scarcity of low-wage sectors in coordinated market economies frequently leads to mass and/or long-term unemployment. The transformation from an industrial to a knowledge/service economy occasions structural changes that confront labor markets and social systems as well as corporatist steering institutions with daunting challenges. Ironically it is often the very institutions created to protect against risks in the labor market that impede adjustments to the new challenges and, with them, reductions in unemployment. This is especially the case in countries where the social insurance system is financed by joint contributions by employers and employees via payroll deductions. This arrangement increases labor costs and has itself become a secondary cause of structural mass unemployment.[44] In a few coordinated economies with highly regulated labor markets and rigid wage systems, such as Germany, there has been increasing social polarization between insiders and outsiders that is quite similar to that found in uncoordinated economies.

Export-dependent sectors can maintain their competitiveness only by continuous innovation in products and processes as well as accompanying cost-cutting. International competition will inevitably raise the productivity of business enterprises, so job opportunities there will be limited even in countries that hold their own in international markets.[45] In fact employment rates in those sectors have decreased in practically every developed economy; most job growth has occurred in protected sectors such as local services.[46] Even in these protected sectors increased employment has occurred mostly in the low-wage sector of the private economy or in publicly delivered social services. These trends have in turn resulted from several factors: the way that the production regime has been socially imbedded; modes of state financing; and political decisions conditioned on the public's willingness to accept a certain level of taxation.

Consequently, coordinated economies will have to respond to the challenges of changing modes of production and new international conditions in different ways than uncoordinated ones. The organization of the social welfare state and its impact on economic processes and results will have to be considered in comparative perspective.

3.7 The social market economy

The term "social market economy" refers to economic systems that have been integrated into social welfare states dedicated to protecting fundamental rights and subjected to regulatory policies designed to achieve full employment.[47] The version of the *Varieties of Capitalism* approach preferred by Kitschelt, Lange, Marks, and Stephans envisages the synthesis of the social welfare and market economy types.[48] The authors begin by noting that the global economy has triggered institutional transformations – especially of political and economic systems – in many national economies. Through an analysis of the reciprocal interactions of the social welfare state and different production regimes, we can distinguish four ideal types of the market/social state complex.

1 *Uncoordinated market economies* combined with *residual* (liberal) *social welfare states* Here, trade unions are perceived by management as impediments to decision-making and play only a minor role in coordinating a firm's activities. In these countries one usually finds a two-party system, divided over questions of economic distribution.
2 *Market economies coordinated at the macro level*, combined with *universalistic*, egalitarian, redistributive, and service-oriented social welfare states marked by a high degree of decommodification These economies, coordinated at the national level, feature top-tier negotiations and consultations between hierarchical organizations of employers and employees on all important issues. In these self-coordinating institutions governments typically play a moderating rather than a directive role. Social democratic parties usually dominate these countries, as bourgeois parties are often fragmented.
3 *Sectorally coordinated market economies* combined with *transfer-oriented social welfare states* preoccupied with employment and incomes policy and displaying a moderate degree of decommodification They facilitate the acquisition of vocational skills on the shop floor or in state-run schools in which labor and business are heavily involved. Trade unions play a major role in determining wages and working

conditions. In these countries a tripartite party system prevails that usually accommodates liberal, Catholic, and social democratic perspectives.
4 *Market economies coordinated by industrial groups* (*keiretsu*) combined with *residual* or *paternalistic* social welfare states The party system in these countries is marked by the hegemony of "bourgeois" parties along with competition among non-ideological clientele parties.

By including welfare state arrangements in the analysis of production regimes in capitalist economies, we discover that a variety of political-economic institutions maintain complicated interactions with the corporatist and political actors favored by existing structures.

The institutional mix

The institutional web that binds together labor market systems, business organization, and the structures of the social welfare state also allows the positive qualities of uncoordinated market economies to be exploited, while their negative aspects are offset by appropriate systems of social security. Thus, for example, by dismantling its job protection scheme, Denmark has achieved a highly flexible labor market now outdone only by those in the United States and Britain.[49] That allows Danish entrepreneurs to expand or reduce their workforces as needed. The insecurity faced by the employee is compensated for by relatively generous unemployment insurance payments, an active labor market policy, and many other social services.

Conversely, production regimes based on an expanded low-wage sector, underdeveloped social security, and a flexible, unregulated labor market generate highly problematic social outcomes from the poverty of low-wage employees to alarming forms of social anomie. In the USA, for example, 1,339,695 people were incarcerated in 1993, a rate of 519 prisoners per 100,000 inhabitants. In Germany the rate of incarceration in that same year was only 80 per 100,000. Western and Beckett have calculated that in Europe the number of unemployed males exceeds that of male prisoners by a ratio of between 20 and 50 to 1. In the United States, by contrast, the ratio between the unemployed and prisoners is a bit less than 3 to 1. If all of these prisoners were included in labor market statistics, the employment rate in Europe during the period from 1976 to 1994 would have been higher than it was in the United States in all but four of those years. In 1995 the official German unemployment rate was 7.1 percent compared to only 5.6 percent in the US; however, these statistics reveal that, if the prison population in both countries were counted, the German unemployment rate would have been 7.4 percent as against 7.5 percent in the United States.[50] Only when system comparisons cast a wide enough net can one judge realistically the true effects of different types of political economy on universal rights.

Choosing the right mix

Let us assume that the highest standards have been met: the requisite economic framework has been politically enacted; the rights of social citizenship have been guaranteed by a universal social welfare state regime; adequate rights of co-determination have been granted; and the primacy of politics over the economy – its right, in principle, to regulate and intervene – has been recognized and anchored in the constitution. Even then, the choice of institutional arrangements for political economy amounts, in practical terms, to only a selection among varieties of welfare capitalism. Two considerations ought to guide political decisions about the specific mix for social democratic theory. *First*, the best aggregate economic outcome that can be expected in light of attainable GDP levels and ecologically responsible rates of growth should be chosen. And, *second*, preferences as to type-specific advantages such as high employment, job security, continuity, productivity, and innovation should be made in politically legitimate ways.

3.8 The social market economy and globalization

Like Hall and Soskice, Kitschelt and his colleagues think of political economies as a framework of incentives and constraints enmeshed in a complex web of institutions and that therefore cannot be fundamentally altered by short-term political decisions. Nevertheless, the pressures emanating from global and socio-cultural constraints may sometimes precipitate changes even in political economies, possibly in the direction of convergence. Yet the *Varieties of Capitalism* authors argue that existing institutional frameworks predispose political economies to react to those pressures in quite different ways. In fact, they claim that the same economic challenges actually intensify institutional differences rather than pushing divergent market economies toward structural alignment. Kitschelt et al. identify five reasons why it is both theoretically and empirically implausible to think that we will see a convergence of modern political economies upon a single, superior model combining markets and political decision-making institutions.

First, despite declining transportation and communication costs, international competition will never be perfect. There will always be a multitude of niches and local production regimes shielded from international competition.

Second, the effects of economic globalization on the domestic economy vary with the blend of economic factors in each. A glance at the "portfolios" of different production regimes reveals a degree of adaptation, but more as a shift of accent within a specific type than between types. Countries, regions, and sectors tend to prefer certain areas of economic activity, and to specialize in markets that are compatible with their institutional advantages.

Third, generalized international competitive pressures will be perceived and managed differently by actors in diverse institutional settings.

Fourth, the expectation that intensified international competition will result in a general convergence of types of market economies presupposes the willingness and capacity of governments to liberalize their markets. However, the extent of economic internationalization is collectively determined by governments and geopolitical regimes with quite distinct preferences and institutional capacities to dismantle trade barriers. Thus, patterns of mutual adjustment are a function not only of economic and organizational trends, but of political logic.

Fifth, the powerful currents of international competition run up against the domestic status quo. The relative strength and organizational skill of producer groups, the configuration of parties, the electoral system, relations between the executive and the legislative branches, and lastly the abilities and territorial-administrative organization of national bureaucracies all weaken or deflect those internationalizing currents. These pre-existing configurations act not just as "dependent variables" forced to adapt to new challenges; they also act like subtle filters influencing the adjustment strategies of the pre-eminent actors.[51]

A brief historical survey reveals certain trends in the evolution of market economies, some toward convergence and others away from it.

The first period, the "golden age" of postwar capitalism between 1950 and 1973, displayed a divergence among types of capitalism resulting from different class compromises and models of growth. However, in this phase one also finds a gradual trend toward a more "organized capitalism." That is, the divergence among already developed structures governing the political allocation of scarce resources remained, although one could also discern a convergence in the direction of stronger political controls over market outcomes.

In the second period, the era of "shocks and crises" from 1973 to 1982, when all postwar paths showed signs of economic and political disequilibrium, newly launched policy experiments continued in a path-dependent trajectory. Countries with organized capitalism such as the nationally coordinated market economies redoubled their efforts to organize their economies. Conversely, comparatively less well-organized countries moved to reduce state organization and regulation, choosing instead to emphasize market relations.

Scholarly interpretations differ about the *third period*, the phase beginning in 1982, in which developed capitalist economies began to change under the impact of globalization.

According to the *neoliberal* view, all types of capitalism now confront powerful market forces that will compel them to restore market relations in areas that had previously been organized by non-market institutions. This *neoliberal model of convergence* downplays the capacity of different institutional patterns to resist the pressure toward evolutionary convergence.

In contrast, the *neo-institutional* approach asserts that institutional divergence not only persists, but has even intensified under the pressure of globalization. To be sure, there has been a tendency for market economies coordinated at the state level to evolve in the direction of sectoral coordination. Those economies have also shown a tendency to reform themselves in order to confront altered political and economic challenges. However, this transformative process has not led to an assimilation of coordinated to uncoordinated market economies. The more coordinated economies remain organized and lean toward intervention and regulation, while continuing to maintain their social protections. When adjustments become necessary, they usually strive to bring about cooperation and concerted action between corporatist actors and governments. By contrast, the uncoordinated market economies become even more libertarian as they weaken social protections and emphasize individual achievement and markets.

The structures of corporatism

At the "meso-level" of political economy, signs of a "dual convergence" are becoming evident: uncoordinated and coordinated economies are moving farther apart, while the latter tend to converge on the model of sectoral coordination. Certain meso-economic variables should be regarded not as passive media that merely transmit external pressures, but as active agents capable of responding to those pressures. This is certainly true for the structure of wage negotiations.[52]

At the beginning of the crisis years, just as the macro-economic turn away from Keynesianism and toward monetarism was occurring, one observes a general retreat from corporatist, state-sponsored wage policies. In the 1990s Great Britain reordered its policy priorities to stress price stability at the expense of full employment, which tended to reduce the role of trade unions. The new ideal guiding policy-making was to encourage market self-regulation, especially in the area of wages and labor relations, and to divest the state of its responsibility for macroeconomic (Keynesian) steering.

Matters evolved quite differently in Sweden. There political-economic developments since World War II have been shaped by a coherent corporatist model. It combines centralized wage negotiations between the powerful trade union federation of industrial workers (LO) and its counterpart in the private sector, the employers' association known as the

SAF; sporadic state intervention in the labor market; and a multitude of social policy measures. This compact form of corporatism allowed social democratic governments to pursue (post-) Keynesian steering until the end of the 1970s in the form of the Rehn–Meidner model.[53] The result has been full employment stoked by a "wage policy of solidarity," active labor market policy, and selective industrial policy.[54] During the 1980s the old patterns of industrial relations and moderate wage demands became increasingly ineffective. For one thing, the Swedish maxim "First growth then redistribution"[55] seemed consigned to oblivion. The LO and SAF relinquished their wage-setting leadership to state actors who allowed inflationary settlements.

Moreover, the solidarity-inspired wage policy no longer could keep pace with the exigencies of post-Fordist, knowledge-based production techniques. Employers, especially exporters, increasingly demanded wage differentiation. The employers' association for mechanical engineering, a key member of the SAF, broke away from centralized wage negotiations in 1983, intending to reach a separate wage agreement with its LO counterpart, the metal workers' union. By the early 1990s the SAF finally decided against negotiations at the highest level. Thus, in the rounds of collective bargaining since then, the issue – both between the SAF and the unions and within the SAF – no longer has been whether there should still be top-tier negotiations, but rather simply how much leeway outcomes in a given industrial sector would leave for agreements in one firm.

In the 1980s the importance of corporatist institutions began to wane just as monetary policy and the role of central banks took center stage relative to other instruments of macro-economic steering. The deregulation of financial markets and wage negotiations correlate. The Swedish case represents a radical "paradigm shift," to some extent even a "regime change"; yet the abandonment of the postwar consensus was far less confrontational and ideologically charged than it was in Britain.[56] The essential elements of Sweden's welfare state and active labor market policies remained untouched by these changes.

There is little reason to expect an end to corporatist self-steering. The break with coordinated incomes policy and the "treaty of Wassenaar" in the Netherlands in 1982 actually inaugurated a new era of consensual coordination. Indeed, the Netherlands is often cited as a case of renascent corporatism. Even in Sweden, a new consensus seems to be taking shape since the mid-1990s about coordinated negotiations at the industry sector level. To be sure, the trade unions had to give up their demands for collective bargaining at the federation level, but at the same time the employers distanced themselves from their demand to bargain exclusively at the firm level. Nevertheless, the Dutch case suggests that the new consensus will not necessarily exclude further decentralization. The employers' demand for decentralized wage negotiations and "wage flexibility" leading to greater productivity, growth, and competitiveness has dominated every capitalist country since the early 1980s, yet the *"organized decentralization"* characteristic of coordinated market economies must be sharply distinguished from the *"disorganized decentralization"* in countries such as the United States and Great Britain.[57]

In light of these experiences, the surmise that we are witnessing a uniform trend toward convergence in industrial relations seems unfounded. Thus, for example, neither Norway nor Finland gives any indication of having embarked on the trend toward decentralization. And in Denmark, once the pattern of wage-setting at the federation level ended in the early 1980s, new kinds of sub-associational collective bargaining institutions arose that yielded wage agreements even more encompassing in some respects than the traditional ones. Sweden, with its unique form of decentralization, is actually the exception within the four Nordic countries.[58]

Thus, within the group of coordinated market economies some cases of institutional stability and some of significant institutional change may be observed. The same is true of uncoordinated economies. In their collective bargaining practices and macro-economic steering policies, countries such as Sweden, Denmark, the Netherlands, and Belgium are converging on the "Rhenish model."[59] Meanwhile, the uncoordinated economies of New Zealand and Great Britain are converging on the American model. What cannot be observed in this dimension is any convergence between the coordinated and uncoordinated economies. But even the German model, toward which the nationally coordinated models are moving, has not been immune to the processes of structural transformation. More and more employers are leaving their associations and thereby abandoning centralized employer negotiations.

Thus, since the 1970s the organizational patterns of wage-setting have changed in rather fundamental ways. These changes may be explained as multi-level processes of adaptation to new conditions of global competition and new forms of production. But that raises the question of why some countries have changed more radically than others – Sweden as compared to Germany – and why such changes have moved the countries in such different directions – Sweden as compared to Great Britain.[60] We may answer the first question by observing that sectoral coordination offers great enough bargaining latitude for employers that they can respond to external market pressures without entirely relinquishing the strategic advantages that coordination brings in high-value production regimes. The answer to the second question is more complicated. Nationally coordinated wage negotiations at the federation level presuppose, first, a high level of coordination and willingness to accept direction within the association. Second, they assume that there is some general arrangement whereby trade unions will attune their negotiating strategy to the maximization of the macro-societal welfare function.[61] Third, and most important, a long-term relationship of trust must have grown up between the actors. To this extent the collapse of the Swedish collective bargaining system is in no sense comparable to the failure of corporatist experiments in countries such as France or Britain in the 1970s or 1980s. The internal associational fragmentation and mutual hostility in those countries meant that they lacked the prerequisites for the success of corporatist negotiations. When instituted under severe economic stress, corporatist arrangements tend to fail, because they have not been shored up by a long history of organizational adaptation and trust-building.[62] The Swedish coordination of labor relations can still count on the traditional corporatist structures; hence, it is efficient for the production regime to modify rather than scrap the mechanisms of wage-setting.

When structures of communication and reconciliation are available in the area of industrial relations, actors also tend to use them. Even though these structures and mechanisms in coordinated market economies have changed over the past two decades, political-economic actors evidently still have confidence in their institutions' capacity for coordination, reconciliation, and communication. For that reason, too, coordinated economies rarely react to the novel challenges of global markets by backing radical moves toward greater flexibility and deregulation of labor relations or the dismantling of social security, but instead opt for *organized* strategies of adjustment.

Contrary to the neoliberal view that uncoordinated market economies can react better to the global integration of markets in goods and financial services, recent experience suggests that coordinated economies have better medium- and long-range prospects. A production regime based principally on the low-wage sector, a rudimentary welfare state, and low taxes can react to global competition *only* by progressively dismantling regulation and social security. By contrast, coordinated economies can react in more subtle ways to this same challenge, and thrive by relying on a well-trained and socially secure workforce as well as high-value, specialized products. Of course, they do have to confront the problem that, given their slight wage differentials, there is no easy way to achieve employment growth in low-skill service jobs.

The primacy of politics

To explain differing institutional forms of capitalist democracy, scholars frequently emphasize certain traditions, sometimes dating to preindustrial times, which supposedly have had the power to shape subsequent economic structures. Among the latter, the following are most often cited as having laid the groundwork for present-day forms of national economy: the role of the church, the influence of guilds, the development of a modern national bureaucracy, the timing of industrialization, the size of domestic markets, and the strength of the organized labor movement.[63] More recently, scholars have proposed a different idea: that social welfare states should be understood not merely as protective reactions against capitalism and the social imperfections of markets, but also as positive components of modern capitalism in their own right.[64] The social welfare state is constructed in reaction to institutional patterns in other areas of the political economy. Market economies and production regimes subsequently adapt to its presence in efficiency-maximizing ways.

The *Varieties of Capitalism* school of thought demonstrates that political economies of the *coordinated* type, *combined with a social welfare state dedicated to protecting fundamental rights*, can survive and thrive in an open market environment, as long as their structures are remade to fit the altered circumstances. Even under the conditions wrought by globalization, social democracy's prospects for imbedding and regulating markets and maintaining the social welfare state are still good. Comparative studies of welfare states contain valuable lessons about which conditions are most favorable to the ongoing regulation of welfare states as well as to their ability to invigorate the economy.[65]

Since the 1990s, extensive political regulation of the economy has become more necessary than ever due to three general social and political trends.[66] For one thing, formerly state-provided services have often been privatized. Second, transnational market integration has opened a chasm between the scope of the externalities generated by the market and the ability of governments to regulate them politically. Finally, risks to the environment and civilization itself have multiplied as a result of unregulated growth. The wave of deregulation that spanned the 1970s and 1980s has meanwhile been replaced by a policy of case-by-case re-regulation.[67] These trends have put the libertarian position on the defensive, according to which regulation should do no more than attempt to maintain competitive conditions in an industry. Consequently, the political economy of social democracy must work out a revised justification for regulatory economic policy. But given the set of national and international problems already depicted, the outlines of that justification appear fairly clear. Be that as it may, the principal tasks will be to develop instruments of regulatory policy and forms of political decision-making that set the goals for their deployment, and to muster the political will to put them into practice in the global arena.[68]

Institutional actors pledged to uphold the fundamental rights of their citizens find the social welfare state to be one of their most powerful political allies. Indeed, social democracy is distinguished by its commitment to make the state serve encompassing social welfare goals. The social welfare state secures the rights to private and political autonomy and of social citizenship by enacting social security measures and enlarging their opportunities for participation in decisions. Yet social welfare regimes can only be sustainable if they enable their economies to perform well.[69] In their symbiosis with free market economies, social welfare regimes must pursue their intrinsic logic with the market, not against or instead of it.

The classical account of the social welfare state was formulated by Asa Briggs:

> A "welfare state" is a state in which organized power is deliberately used [. . .] in an effort to modify the play of the market forces in at least three main directions – first, by guaranteeing individuals and families a minimum income irrespective of the market value of their work or property; second, narrowing the extent of insecurity by enabling individuals and families to meet certain social contingencies (for example, sickness, old age and unemployment) which lead otherwise to individual and family crises; and third, by insuring that all citizens without distinction of status or class are offered the best standards available in relation to a certain agreed range of social services.[70]

While far from perfect, Briggs's definition is a good starting point for a theory of social democracy. It assumes that the uncertainties and marginalization occasioned by free market capitalism ought to be mitigated by state-provided *security guarantees* and *opportunities for participation* that are independent of the market. Social democratic theory would add that the type, level, and spheres of security benefits should be tied to the state's guarantee of fundamental rights. The UN Human Rights Covenant does not leave it up to the discretion of individual nation-states *whether* to protect the social and economic rights derived from it. It simply declares that each government must decide, given its resources, *how* and to what extent to protect those rights. Even the social welfare state has no obligation to do what exceeds its capacities. But since equal rights are at stake here, the state's obligations to underwrite social security, education, labor rights, health care, and employment opportunities must be met to the greatest economically feasible extent.

In this sense fundamental rights impose a universal obligation to provide welfare state services. But decisions about how to provide them – and at what level – are up to the policy-makers. Indeed, even the way that social security should be offered by the welfare state is a political question. The level of security offered by the welfare state will thus hinge on several factors: the magnitude of GDP, labor productivity, political culture(s), and the constellation of political actors. The social democratic viewpoint would add that it ought to follow the basic democratic principle (also the condition for social autonomy) that citizens should always obey rules they have made for themselves. That is, the beneficiaries must be given ample opportunity to participate in the structures of decision-making about social services and their provision. The social welfare state must be internally democratic.

There is a scholarly consensus that the social welfare state should exempt certain spheres from the play of market forces, and substitute politically defined guarantees for these. These, the "big five," consist of health, education, housing, social security, and personal services. More recently, other such spheres have been added: the environment, leisure time, and transportation, as well as urban and landscape planning.[71] Theory has not yet solved the problem of where to set the minimum level of services so that it meets the standards implicit in fundamental rights. But scholars have described how social welfare states actually work, and how far existing welfare regimes go in satisfying the claims of fundamental rights.

In respect to the structures of the social welfare state, the classic dichotomy of goals and instruments runs up against inherent limits set by the principle of social autonomy.

First, in one sense full employment is only a means to finance the rest of the programs offered by the social welfare state. But employment also counts as one of the values supported by fundamental rights, so it is in that respect an end in itself.

Second, social security benefits should not be provided in a way that contradicts the goal of maintaining human dignity.

Third, the structures that define and guarantee social security must permit and encourage democratic participation.

With these qualifications in mind, we can analyze the goals and instruments typical of the social welfare state. But let us note that few of the possible instruments of welfare state organization can ever be completely neutral vis-à-vis the state's goals as understood by social democracy. Most instruments, such as tax policy, have repercussions on the goals themselves.

4

A Rights-Based Welfare State

4.1 Social security regimes

Dimensions of the social welfare state

Anton Hemerijck has analyzed the factors that may vary from one welfare state to another. His research yields a sophisticated tableau of organizational possibilities, namely:[1]

- *eligibility for benefits and the spectrum of covered risks* Access to social services may depend on citizenship or on need, on job-related insurance contributions or on private contracts.
- *the structure of service-provision and the generosity of benefits* Services can be either minimal or generous; they may be based on income or wealth qualifications. They may grant unitary basic services, or make benefits depend on income or contributions. The service structure is geared to each country's social protection goals, whether these involve income floors, anti-poverty efforts, or equality.
- *methods of financing* Social services can be financed from general revenue, wage-based contributions, user fees, or some combination of the above.
- *the intensity of services* Social services can be delivered either by professional (public) providers, by the market, or in informal ways by the (extended) family.
- *family policy* This may be passive, emphasizing cash payments toward the support of the family headed by a male breadwinner, or it can actively promote gender equality by subsidizing publicly provided daycare and generous family leave allowances.
- *labor market policy* These may include everything from employee and union rights to regulations governing job dismissal, minimum

wages, collective bargaining rights and procedures, works' councils, and numerous other variants of active labor market policies.

- *the logic of governance* Responsibility for the management of welfare state and employment policies is not necessarily always vested in public administration. Other possibilities might include devolving the management and provision of welfare state services upon local authorities, and cooperative arrangements between social partners and/or private or third-sector parties.

- *Industrial relations* The breadth and coordination of industrial relations are closely connected with employment policies, labor market regulation, and the logic of the social welfare state generally. The spectrum ranges from fragmented, uncoordinated systems of sectoral negotiations up to centralized coordination. The coordination of industrial relations crucially affects employment, income distribution, and solutions to problems such as inflation and unemployment.

In now-classic fashion, Esping-Andersen has compared the welfare regimes that emerged in the last quarter of the twentieth century, identifying three ideal types: the *liberal, conservative,* and *social democratic.*[2] Their chief distinguishing criterion is whether and to what degree they have institutionalized social rights. Here the most significant boundary separating Esping-Andersen's three types of welfare regimes runs between the latter two types of social welfare state based on those rights, and the liberal states that fail to institutionalize social civil rights. These rely heavily on need-based poor relief that recognizes no legal entitlement to support and generally treats the market as the sole source of welfare for their citizens. Liberal welfare regimes thus do not meet the standards of social democracy, whereas the other two variants do, since they have institutionalized social civil rights. The provision of welfare in the social democratic type rests with the state; in the corporatist model, responsibility is assigned mainly to the family and society.

The ***universalistic (social democratic) social welfare states of the Scandinavian type*** are distinguished by the following features.

1 Legal entitlements to most social services depend on the status of social citizenship which is recognized in social rights.
2 Wage-replacement benefits in many transfer programs are nearly high enough to approach the claimant's previous income level.
3 The social welfare state is overwhelmingly financed from general revenues.
4 Apart from the health and education sectors, the system offers many other social services, for example in care of the elderly and morning-until-evening daycare.

5 An active family policy aims to allow women to enter the labor market on equal terms with men by providing complete daycare for their children and other supplementary services.
6 Job protection policies vary from the low (Denmark) to the high end (Sweden). They are generally supported by active labor market and adult education policies.
7 Corporatist industrial relations tend to centralize collective bargaining; thus, contracts negotiated at the highest level set the standard for most businesses and employees.
8 The state obliges itself to pursue a macro-economic policy of full employment.

Secondly, the *conservative social welfare state regime*, widely practiced on the European continent, evinces the following characteristics, which may be more corporatist or family-centered, depending on the traditions in individual countries.

1 The entire system features employment-based social insurance centered on occupational and status groups.
2 There are significant inequalities in the transfer levels of different programs. For example, high wage-replacement levels in old-age pensions may be combined with low wage-replacement rates for unemployment insurance, as in Italy.
3 The social welfare state is financed mainly by wage-based contributions.
4 Aside from health care and education, very few benefits are provided for low-income recipients. The third sector and private employers take up the slack.
5 Family policy tends to be passive, and tailored to the male breadwinner model; the employment rate for women is relatively low.
6 Extensive job protection guarantees are combined with passive labor market policies.
7 Comprehensive vocational training programs extend beyond individual industries.
8 There is a rigidly organized system of social partnership for parties to collective bargaining.
9 Industrial relations are coordinated. Sectoral wage negotiations often set industry-wide standards.

By contrast, *the liberal, Anglo-Saxon social welfare regime* is characterized by the predominance of market principles, and rests on the following foundations.

1 Programs are targeted to particular groups. Applicants usually must demonstrate need to qualify for benefits.

2 In most programs wage-replacement levels are low.
3 Programs are financed mainly from general revenues.
4 There are very few entitlements to social services except for health care and education.
5 Family policy is weakly developed.
6 Job protection is rudimentary. Labor market policy is passive, while the vocational education system is underdeveloped.
7 Industrial relations are uncoordinated and usually respond to market conditions. Trade unions are moderately strong, but collective bargaining is decentralized and sets standards for only a portion of the workforce.

In spite of their institutional differences, the conservative and social democratic welfare regimes are both based on constitutionally protected social rights. Yet they do differ in respect to coverage (universal or not), social benefits, financing, and the status of beneficiaries. The social democratic ideal type is distinguished by its willingness to extend basic security to everyone, regardless of the recipients' previous income level, contributions, or job performance. This universalistic model aims to achieve equality of status. Solidarity between classes is supposed to be encouraged by equal rights for all. Social service systems are tax-supported. By contrast, the conservative ideal type is marked by the imposition of compulsory social insurance. The provision of services depends on previous contributions into the system. To receive a reasonable level of social benefits, a person must have contributed large sums over many years. Such a system has the effect of reinforcing social stratification, and maintaining it whenever social risks occur.

Esping-Andersen himself has emphasized that the welfare regimes he describes are ideal types that epitomize a variety of characteristics. Individual countries are at various removes from the ideal types. In fact, social welfare regimes in many of them, such as Germany, France, and Great Britain, display features of several different ideal types. Actual social welfare states are distinguished, among other things, by the way they institutionalize the basic eligibility requirements citizens must meet to qualify for social benefits. These may take the form of legitimate entitlements to civil rights, need, or contributions rendered. As far as need-based aid is concerned, claimants have no legal entitlement to social benefits, much less to a specific amount. In the case of contribution-linked benefits, only those who have contributed have a legal claim to receive the appropriate benefits in their full amount. In respect to the civil right to social services, constitutional law itself supports a person's legitimate claim to them. Three criteria ought to be considered in evaluating normatively the different justifications of entitlement:

1 the legal status of social services as a constitutionally guaranteed civil right
2 the kind and extent of services in view of their possible contribution to securing positive liberties and opportunities for private and political autonomy
3 the way in which services are rendered considering the conditions for social autonomy.

Empirical research allows us to set priorities for combining the civil rights criterion with an adequate spectrum of social services. In light of the basic right to protection against risk, the *level* of legally guaranteed social benefits must be set at least high enough so that, if social-structural risks actually occur, the victims' claims will still be met. The third criterion, social autonomy, implies that democratic procedures should help determine the level of benefits. Citizens should be included in decision-making about the provision of services and, if possible, be given some direct role in the latter. It would contradict the terms of rights-based legitimacy to arrange a trade-off in which the state might support social services generously, while refusing to institutionalize claims to them as civil entitlements and/or not implementing them in a way that respected the beneficiaries' social autonomy.

The social welfare state in the context of political autonomy

The theory of social democracy expects two things from the social welfare state, both to be guaranteed by its mode of organization and service delivery.

First, it should achieve *social justice*. By preventing and compensating for risk, the welfare state should be able to secure the just distribution of life chances and see to it that basic rights are honored equally for everyone in practice. In this sense it is social democracy's chief response to politically optional risks, and as such it is defined by its normative contribution to securing basic rights.

Second, it must promote *economic efficiency* and growth. The social welfare state can do this indirectly, by contributing to social justice, and directly, by the way it distributes social benefits. The economic objectives may be achieved in several ways: by (1) the motivation that a just social order instills in citizens; (2) the enhanced willingness of citizens to accept social and economic change when their social security is guaranteed; (3) their contribution to the training and retraining of the workforce; and (4) the countercyclical effects of the state's income security policies.[3] By offering citizens the experience of a nearly just distribution of life chances and by providing public goods to all of them, the social welfare state can make a vital contribution to social cohesion and political stability.[4]

History has not yet resolved the issue of whether the residual liberal welfare regime on the one hand and the rights-oriented models on the other embody different stages in the actualization of social democracy or the enduring outcomes of fundamentally divergent social and political paths in individual countries. Several factors seem to indicate that the entrenched differences will endure. First, as noted, the pre-democratic history of each country has bequeathed to it a unique set of institutions, constellation of actors, and cultural-political traditions. Second, these initial conditions led to the crystallization of quite different models in each case, while path-dependency kept the inherited model on the same trajectory for over a century.[5] On the other hand there are indications that increasing pressures of globalization may constrain many countries to emulate the most successful models.[6]

Esping-Andersen explains the differences among these types by citing contingent historical factors such as differences in political culture, party constellations, the size of the respective country and its economy, the degree of its dependence on outside influences, and its democratic pre-democratic history. However, one has to assume that self-interest alone enables actors to learn social and political lessons and act on them. Therefore, the specific constellation of actors that prevailed in the early phase of a country's development cannot be viewed as a permanent constraint limiting the actors' latitude to act in new ways in the future. Rather, so-called path-dependency is itself conditional on changeable constellations of actors.

Furthermore, as each model develops, there is an increasing tendency for it to "borrow" elements of competing models.[7] This is particularly evident in the respective fates of the welfare state models exemplified by the United States and Sweden. In the United States the pendulum first swung toward a more social democratically oriented welfare state model under the impact of the Great Depression. But later, even under a Democratic president, it swung back quite strongly toward the earlier residual model.[8] By contrast, Sweden began dismantling its social democratic model during the 1970s, but in the 1990s it was compelled to restore many of the social services it had once granted.[9] The most recent wave of social welfare state reform beginning in the 1980s can be interpreted as a process of benchmarking, whereby successful solutions offer general guidance for other countries.

Variations in the models

No particular welfare regime model can be derived from the theory of social democracy. Nevertheless, we can infer a set of concrete norms that rate the capacity of various models to provide legitimacy and establish institutions or policies most likely to achieve social democratic goals. The social welfare state envisaged by social democracy is open to model variations within the limits allowed by the protection of basic rights. At this point, we can discern only the outlines of a future social welfare state, not its outcome. The two most important criteria are:

1 a system that grants and guarantees social and economic rights across the board
2 the inclusion, via adequate participatory rights, of social benefit recipients qua incumbents of social rights in the structures of decision-making.

As the paradigm cases of Sweden and Germany demonstrate, these criteria can be met by either model. Previous research has offered important insights into what must be done to consolidate a comprehensive system of social rights. One important factor is that the market-friendly and compensatory functions in the welfare state should complement one another.[10] A second involves the reciprocity that may exist between the type of social welfare state and the interests of the set of actors that support it. A third factor centers on whether political discourses on civil rights and their implications for the social welfare state are rigorous and deeply rooted in the country's political culture.[11]

The problem of decommodification

The notion of decommodification plays a key role in Esping-Andersen's typology of the welfare state. Among other things, the type and quality of the various welfare state models is measured by the degree of decommodification embodied in the organizational forms and eligibility requirements for the main social welfare programs, especially pensions, health care, and unemployment compensation. Esping-Andersen assesses the degree of decommodification on the basis of his judgment about "the ease with which the average person can opt out of the market."[12] But this criterion seems dubious. According to Esping-Andersen, the degree of decommodification brings into play several elements of particular importance to the idea of social democracy: the scope, intensity, and arrangement of social citizenship rights.

As soon as the *complementarity of rights and duties* is introduced into the discussion, it becomes apparent that the ease of evading market constraints cannot be a measure of the real-world efficacy of social rights. That would work only if individual *rights* were taken to be the exclusive normative criterion. But even then any unjustified refusal of able-bodied people to accept employment would normally violate the social rights of third parties, since the former would end up consuming resources needed by others. As noted already, the decision to grant equal social and economic rights implicitly obliges each person to take account of others' rights as well as those of the whole community to secure its social and economic reproduction.[13] If too many people made unjustified claims on the right of exit from market constraints, they would soon use up society's resources at such an alarming rate that either the society-wide standard of living would decline or else eventually future applicants for social aid could not be provided for in the same way as before.[14] In sum, the incumbents of rights have a correlative duty to take advantage of social rights only to the extent necessary and to do their fair share to uphold the system of rights as a whole.

In order to shore up the welfare state's finances and reaffirm political consent for it (which had become shaky on account of the violation of the previously stated condition), Dutch welfare reforms of the 1990s canceled some of the market-exit options that were being perceived as overly generous.[15] The introduction of unpaid sick-leave days into the Swedish health-care system, also in the 1990s, as well as equivalent reforms in other countries, follows the same principle of rebalancing rights and duties. The inclusion of the norms of duty and primary self-reliance implies a further tilt away from Esping-Andersen's view of how decommodification should be understood. Assuming that universal rights and duties have equal status, one can argue that every person who is able to work while maintaining his or her human dignity is not only entitled, but actually obliged, to do so. Only when it can be demonstrated that a person cannot earn an adequate income via self-reliant action in the market is he or she entitled to a replacement income on civil rights grounds. In that case certain risks, including unemployment, old age, illness, and the inability to earn a living, will likely jeopardize the person's enjoyment of fundamental rights. Then social insurance guaranteeing those rights must kick in, assuring the person of roughly the same income he or she could have earned in the market. This entitlement holds for a long enough time to allow the person to find suitable employment again or revise his/her life plan in light of changed circumstances. We can still talk about decommodification when the person's social benefits are taken away or reduced for failure to perform the expected social duty of primary self-reliance. In this case the affected person is not cast on the mercy of the market, but is referred to the market to the extent that acceptable opportunities exist there for him or her. Here the Danish labor market reforms of the 1990s have exemplary significance, since they enact as many measures as possible to encourage employable people to work, and impose sanctions for non-compliance.[16]

Rights and duties

In Denmark the supply of jobs was expanded through measures such as job rotation,[17] more opportunities for leaves of absence, including special leaves (for parenting, education, sabbaticals, etc.),[18] and new regulations on early retirement. The maximum period for drawing unemployment compensation was reduced from nine years to four. But in return, the unemployed were entitled to enter a three-year-long retraining program as part of the four-year unemployment period. That program ran under the rubric of "rights and duties" and provided for cooperation between the jobless person and a state-run unemployment agency to develop an action plan that would eventually bring the person back into the workforce. If out-of-work persons refuse to accept reasonable job offers, they will have to reckon with cuts in or loss of their benefits.[19] The definitions of what should count as an "acceptable" job offer are drawn very broadly in the Danish case.[20] In this model, continuing vocational education, especially for youth and the less skilled, plays a large role. It is usually done through wage subsidies and state support of continuing education. After they have been out of work for six months, young people under twenty-five are supposed to receive either a job or a spot in a vocational training program of at least eighteen months' duration. In that period they draw education subsidy payments or half the amount of normal unemployment compensation. If they refuse to accept either one, their support is halved.

In the wake of these reforms long-term unemployment fell by 70 percent, while youth unemployment (among those under twenty-five) declined by more than 60 percent between 1996 and 2001. More than 200,000 new jobs were created in the private sector, and the employment rate for women thereafter was scarcely below that for men. The latter phenomenon can be traced back to a rising supply of childcare providers, day care centers, kindergartens, and after-school programs, which evidently met an unfilled need. Furthermore, special programs were designed to help people find work who would probably not be able to meet the demands of a "normal" job, for example, refugees and immigrants and those with handicaps. Another reform package, passed in 2002 under the banner of "more people working," contained the following points: an integrated labor market system, faster and more direct job placement, incentives to "activate" the unemployed, aid to make the less skilled more employable, simplification of the labor administration, and the inauguration of an employment council to coordinate all these measures.

This program combines the job-creation measures of local governments and state-run employment centers, investing both with the same rights and duties to implement control mechanisms and rules. The unemployed are supposed to return to the workforce as quickly as possible, a goal supported by more effective job-placement, counselling, and personal attention. Work has priority over job-preparation, and the acceptance of an available position takes precedence over training measures. In addition to local governments and state employment centers, public and private enterprises, training institutes, and unemployment insurance funds are also all obliged to emphasize job-placement and continuing education. If, in spite of all these programs, people still cannot survive in the labor market, they are entitled to claim generous wage-replacement payments. But if they violate their duties of self-reliance as they participate in employment-preparation programs and/or refuse to take acceptable work, they must expect sanctions.

The Swedish welfare state has long pursued an active labor market policy, featuring strategies that combine three distinct and not always compatible goals:

1 shifting jobs from unproductive into productive branches of industry
2 intensive training of workers in branches that have grown unproductive, to prepare them for jobs in the more productive sectors
3 obligations imposed on the beneficiaries of such programs to relocate if necessary.

Labor market policies of this nature combine the goals of economic productivity, social security, and balancing individual rights and duties. They seem to be a more attractive alternative for protecting rights than simply doling out transfer payments to the unemployed. The Swedish and Danish models demonstrate how the complementarity of rights and duties and of a flexible economy and social security can be embodied politically, so that the objectives of social democracy can be very nearly attained.

In sum, the idea of decommodification should not imply the uncoupling of social services from market performance, as with Esping-Andersen. It might even be politically justified at times to make recipients of a social minimum income prove that they really do want to participate in the economic life of their societies.[21]

One idea that has recently gained currency after it was proposed by Van Parijs would grant a subsistence income to every citizen with no strings attached, regardless of whether recipients chose to go to work or go surfing. His proposal cannot be justified on the basis of either social rights or universal norms of justice. If it were ever put into practice, it would ineluctably distribute the liberties and opportunities of citizens, not to mention their rights and duties, extremely unequally.[22] His model does enjoy the apparent advantage of guaranteeing to every citizen a basic right to social security, and does so at a time when the employment situation has become increasingly precarious. However, it is equally possible to provide this kind of guarantee while tying it to the prior performance of duties that every citizen *can* carry out. Thus, three powerful arguments weigh in against the model of an unconditional citizen income.

1 It is not universalizable, because it presupposes that only a limited number of citizens will actually take advantage of it.
2 In practice it could never work sustainably, because experience shows that it would offer too much motivation for an excessive number of claims.
3 It conflicts with the complementarity of rights and duties anchored in the nature of fundamental rights, unless it is expressly approved by the juridical community of citizens under certain contingent conditions.

In every current model of the social welfare state, including the Scandinavian, which approximates most closely to the social democratic ideal type, the magnitude of wage-replacement benefits depends on the recipients' ability to prove that they could not provide for themselves through successful market activities. In this limited sense one can speak of a decommodification of their social status, but not as though they were unconditionally relieved of the burdens and pressures of self-marketing. On the contrary, all of these social security systems are designed to oblige the individual person to earn their own living in the marketplace. Only when they cannot do so should social services compensate for the incipient risks. The decommodification effect of social security systems was not intended to offer people an alternative to the market, but rather to make sure that their fundamental rights would be protected if and when risks occurred.

As the example of Denmark shows, the most advanced social security systems operating at the highest material level have been most determined to bring those who have failed in the labor market back into it as quickly as possible. As part of their efforts to reform the social welfare state, several countries have tightened testing requirements for granting social benefits. But there is no conflict between those tougher standards and social rights. Rather, they could be justified as a step toward maintaining the air of legitimacy surrounding the programs, and as a way to secure permanently the material resources on which social services depend.

However, a dilemma does arise when those who violate their duty to accept gainful employment find their subsidies reduced so drastically that they fall below the threshold of a socially acceptable, dignified human existence. It is a crucial feature of social rights to prevent such occurrences at all costs. The extent to which a welfare state pushes decommodification and "activation" depends primarily on its institutionalized conceptions of justice and cultural traditions. The narratives of the social welfare state, based on those traditions, ultimately determine the arrangements and levels of national social policies. They draw partly on universalistic notions of rights, but also on the collective ethics and specific experiences of a concrete society.

4.2 Welfare state and welfare society

The market, the state, and the family all provide welfare benefits, but then so too does civil society. The concept of a *"welfare society"* expresses this social function of civil society, though it needn't imply any competition between it and the welfare state. For example, a welfare society can accommodate mixed economies in which civil society's contributions to social welfare supplement the services provided by the state.[23] To the extent that the idea of a welfare society is used polemically, in pointed contrast to the welfare *state*, it presupposes a libertarian or communitarian persuasion. Both claim that social security should not be assigned to citizens as a legal right that they can validate against the state, but rather as charitable initiatives of civil society undertaken voluntarily and from motives of neighborliness and sympathy.[24]

The welfare society of the United States offers the best empirical case study of this idea. It delivers a volume of social services nearly as great as those of European states, although predominantly through the voluntary services and activities of benevolent private associations.[25] At first glance, a welfare society strategy such as this appears ethically neutral, since authors of very different persuasions, ranging from conservative to liberal to grass-roots democratic, could go along with it. Plausible arguments can be adduced in support of the project of a welfare society, all of which have links to social rights.[26] These include the greater proximity of aid recipients to donors; lower costs to achieve the same performance efficiency; the encouragement of civic solidarity and engagement; less state control over the recipients; unburdening of state budgets; reining in of political alienation on the part of the citizens who are compelled to finance the welfare state; and prevention of the emergence of a culture of dependency on the part of subsidy recipients because of their "entitlement mentality." But serious objections can be made against this attempt to build the welfare society position on a foundation of fundamental rights.

First, the humiliating experience of social insecurity is not eliminated by a strategy of risk minimization that leaves the individual in doubt about whether he or she can rely on the benefits, or what their type and scope might be. The problem here is that the individual does not have any *rights* to social support.

Second, depending on the good will of private individuals and organizations may undermine people's self-esteem and social respectability in the eyes of others. This differs profoundly from the experience of redeeming a legal claim of which one is the co-author qua citizen. The former approach violates the basic conditions of autonomy and recognition.

Third, in large countries, the principle of a welfare society leads to substantial and illegitimate geographic disparities, because the benefits it provides depend on the social activism and generosity of local welfare initiatives.

Hence, in contrast to the welfare state solution to social security, the welfare society strategy of social protection can be at best a stopgap or supplemental solution. It is significant mainly as part of a transition to the construction of law-based social welfare state structures and/or as a way to supplement the latter.[27] Social democracy should not regard the welfare society as the primary provider of social risk insurance, one that would usurp the role of the social welfare state and of guaranteed social rights.

4.3 Labor and human dignity

Globalization, changing gender roles, and the rise of the knowledge economy and the tertiary sector are transforming the nature of work everywhere.[28] Many observers predict that labor markets in a globalized economy will rarely accommodate uninterrupted, meaningful careers.[29] Rather, a discontinuous, fragmented career pattern will become the norm, with phases of voluntary or involuntary part-time work punctuated by temporary or long-term unemployment. This precarious employment history has been dubbed the "Brazilianization"[30] of working life. Economic globalization and accelerated technological change in the knowledge society lead to hastened structural transformation, transfers to new job locations, and the rapid obsolescence of hard-won vocational knowledge. Employees in advanced service economies may have to relearn vocational skills and knowledge six to eight times during their careers.

All this carries far-reaching implications. It means lifelong learning for everyone, even for highly qualified workers, the winners in modernization. Even the qualifications that people will have to acquire throughout a lifetime of continuing education will not protect them against the uncertainties associated with unpredictable forces of change. At best they will smooth the way for a transition into the next phase of work. By contrast, the less successful and qualified workers will assemble "patchwork" employment histories during their careers. Their fate will be an uncertain sequence of temporary employment in one profession, followed by temporary unemployment, retraining, part-time work, renewed bouts of unemployment, and ephemeral phases of full-time employment again in some new field. They will have difficulty exerting any control over the entire process.

One alternative to the dwindling stock of employment opportunities would emphasize a kind of "communitarian" civic work.[31] It would be self-organized, equivalent to gainful employment, socially recognized, and rewarded (not compensated) with a kind of citizen salary. Three objectives could be attained by means of a single instrument of labor policy. "Communitarian" civic engagement would be affirmed and stabilized by an explicit reward. Unemployment would be eliminated through the reconceptualization of work. And some of the most explosive problems of the social life-world, for example in schools, child and elderly care, the neighborhood and natural environments, could be resolved by the increased supply of civic work. Moreover, the solutions would be cheap and closely attuned to lived experience.

In practice this sort of model would encounter serious problems. *First*, the people who are most willing to perform "communitarian" civic tasks are those with a stable place in the working world. *Second*, it is hard to imagine a mechanism that would allow civic activities to be classified precisely enough that we could decide which type of work deserved what kind of reward. *Third*, the free-rider effects would probably be enormous, because people would volunteer for trivial duties while demanding a full measure of its rewards. Unfortunately, only cumbersome oversight bureaucracies could discourage such free-riding.

Employment and human dignity

If it does nothing else, a social democratic political economy must try to provide equal opportunities for everyone to locate gainful employment.[32] It alone creates the conditions that nurture individual self-esteem and social recognition, which reaffirm human dignity.[33] *Hence, the opportunity to share in the work of society is rightly considered a fundamental economic right, for it opens the way to the enjoyment of other social and economic rights.* All reform projects that give up on such employment, hoping instead to rely on alternative forms of making a living, come up short. Likewise, the idea of a universal *citizen income* is acceptable only if it is intended to ease transitions from one job to another, not to function as an alternative to gainful employment.

Human dignity and social citizenship justify the rights of the individual to share in systems of social action that are essential to his or her self-esteem and social recognition.[34] It is primarily up to individuals to find entrée into those systems by dint of their own exertions in civil society, business, etc. The state has several obligations here: to open up appropriate opportunities, reduce barriers to access, and facilitate the equal treatment of all citizens. In modern societies this entitlement justifies a *right to work*. But under market conditions that right must be hedged in with qualifications. It does not imply that everyone has a guaranteed right to keep the job he or she already has. Nor does it justify a legal right to employment for every single person in every conceivable situation. Rather, it entails two political imperatives imposed on state action:

1 to work toward full employment
2 to guarantee all citizens a level of social security that is not drastically less than the income they would receive from work, provided that they have made the maximum effort to locate a job on their own. Furthermore, the state must provide whatever assistance the citizens need to find employment again.

The state should also be undogmatic about the means needed to put these rights into effect. In regard to employment, this principle suggests two restrictions on potential legal claims. In modern service-oriented societies a sea change is occurring in the mentality of certain subcultures, one that tends to devalue employment as the source of a person's social identity. This is probably a reaction to the fact that one's chances of finding employment are becoming less and less predictable. Second, it is likely that other forms of social activity will be upgraded, and eventually ranked as equivalent to traditional employment in society's cultural self-consciousness. These activities would then fulfill the same need for recognition and self-esteem that was once reserved for gainful work.

Nevertheless, the right and the duty to accept gainful employment are central social values. There is no substitute for access to properly remunerated employment as a social right. Comparative studies suggest that this goal is attainable even in a globalized economy, given the right set of institutional conditions.[35] In Germany, for example, only a slight decrease in normal work relationships was registered during the 1980s and 1990s. That gradual decline has continued, although a trend toward more flexible job descriptions and work schedules may be observed.[36] OECD research also attests to the value of increasing the rate of labor-force participation; indeed it is probably possible to reduce unemployment to the "natural" level of roughly 4 percent. For demographic reasons Germany is even predicted to have a labor shortage from 2010 on.[37]

The social democratic project now has to contend with two formidable challenges. How can gainful employment still be offered to everyone, and how can the inevitable move to greater flexibility in the workplace be made compatible with social security and continuity? Comparative research shows that an "anti-market" policy is doomed to fail in an open market environment. Nor would it attract much support in any present-day democracy on account of the massive decline in the general welfare that it would entail. On the other hand a "pro-market" policy, one that expected the market to heal the wounds it had itself caused, would lead to discrimination against the lower-income strata, as is confirmed in the case of the Anglo-Saxon countries, where that policy is practiced. It contradicts the basic right to a level of income sufficient to insure a socially acceptable standard of living. The most promising labor policy is one that works "with markets." The declining appeal of Keynesian demand management and economic planning by nation-states as a means of insuring full employment does not spell the end of opportunities to shape the political-economic landscape. An employment policy that works with markets at the nation-state level, as evidenced by the successes of the Netherlands, Austria, and Denmark, still has considerable room to experiment. There are five reasons to think that their success can point the way toward realistic, well-tested strategies.[38]

First, sectors of the economy most exposed to the brunt of global competition will not contribute much to the goal of reaching full employment in a developed economy. They can adapt to transnational competition by rationalization as well as technological and product innovation, but then they will at best maintain their current level of employment, as the most successful OECD countries have done. The spheres that are most crucial to full employment are the ones sheltered from global competition, the sectors in which personal services predominate. It is not clear whether the full employment potential of these sectors has been tapped; that depends on political decisions concerning tax rates, payroll deductions for social programs, and low-wage subsidies.

Second, since the 1990s the Netherlands' "employment miracle" has drawn attention to that country's techniques for reducing joblessness without overburdening either the national budget or the budgets of specific social programs. These involve a combination of part-time work, insistence on normal eligibility periods for drawing social benefits and pensions, and boosting women's labor-force participation rate.

Third, social-liberal policy in Denmark since the 1990s has demonstrated how increased economic flexibility can be combined with the maintenance of higher social security standards without causing socially unprotected mobility.[39] When compulsion to seek retraining and take an acceptable job is coupled with generous social security, and temporary openings are filled through well-organized job rotation, several goals at once can be attained. These programs can satisfy the economy's fast-changing demand for qualifications, protect the individual's social security, and promote social integration.

Fourth, in countries where the labor-force participation rate is generally high, unemployment tends to be low. That is the case whenever women's employment rate is high (birth rates then also tend to be above average). Thus a family-friendly social policy that respects most women's wishes to have children *and* a career would contribute to the just distribution of gainful work and the reduction of unemployment.

Fifth, besides policies to support innovation, technological development, and growth, the best thing governments can do to approach full employment is to promote job-creation in sectors with high demand for personal services. Like the other strategies listed here, that is mostly a project for welfare state reform.

Wage subsidies in the low-wage sector

In developed service economies, the goal of full employment can be most closely approximated by fully exploiting the job-creating potential of the low-wage end of the less productive human services. This is compatible with the goals of social democracy under two conditions. Either income inequalities must not exceed a certain legitimate threshold, or the actual incomes earned in this sphere should not fall below the minimum socially acceptable living standard. But a policy targeting expansion of the low-wage sector harbors perils for social rights.

1 Those employed in the low-wage sector under pure market conditions would not earn enough income to have a dignified life.
2 If the wage that a person earned in the low-wage sector fell below the level of transfer payments, then he/she would have no incentive to accept that kind of job in the first place.
3 There is a well-recognized connection between employment in the less productive service sector and excessive wage differentials in the lower range of a society's income distribution.

One way to overcome the unemployment trap and the problem of socially inadequate income is to subsidize the low-wage sector. Many countries have adopted a range of wage-subsidy programs, for instance by enacting a negative income tax, earned-income tax credits, or other forms of income support combining private-sector earnings with the subsidy.

4.4 Education as a crucial resource

The right to an equally good education for all citizens is crucial to social democracy. Education influences the future opportunities of every citizen. Furthermore, it lays the groundwork for a self-directed, self-aware life, and discloses new perspectives and choices. Education is likewise one of the keys to a socially just and economically successful society. In the knowledge society, a highly qualified workforce, always able and willing to be retrained, is a prerequisite for productivity and economic progress. Since education is the decisive resource alike for human, social, and political capital, it enhances civil society and democracy while securing social opportunities.[40] Education is also becoming the best personal insurance policy against unemployment. People who have not completed advanced vocational or professional training are more likely to suffer unemployment than those who have.

Social democracy thus imposes an obligation on the state to lay the educational foundations – both formal and material – for the free and equal development of all citizens. One core element of a "preventive" social welfare state is an education policy designed to *equalize opportunity*. Investments in education are simultaneously investments in personal liberties, potential social development, and democratic integration.

OECD studies show that improvements in the educational attainments of the employed population increase labor productivity.[41] In industrialized nations improvements in the quantity and quality of education among the employed population lead to increases in GDP. In short, investments in education have an economic pay-off. However, their effects frequently show up only after a fairly long interval or lag-time.[42]

As noted, the theory of social democracy is committed to the principle of pragmatism in social steering. Accordingly, even in such a normatively crucial sphere as education, the theory would not insist on specific types of public institutions and arrangements. Even a mixed system with a substantial share of private educational institutions, such as the American system of higher education, *can* satisfy the requirements of social democracy as long as adequate scholarship programs exist. The moderately egalitarian standards of social democracy are met as long as no applicant is prevented from getting the education for which he/she is qualified. Thus, for example, an elite university such as Harvard may decide to charge wealthy applicants high tuition, while also accepting and financing the education of less well-off applicants, without violating the conditions of equality of opportunity.

The PISA studies have turned up correlations in the realm of educational practices which should be consulted in any discussion of strategies for achieving equality of opportunity in society.[43] *These studies prove that equality of social opportunity and learning success correlate highly with two factors: beginning pedagogical care at the earliest possible point in the pre-school years, and initiating "tracking" into different types of schools at the latest possible point.*

Encouraging early childhood learning

Human beings make the greatest strides in their development during early childhood. Later on their ability to learn will never again be as high. Efforts at remedial education in later life usually fail unless the learner brings along the relevant cognitive skills that were supposed to have been acquired earlier. Thus, support for programs that improve early learning seems likely to have a positive effect on later educational attainments and social equalization.[44]

Research confirms that early childhood is by far the most critical phase for acquiring "cognitive skills."[45] That term actually has two meanings: first, the ability to understand, interpret, and process information; second, the ability to learn again, quickly and effectively. Cognitive skills are fundamental in a knowledge economy, with its high rate of technological innovation and recurring demand for new skills. Pupils who do well in tests of cognitive skills will probably make a successful transition from secondary to tertiary education.

A child's cognitive development is strongly influenced by his or her social background and the educational attainments of the parents. Therefore, an educational system committed to achieving equal opportunity for all children regardless of their social background will have to equip them with the means to acquire these cognitive skills. The goal of equal opportunity must therefore attempt to sever the links between the parents' social status and the child's learning. In countries such as the United States, Britain, and Germany, existing educational systems rarely succeed in doing this. By contrast, Sweden, Denmark, and Norway present a positive balance sheet. Today, the father's educational level there no longer has any measurable influence on the child's development of cognitive skills and school achievement. Several decades ago they instituted universal pre-school care and education. Children from economically and/or culturally disadvantaged households receive roughly the same cognitive stimulation as children from privileged social backgrounds. For that reason, when Scandinavian children start school they have good cognitive skills regardless of their social origins. Those skills sustain them throughout their entire educational career and make the learning process more efficient, because teachers can assume that all the children start on the same footing. Thus, investments in the support of early childhood education are crucial to genuine equality of opportunity. Accordingly, fees for such institutions should be kept as low as possible or else be income-adjusted, so that no one must incur early childhood education deficits for financial reasons. In Scandinavian countries today care and education are provided for virtually every child under three years old.[46] A system of incentives or even requirements might be introduced to draw immigrant children too into the same system of early education, enabling them to attend kindergarten starting at age three.

Primary and secondary school education

Hitherto, social origin has affected not only the development of cognitive skills, but also one's chances to get an education or graduate from school with a certain kind of diploma. When tracking begins early in the school system, it is more difficult to weaken the links between the pupils' family background and their level of educational attainment.[47] International experience teaches that the comprehensive school is an especially effective tool for reducing educational handicaps. Comprehensive school systems have the advantage that the stronger students can help the weaker ones to learn. And by supporting the slower students, the more gifted ones acquire social skills as well.

Equally important for creating more equality of opportunity in education is the all-day school. It helps improve the overall level of achievement among lower social strata, enables parents to participate more fully in public life, and allows women to hold full-time jobs, thus proming greater equality between the sexes.[48] Schools designed to build character and foster the ideals of self-reliance and autonomy best satisfy the principles of social democracy. Every human being should be trained to take responsibility for his or her own learning and actions. Moreover, educational institutions have to do their work in a self-reliant way.[49] Curriculum development, for example, can be shifted from the state to those who are directly involved, including school students and parents. A self-governing school becomes a learning environment that carries on information exchanges with its social milieu. It can incorporate and respond to regional and local conditions, while taking into account the pupils' individual situations and needs.

Vocational education

A solid vocational education is the indispensable prerequisite for all citizens to find gainful employment and fulfill their responsibility to self. All young people deserve a legal entitlement to a quality vocational education that equips them with marketable skills. There are several principles that could be adopted for a policy of vocational education.

1 All applicants for places in training programs, including the least promising, have a right to vocational training.
2 Individuals must be given options among several different avenues of professional development.
3 Training standards are subject to public accountability.
4 Responsibility for vocational education should be shared by the state and private industry.
5 National training systems should be linked to international standards and expectations.

Principles of social democracy in education policy

Educational policy is still not always considered a part of social policy, even though the educational system has an enormous influence on the distribution of opportunities and should be regarded as vital in the campaign against social inequality. Educational policy must encourage self-directed learning, reinforce the individual's powers of judgment, and educate people to think independently, but always with an eye to its effects on distributive justice. Thus, for example, no stigma should be attached to higher education degrees obtained in non-traditional ways, e.g., via continuing education classes.

The theory of social democracy endorses the following principles of education policy. *First*, all citizens have a right to a basic education that enables them to make full use of their rights and duties. *Second*, every person has a right to a vocational education that improves his or her prospects of employment. *Third*, it is the responsibility of the state to make sure that these rights can be practiced effectively.

The right to education has three aspects. First of all it is a *basic social right* of all citizens. Second, it touches on *equality of opportunity*; no group may be given special privileges or disadvantages. Third, it defends the state's obligation to pursue an *active education policy*.

The entire range of educational opportunities should be provided as a public good. But that does not entail that education should be offered free of charge, only that no one should be denied an education merely on account of financial need. Even if it is deemed desirable to offer education as a free and equal good, at no cost to the student, it would probably be extremely difficult to finance such a plan entirely from public budgets. There is no conflict between fundamental rights and notions of justice on the one hand, and a system of financial contributions adjusted to income and wealth on the other, especially in the higher stages of education in which professional credentials are earned. That is particularly true of university studies, the successful completion of which usually lead to above-average incomes. Thus, it is not hard to justify the shifting of tuition charges or loan repayments to post-graduate years, as is done in Australia and the US, especially when we recall that fees are charged for many other kinds of professional and continuing education.

4.5 Perspectives on sustainability

The social welfare state

Free market conditions have bestowed on the social welfare states of the developed world a host of vexing new problems, especially to the extent that they maintain their commitments to uphold universal basic rights. Yet if governments seek to renounce such burdensome commitments, they risk precipitating far-reaching crises of stability and integration. The latter may eventually undermine citizens' willingness to participate, weaken social cohesion, or imperil the legitimacy of the political system.

Liberal welfare states, by reducing support levels and shifting social insurance provision to the private sector, may have made themselves more viable in an economic sense, but at a high price. Their unresolved problems of inequality and poverty confront them with dilemmas of normative legitimation.[50]

Social democratic welfare states, beset by claims for social services, have likewise lowered standards and reaffirmed the principle of personal responsibility, gradually putting themselves on a sustainable footing. They have benefited from broad public acceptance of a high level of taxation, expansion of employment opportunities in the social service branches of the public sector, and a business-friendly dual taxation system. As long as these countries' citizens voluntarily continue to bear a high tax burden, they will have only one really serious social justice problem to confront. To attain the goal of full employment, they have had to create many new jobs in the social services branch of the public sector. But since these are mostly only low-skilled, poorly paid jobs, ever greater wage differentials separate low-end employment from higher-income occupations. Yet this trend conflicts with the traditional egalitarianism that social democratically governed countries value, and therefore incurs political costs.

The *conservative* welfare states of continental Europe face a plethora of unresolved problems. Among these are a tax structure that discourages business and employment; the unsustainable financial basis of their social welfare systems; and barriers that protect incumbent job-holders while disadvantaging job-seekers.

All social welfare states must try to approach full employment, since that is both normatively mandated and the most important precondition for the financial sustainability of the entire social welfare edifice. Unfortunately, full employment has become more difficult to achieve as a result of demographic shifts and open market pressures. The project of social democracy itself forecloses two options that have been adopted elsewhere: reducing the social welfare state to a residual minimum and allowing the market to drive wages lower. So, to resolve its problems in a way consistent with its normative standards, the social welfare state must adopt strategies successfully tested in certain "cutting-edge" countries.

First: Taxing income rather than imposing a system of wage-based contributions is the best way to finance the welfare state. Such contributions effectively increase the costs of labor by the additional amount that employers must pay to support the social insurance system. Hence, they discourage job-creation, especially in less productive, low-income sectors, while setting a long-term trap for the social welfare state. In times of economic crisis, when its services are most urgently needed, the state finds its financial solvency undermined by increasing unemployment and declining revenues from wage-related contributions. Moreover, social welfare states are especially vulnerable to demographic shifts (e.g., the declining base of active wage earners that must support an increasing number of benefit recipients). Then, too, they have trouble adapting to changing gender roles in either the family or the workplace.

Second: The optimal solution to the problem of old-age insurance is a tax-financed basic pension that would be both financially sustainable and devoid of negative side effects on labor markets. This arrangement also resolves intergenerational distributive conflicts in a way that is fair to all generations.

Third: As we pointed out earlier, the members of society should be given a chance at gainful employment. Consequently, programs that make them employable or offer continuing education for the job market as well as "activating" social services should be given precedence over transfer payments and measures designed merely to protect the status of current job-holders. In other words, the principle of "making work pay" is given special legitimacy by the theory of social democracy.

Fourth: Both the goal of full employment and considerations of fairness favor a desegmentation of labor markets. This can best be achieved by protecting workers against termination, while encouraging job-creation and assimilating the many different occupational categories to a single set of standards. All this presupposes some system of unemployment insurance that allows the recently unemployed to maintain their previous standard of living for a stipulated period of time, while offering the best possible package of incentives to expedite their return to the workforce.

Fifth: New forms of employment created by the knowledge economy, such as outsourcing, freelancing, and part-time jobs, should be granted social protection equivalent to that enjoyed by traditional, "normal" work relationships, even where old-age insurance is involved, since that is the optimal prerequisite for extracting the maximum benefit from their job-creating potential. The protection afforded to such new work relationships would allow society to inch closer to the goal of full employment while providing the same minimal insurance coverage for everyone.

Sixth: A child- and family-centered reform of the social insurance system seems the best way of fulfilling the classical desideratum of social democracy: to organize the social insurance system so that it simultaneously contributes productively to economic development, promotes social justice, and operates sustainably.

The innovative side of sustainable welfare state reform combines family-centered with education-centered strategies. Experience shows that full-day childcare starting from the earliest feasible pre-school age, financed by a graduated, means-adjusted scale of contributions, can be expected to produce a number of benefits:

1 an increase in the rate of female participation in the workforce
2 enhancement of equality of opportunity accomplished by overcoming the effects of inherited status
3 a significant increase in birth rates.

In this manner several goals are served at the same time and via the same institutional sources: equality of social opportunities, sustainable financing of the welfare state, and foundation-laying for a "policy of second chances."

A social welfare state can be regarded as well founded when it fulfills the following conditions.

First: All citizens have a basic right to secure an adequate standard of living no matter what risks may arise, as long as they take primary responsibility for themselves.

Second: In cases where risks arising from the social structure itself jeopardize the enjoyment of basic rights, those affected must be assured that their accustomed way of life will be preserved for a reasonable period and at an adequate level.

Third: In the longer term it is enough for the welfare state to provide equal basic insurance. Neither justice nor social rights requires anything more. If some people want a greater degree of security against risk, they should be responsible for arranging it themselves.

Fourth: Social insurance schemes that exceed these standards may be justified in light of the notions of justice prevailing in some societies.

Fifth: The experiences of European welfare states such as the Netherlands in the 1990s or Germany after the year 2000 lend credence to the suspicion that structural path-dependency is a politically relative factor, not an absolute limitation. Under the pressure of exogenous or endogenous crises, even the most hidebound societies seem able to carry out reforms inspired by the successful models tried in comparable countries.

Part III

The Politics of Globalization

5

Progressive Globalization

5.1 Social democracy and globalization

Globalization as a risk to democracy

There are myriad competing paradigms in current theories of globalization. The notion of "fair" globalization adumbrated below has been influenced by several of them, each explicitly cited in the appropriate context. But above all the pioneering work of David Held and Keohane and Nye has shaped our approach.[1] "*Globalization*" is neither a monolithic nor a teleological phenomenon, but it is one that poses special problems for democracy, the rights of citizenship, and the social democratic project itself.[2] Debates in democratic theory have yielded agreement about the nature of those problems on the following points.[3]

First: whereas markets, environmental deterioration, migration, organized crime, and electronic mass communications increasingly transcend national borders, democracy is still limited to acting within the framework of the nation-state. World society has not responded vigorously to those challenges, especially their impact on universal basic rights. The European Union offers a partial exception to this generalization, at least within its own regional sphere of influence. But typically economic globalization vitiates democracy and the rights of citizenship, consequently eroding even their claims to legitimacy.

Second: beginning in the nineteenth century, social and even sometimes liberal democracies worked to imbed markets and "tame" capitalism in the economically advanced countries. They eventually succeeded in aligning market behavior more closely with the principles of liberal democracy.[4] In fact, most European countries owe their political legitimation to this historic compromise between capitalism and democracy. But in its current "negative" phase, globalization has lowered accustomed levels of market imbedding, especially where ecology, culture, and social protections are concerned. Thus, it indirectly weakens democracy's implicit claim to legitimate authority. As national welfare states face intensified economic competition from abroad, those trends should accelerate.[5]

Third: market-led modernization, driven by the pressure of economic globalization, is gradually abandoning its commitments to political and social rights. The most powerful forces behind this development increasingly elude political control and accountability.

Fourth: we are witnessing the loss of what Streeck has dubbed the "co-extension" between effective democratic action and limited national territoriality.[6] The fates of national political societies are beginning to intersect, as all confront common, border-transcending problems. David Held has described this transnational confluence as the emergence of *"overlapping communities of fate."*[7] Negative globalization has proved to be a "meta-risk" to the real-world efficacy of universal rights, because it dramatically increases the scope and intensity of even fairly easily managed social risks. Yet, at the same time, it disempowers the structures of political action that might forestall them.[8]

Negative and positive globalization

We may follow Jan Tinbergen in calling that kind of globalization "negative," especially in view of its effects on democracy and citizenship.[9] To restore the efficacy of political action, we need to create *positive* globalization. Only thus can we secure the rights of citizens, close the gaps that have arisen in legitimation and political action, and create transnational forms of political accountability, deliberation, and decision-making.

Negative globalization poses several challenges for democratic theory and policy. First, we have to elucidate how the legitimation of democracy and basic rights can be maintained now that the accustomed *co-extension* between the arena of political problems and potential democratic intervention has been displaced. This dilemma touches the deepest sources of democratic legitimation in an age of globalization. Second, actor theory suggests a further question: which transnational institutions can be relied on to counteract the global democratic deficit? Finally, what *limitations, resources, and actors* might help implement the structures of transnational regulation?

The democratic legitimation crisis

The legitimation deficit from which the global political and economic status quo suffers developed during the last two decades of the twentieth century as negative globalization proceeded apace. It is not limited to the global theater, but extends as well to the internal legitimation of democratic nation-states by disrupting their domestic policy-making capacity. The flip side of the global loss of political sovereignty is thus a loss of sovereignty in internal affairs by constitutional democratic nation-states.[10] So when we ponder how to eliminate the democratic deficit created by negative globalization, the answer is not simply to launch an ambitious project of expanding democracy into the transnational arena. Since the chain of global problems extends into the domestic arena too, the future of democracy itself is at risk.[11]

Modern democratic theory suggests that the search for answers to the question of democratic legitimacy should build on two premises.

1 Those problems that are inherently of a political nature, whether transnational or located in a national society, have to be resolved through politically legitimate procedures.
2 Politically legitimate decision-making procedures must be *democratic* and must respect the norms of *fundamental rights*.

Two criteria have emerged in contemporary discourses of legitimation to distinguish political from private issues.[12] Social actions and their consequences are political when they ineluctably give rise to rules or circumstances affecting all members of society, i.e., that admit of no private exit options. At issue here are laws, programs, and public goods, as well as externalities that inevitably entail compulsory consumption for the entire society or large collectivities. Matters of this kind are by their very nature political, because they can be dealt with only through collective political action.

Second, an intrisically *political* problem – one that demands a political solution – arises whenever the universal rights of individuals or groups are violated. Although this general rule holds for all five categories of rights, the obligation to intervene politically when civil and political rights are violated is direct and immediate. By contrast, when social, cultural, and economic rights are violated, we should contemplate longer-term solutions. In any case, whenever fundamental rights are violated, whether by deliberate actions of state actors or through externalities, political problems emerge that call for politically legitimate solutions.

Globalization and social democracy

The theory of social democracy has a great deal at stake in the project of democratizing the global arena. The conceptual challenge it faces is fourfold.

1 It must find a way to insure that liberal democracy's procedures for decision-making and intervention can deal successfully with all of

the politically defined social risks and problems that crop up on the global level.

2 It must maintain the decision-making authority of liberal democracy over all problems that can still be resolved at the level of the nation-state.

3 It must work to imbed free markets socially, politically, and ecologically to protect the fundamental rights of those adversely affected by market outcomes.

4 It must do the political spadework that will enable social democratic projects to be carried out in each country.

The first steps toward *global governance* demonstrate that even negative globalization can be partially imbedded in a matrix of political policy-making. Tony Blair was wrong to claim that it is simply a fact of life and that social and political actors just have to cope with it.[13] To the contrary, it is malleable within certain limits that have yet to be defined. At this point we have no way of predicting which of the two possible strategies – coping and shaping – will predominate as democracies try to manage the problems of globalization. To offer even a preliminary answer would require greater clarity about several conditions affecting the projects of "positive" globalization linked to a reasonably democratic vision of global governance. Those conditions involve three distinct issues: *norms, the logic of the system,* and *the theory of actors.* On the normative front, we must clarify the claim that people have a right to world citizenship. As far as system logic is concerned, we need to determine whether there are any realistic prospects for transnational democratization. Actor theory should analyze the asymmetric interests and resources held by states and actors on the global stage.

The interaction among three factors will help decide whether social democracy can be constructed in the global political arena. One is the recognition that ecological crises will jeopardize the continued physical existence of every society unless there is a minimal commitment to social democracy. Second, recessions arising from insufficiently regulated financial markets often begin to resemble wildfires from which even non-cooperators cannot escape. Finally, those groups adversely affected by negative globalization will organize trans-border protection schemes that may strengthen their hand. In that case, national actors may find that the political price of non-cooperation eventually exceeds the costs of cooperation.

Because its own dogma commits it to non-intervention in the marketplace, the libertarian alternative has tied its own hands and can offer no plausible solutions. By contrast, social democracy should be able to rally a broad coalition of actors behind its program. Those considerations make even idealistic constructs seem relevant and politically feasible, such as the notion of the political philosopher Otfried Höffe of a subsidiary, federal world republic based on cosmopolitan citizenship rights. Of course, his vision could not become a reality anytime soon, but it might point in the direction we need to go or serve as a model for designing something more practicable.[14] To democratize the global order, there is no need to invent idealistic schemes for a unitary, harmonious society. Rather, it is sufficient to build on the "realistic" deepening of the transnational cooperation already underway, since that is grounded on the self-interest of all participating actors. The challenge is to devise reliable political steering instruments to tame negative globalization and create a universally legitimized set of rules to guide positive globalization. Democratization means giving priority to democratically legitimized political actors to shape the global environment and, if necessary, to override private decisions about economic and social development.

Under current conditions the only approaches in democratic theory that deserve the name "realistic" are those that do justice to Giddens's criterion of "utopian realism." In other words, they can be justified in terms of all three logical dimensions, the normative, actor-theoretical, and systems-theoretical.

5.2 Global citizenship

Globalization and fundamental rights

At a minimum, universal basic rights implicitly endow each person with the rights of passive global citizenship.[15] But those rights must be supplemented by an entitlement to active global citizenship as well, since globalization has occasioned planetary-scale rights violations.[16] That status would entitle world citizens to participate in decisions that affect their fundamental rights.[17] The idea of enacting cosmopolitan citizenship, which goes back to Immanuel Kant, has surfaced again since globalization and its political fallout have reignited the debate Kant originally launched.[18] In an interdependent world the rights and vital interests of human beings, regardless of the political community to which they belong, can be directly infringed by the actions of people in other countries. To protect themselves they must learn to cooperate effectively with other actors. The political status of global citizenship confers a right to such defensive cooperation, while simultaneously imposing obligations on all actors who can rectify rights violations.[19] To put this principle into practical effect would require a form of cosmopolitan society capable of effective decision-making. The theories of democracy and fundamental rights both justify the principle, though they say little about the forms it should take.

World citizenship

We must suppose a contract that lays the groundwork for the responsible co-existence of all autonomous persons in world society, and in which all human beings mutually recognize one another as incumbents of legal rights and as citizens. But due to de facto globalization, the contract must be extended to include the civil rights through which they recognize their equal autonomy as members of the politically sovereign body with power to decide on matters that concern them all.[20] In principle, all persons have an equal right to share in making decisions that create a binding framework of rules defining their collective life-situation, i.e., that determine the actual worth of human rights they enjoy. Otfried Höffe speaks of a graded citizen status in respect to the political rights of world citizenship.[21] An individual is first of all the citizen of his or her own country, then of his or her region, and finally of the world. These identities do not compete; rather, they complement one another, depending on which level of political authority is the appropriate one in which to participate.

Citizenship can be understood as a form of collaboration among persons who reach agreement about a framework of rules that will govern them in their future co-existence.[22] At bottom citizenship is a reciprocal guarantee of equal rights, obligations, and opportunities to participate in political decisions that affect everyone. Positive globalization, however, suggests a further question about it: can we embrace a new vision of citizenship at the global level? If there is to be such a right of world citizenship, then it calls for a subsidiary global democratization, so that suitable forms of political decision-making can be instituted at all levels of global society where they are needed to safeguard fundamental human rights. This democratization, mandated by the principles of human rights, should be subsidiary in the sense that it delegates decisions to a higher and more remote level (from the viewpoint of the co-sovereign) only when that is the only venue in which they can be properly addressed. Although the demand for global democratization follows from the right of world citizenship itself, it does not stipulate how the former should be carried out. Therefore, the right of world citizenship entails the planetary priority of democracy over economic and social power, but does not require that an institutionally closed world state be created.

Cosmopolitan rights and their corresponding duties call for the establishment of a world political order in which the human rights of every individual would be protected.[23] Cosmopolitan rights also imply a cosmopolitan duty, incumbent on all human beings and states that are sufficiently well off materially, to undertake a planetary project of compensation from motives of human solidarity. It would have to go at least far enough to insure the validity of human rights at some appropriate minimum level in every corner of the globe.[24]

But without a well-developed regional and global political identity, the process of positive globalization qua active democratization will scarcely be possible. Hence, a new kind of multi-level political identity, a new form of citizenship that embraces national, regional, and global tiers, must emerge. It may already be taking shape among the actors of transnational civil society, but apart from them it has been at best a vague political hope.

Following Held, we may regard world citizenship as a form of human multi-level citizenship that addresses different levels of political decision-making. Political cosmopolitans of course remain citizens of their own nation-states, but they are also often citizens of regional systems of political cooperation such as the EU. Additionally, they are citizens of the global commonwealth, the laws and regulations of which increasingly affect their lives. Hence, they have a civil right to participate in the making of those laws. Furthermore, they hold other rights enacted by world institutions and in some cases reinforced by sanctions. Even universal human and civil rights establish a kind of cosmopolitan political status in whatever form they exist and despite the weak sanctions that presently back them.

World citizenship embraces not only political and civil but also social and economic rights. It is a new form of "post-communal," multi-dimensional citizenship. But it is also post-liberal, because it adds social and economic rights to the traditional liberal list. Global multi-level citizenship is, as noted, enriched by an additional dimension: the right to political action on the global stage.[25] Global democratization begins a process through which world citizens secure their rights at the most appropriate level. As occurred when national citizenship developed, so also on the transnational plane we should anticipate a process of circular causality. As citizens reach agreement in public regional and local forums about how to exercise their rights in common, they are in the first, embryonic stage of developing a political identity. That emergent identity will in turn intensify the activities and communications that advance the construction of institutions of collective global action.

Social standards and universal basic rights

As noted, civil and political rights on one hand and social and economic rights on the other are treated differently by the enforcement protocols of the United Nations. But that distinction does not mean that world citizenship is inherently dichotomous.[26] Nor does the distinction between the two types of rights suggest any logical inconsistency in the institutions and procedures of the United Nations. But paradoxes would ensue the moment that the social and economic rights – or the portion of them above and beyond basic labor rights – were actually implemented globally. Clearly, the most crucial workers' rights are closely linked to the core principles of fundamental human rights themselves; besides, they have a causal connection to economic and social progress in each country. Yet the full complement of workers' rights hinges on the developmental stage of each particular country. Hence, they are logically valid only as obligations of conduct.

Elementary workers' rights help to create markets and keep them functioning properly; thus, they should normally be seen as contributing to economic growth and greater efficiency. This fact, together with their close connection to human rights generally, suggests that the enactment of workers' rights should be subject to the same strict regimen of implementation and enforcement that the contractual apparatus of the UN foresees for civil rights. Of course, each country must decide how to actualize more extensive social and economic rights in light of its level of economic development. To impose on a country expectations unsuited to its economic situation could trigger a severe recession. In turn, an economic crisis could easily undermine the real-world efficacy of even the most elementary workers' rights.

From this economic perspective one can draw some practical inferences about the project of global social democracy. The core labor rights can and should be given essentially the same institutional form as civil and political rights. Violations of either kind should evoke immediate responses, whereas enforcement of economic and social rights must be left to the discretion of individual countries. It would be sensible for the international community to pressure recalcitrant regimes to enforce the civil and political rights first, in the expectation that this would eventually create a more favorable climate for economic and social rights as well. In this respect, cosmopolitan rights do differ internally in the manner described, but they are not split into two distinct groups, one valid absolutely and the other only relatively. Cosmopolitan citizenship is thus also *world social citizenship*.

5.3 Global governance

"Negative" globalization has weakened democracy by abetting two long-term trends. It has undermined the legitimacy of democratic regimes and eroded their sovereignty, both of which trends pose serious challenges to social democracy. The proper response is to construct a counter-model of "positive" globalization that is achievable, while still meeting the standards of legitimacy associated with democracy and the protection of human rights. Of course, these challenges confront liberal democracy too, but they affect social democracy more directly on account of its more elaborate notion of fundamental rights. In the scholarly literature, there are basically four competing responses to these challenges.

First, advocates of grass-roots democracy such as the American political scientist Benjamin Barber expect global capitalism to be reimbedded only by a global civil society.[27] He claims that the traditional institutions of representative democracy are no longer very useful, because they so often ignore the real interests of citizens and because transnational economic interests can easily block their initiatives. In and of themselves, they cannot create an effective system of global political regulation. Transnational networks and the activities of civil society must continue to be crucial elements in planetary democracy. They can improve the effectiveness of transnational institutions, regional systems of cooperation, and global regulatory regimes. And they can make sure that these systems remain or become receptive to the interests and life experiences of the ordinary people most affected by their decisions. But because civil society's networks lack complex organization, a permanent presence, and the power to impose sanctions, they can never replace transnational institutions.

Second, libertarian democrats see in the primacy of global markets vis-à-vis politics and the decreasing influence of regulation a significant advance in rationality over what they believe to be the short-sighted, redistribution-obsessed mentality of democratic politicians.[28] Their ambition is to dismantle transnational regulatory institutions so that self-regulating markets will gradually improve living conditions everywhere. They hope that the impartiality of economic logic will overcome the flaws of democratic politics. They have little confidence that political regulation would alleviate the destructive consequences of markets on the environment, of global financial speculation on standards of living and employment, or of the grossly unjust distribution of opportunities. Indeed, they might not admit that all of these phenomena are problems in the first place. In sum, the libertarian democrats would trust in the logic of the market, and seek to eliminate obstacles to its complete ascendancy. Of course, from the perspective of social democracy, that would only lead to an intensification of economic crises and ecological destruction, violate the cosmopolitan right to democratic self-determination, and make it harder to secure civic rights for all.

Third, Otfried Höffe has framed a detailed rationale for world citizenship rights on both the political and economic levels. His argument culminates in the proposal for a subsidiary, federal world republic, which might be a promising idea as long as we treat it as a heuristic symbol for the complex processes of global democratization.[29] His argument and the problems of global citizenship have already been considered in the previous two chapters.

Fourth, despite the trend toward globalization, the "realist" school of international relations still sees in individual sovereign states the only serious international political actors. Its adherents therefore repudiate all projects that transcend the framework of sovereign politics carried on by territorial states. In short, schemes for global governance appear to the realists as an empty "politics of declamation" without real-world consequences.[30] But that would be a mistaken impression, as we have argued already in earlier chapters. It is certainly a realistic endeavour to build on the forms of transnational cooperation already established, since that only requires major actors to continue to pursue their own self-interest in enlightened ways.

Liberal globalization

David Held argues that democracy was established in stages, over several millennia of Western history. In the first stage, the ancient Greek city-states were democratized; in the second or Enlightenment phase, modern nation-states gradually became more democratic, beginning in the eighteenth century. The time has now arrived to make still another advance in democracy, different from the previous ones because of its global dimension yet rivaling them in world historical significance.[31] There is a great deal at stake for the project of social democracy in the quest to design workable structures for liberal democratic deliberation and decision-making in the global political arena. Unlike libertarian democracy, the latter must therefore treat the enhancement of liberal democracy on a global scale as critical to its success. The theorists of libertarian democracy may consider the decline of transnational regulative capabilities as an irrevocable trend spurred by economic modernization. Social democracy cannot be so nonchalant. It defends the liberal democratic framework by universalistic arguments. Social democratic theory especially challenges the libertarian claim that the ongoing erosion of global political sovereignty will yield a more rational social order, because (it is claimed) dimished global political authority reduces the chances for political mismanagement, and so expands the autonomy of all the world's citizens.[32]

As Anthony Giddens has shown, it would be theoretically irresponsible to brand as "utopian" projects of global democratization that seek a higher ground of political legitimacy. As long as these are empirically solid, the so-called realists and libertarians have no credible reasons for attacking them.[33] Democratic theory, especially its social democratic variant, must constantly adapt to the protean shifts of globalization. It is therefore obliged, by the moral principles of *utopian realism*, to guide the design of new, transnational forms of democracy that might overcome the "democratic deficits" of negative globalization.

Elements of an integrated world society are starting to emerge in the present-day patterns of transnational political cooperation. But in their existing forms these evince clear contradictions. In some cases, for example those of the World Bank and the world trade agreements, their ability to control events and find acceptance for their policies has been seriously compromised by a tendency to exclude or under-represent important actors and interests.

Overlapping elements

As we attempt to evaluate these models' prospective contributions to the political evolution of social democracy, we might usefully employ three criteria drawn from the theory of actors. The first concerns the models' normative position within the theory of democracy, the second, the appropriateness of their institutional design to confront the political problems of negative globalization, and the third, the practicability of their aspirations in the world as we know it.

None of the models, taken in isolation, can claim to have mapped out a route to positive globalization. They can explain neither how transnational political institutions could acquire the power to act in democratic ways, nor how to insure the social and ecological imbedding of the world market. Only by combining selected elements of all these models can a normatively and institutionally appropriate political sphere be created. This effort could build on the obvious consensus of all models about the initial conditions and structural elements of global democratization. The latter would include:

- an analysis of the existing situation itself: in order to regain their political legitimacy, democracies within nation-states and in the emerging world society require a new form of symmetry between the kind of trans-border problems they face and their (limited) capacity to take action and be held accountable for the results.
- a definite idea of cosmopolitan citizenship: it must empower citizens in every corner of the world to participate in political deliberations and decision-making at every level of the world's political society at which their interests are at stake – the local, national, regional, and global.
- the conviction that global democracy must demand the social, cultural, and ecological reimbedding of global markets, while making the world economy more accountable
- the necessity of reforming already existing institutions of transnational political coordination – above all the UN and its affiliated bodies – to make them more representative, accountable, and effective
- emphasis on the role of transnational civil society and its networks in the process of democratic globalization
- the invention of new supranational political institutions
- the conviction that global democracy can only be launched as a new form of complex political interaction between institutional and non-institutional actors

All the authors except Höffe concur that a vision of positive globalization should not culminate in the prospect of a world state. Neither the multiplicity of regulatory schemes nor the principle of democratic subsidiarity would allow that.

Open methods of global democratization

An *open method of global political coordination* ought to be normatively defensible, institutionally appropriate, and achievable by actors who have sound reasons to support it. It must therefore rely on the concert of six strategic elements.

First, cosmopolitan citizenship, which would authorize citizens to take an active part in the political decisions that affect them wherever they may be.

Second, the democratization, expansion, and deepening of existing *transnational and supranational political institutions,* particularly the United Nations and its affiliates. Two especially promising proposals are the founding of a Chamber of Nations and of an Economic Security Council with power to regulate economic processes.

Third, the expansion and internal democratization of *regional systems of political cooperation* such as the European Union, ASEAN, SAARC, NAFTA, Mercosur. They are the building blocks of global democratization.

Fourth, the democratization of functional regulations in important sectors of the world economy and world society such as trade and the environment. This could be achieved by expanding existing transnational accords, for example the Kyoto Treaty, and agreements made by the International Labour Organization (ILO) and the World Trade Organization (WTO).

Fifth, transnational civil society needs stronger support from political institutions and deserves a place at the table when the global political community makes decisions. Its input is indispensable in certain areas, such as protection of human rights, guarantees of more humane working conditions, environmental protection, and gender equalization.

Sixth, the global public has a crucial function in the emergence of cosmopolitan citizenship and oversight of global actors. A shared awareness of cosmopolitan citizenship may emerge from the deliberations of a global public.

The globalization of social democracy

Given the scope of the problems, it is a daunting, complex task to reimagine social democracy in the shadow of globalization. But its advocates need not pin all their hopes on normative theories. Globalized social democracy actually dovetails with the interests of influential global actors. Moreover, it draws strength from trends in the evolution of world society and the community of nation-states. Lending support to this more optimistic scenario are the gains that have already been achieved in transnational governance. Social democratic politics in a global arena demands that all four crucial transnational decision-making levels be expanded and networked to make them more effective and better suited to promote cosmopolitan ends. The principle of subsidiarity determines the distribution of decision-making among these levels.

5.4 The global imbedding of markets

The political contours of social reimbedding

Integrated markets must be reimbedded, especially in the spheres where negative globalization is already generating externalities. Besides markets for goods and services, the latter would certainly include financial markets, direct investment by transnational corporations, and "global sourcing," the outsourcing of production and service components to the most favorable locations worldwide.

In the last quarter of the twentieth century, extensive liberalization of world trade under the aegis of the GATT and WTO treaties dismantled or reduced national trade barriers.[34] In the same period, transportation and communication costs fell so much that most producers can now sell their products in markets all over the world. National and regional markets once sheltered by tariffs and non-tariff barriers are now globally integrated and have coalesced into a single world mega-market. In principle, price, quality, and cost competition have superseded all those limits, and that profoundly alters the competitive situation. Now low-wage countries have greater opportunities to sell their products in high-wage countries, while leading firms in the strongest economies can expand their market dominance across the globe. Also, the division of labor is being transformed by the rules of comparative advantage in production costs. The export-dependent and import-sensitive sectors of high-wage countries can only survive and prosper by offering innovative, high-tech products that give them a competitive advantage in global markets. Conversely, they have to abandon production of goods that can be made in low-wage countries with equal quality but lower costs of production, since they cannot compete with those in either export or import markets. While this state of affairs entails structural adjustments and temporary job losses in sectors hard hit by shifts in the world division of labor, it nevertheless has the potential to generate a win–win situation in the long run, one in which GDP and job growth both improve.[35]

Three challenges to social democracy emerge as a result of globalization.[36]

First: the rules of world trade under the WTO regime have to be purged of all remaining trade barriers that principally disadvantage developing countries.

Second: the norms for a dignified work life elaborated by the ILO should be implemented everywhere in the world. This could be partially achieved by labeling products on the market that conform to its standards.

Third: progress should be made in creating a global regime, analogous to the WTO, that would set ecological standards for products and production methods far exceeding the existing ecological regulations. Full compliance with the Kyoto Protocols would be a cornerstone in this edifice.

Failure to imbed *financial markets* in reliable forms of transnational political accountability and control is the most serious defect that has arisen from the current wave of economic globalization.[37] Instruments for insuring financial transactions against investment and currency fluctuation risks, together with the concentration of billions of dollars in the hands of a small number of investment and pension funds, have tended to insulate the finance capital floating around daily on international stock exchanges from ordinary trade flows and rendered it largely independent of control. When the volume of financial transactions initiated by the biggest funds sometimes exceeds the entire GDP of small countries, abrupt in- and outflows of capital can plunge entire economies into crisis almost overnight. Chain reactions may be unleashed that engulf whole regions, largely depriving them of the capacity to respond politically. The predominantly libertarian architecture of today's global financial markets has made possible the accumulation of enormous private advantages at the expense of higher living standards and jobs. The consequences not only affect individual economies directly victimized by abrupt capital flight; they can even engulf portions of the global economy. They are linked to violations of elementary rights, both the negative liberties of autonomous self-determination in economically weaker nations, and the positive liberties that involve the social prerequisites of human self-determination throughout the world.

Diminishing political control over markets entails serious rights violations, while weakening the social and cultural fabric of a durable democratic order by continually revealing democracy's powerlessness to secure a decent life for large segments of a country's population.[38]

Elements and strategies

Social democracy needs to design a global financial architecture featuring checks and balances sufficient to insure the primacy of democracy and rights over the externalities generated by integrated markets, but without disturbing those markets' intrinsic logic. Policy debates among political actors have revealed the outlines of a plan that would achieve some of this. First, world markets would be imbedded so as to avoid, as far as possible, the occurrence of the usual risks. Second, global security policy would be mainly preventive.[39] Risk analysis of the previous trends in negative globalization suggests the following strategic elements.

Global *development policy* should pursue two interconnected objectives. First, it should solicit aid from wealthier nations and the world community to guarantee the elementary rights of people everywhere in the world. Second, it should work to eliminate the extreme disparities of wealth between rich and poor countries.

The United Nations *millennium goals* provide a platform allowing the rich countries to cooperate to realize these aims.[40] Both points are involved here: guarantees of basic rights and preventive security policies to provide a reasonable measure of stability in global relations. This approach to development policy promises to staunch the flow of refugees, address their great suffering, and confront the integration problems experienced by their host countries.[41]

What must be avoided, however, is the temptation merely to distribute aid funds among the budgets of developing countries. That would likely stabilize existing conditions and reduce the political and administrative quality of the ruling regimes by promoting corruption, reinforcing the privileges of state elites, and fostering rent-seeking behavior contrary to those nations' interests in economic development.[42] Development aid ought to focus on guarantees of public goods that promote opportunity and human development, such as health care, education, and of course employment.[43]

The key to attaining these goals is to be found in the structures of world trade. As attested by the Brandt Report, it would be in the long-term interest of the trading nations to meet the conditions of fairness in world trade specified by the Doha sustainability agenda for reform of the WTO.[44] The most radical changes in trade policy should be undertaken in agricultural commodities. In almost all developing countries, the agriculture sector will have a vital role to play in economic development and job-creation for the foreseeable future. A successful employment strategy for the developing nations would ease restrictions on agricultural imports into the rich countries, which can only be accomplished by lowering farm subsidies there.[45]

To bring about reforms of this kind and insure a permanently fair control of changed conditions, we need to open up the WTO itself and democratize its decision-making and oversight procedures. The Johannesburg Summit of 2003 provided both poor and rich countries with guidelines for a sustainable development strategy. The linchpin is the transfer of environmentally friendly technology from the rich to the poor world, to achieve faster growth coupled with improved environmental protection.

Promoting democracy

The causal connection between underdevelopment and political instability shows up in the empirical finding that most poor countries have at best established defective democracies, at worst, autocracies.[46] The model of circular causality offers the most plausible explanation for this. While democracy and democratization support economic and social development and the fair distribution of the wealth it generates, so too successful development provides stable foundations for democracy and political participation.[47] Consequently, pro-democracy development policy should focus on both sets of causes at once, promoting both democracy and development. The democratization of transnational regimes, institutions, and organizations contributes to the same end. A global tax that financed such a pro-rights and pro-democracy development policy could support that process and enhance the capacities of transnational actors working toward democratization.[48]

Global public goods

The imbedding of the world market is intended to guarantee the supply of public goods indispensable to the achievement of universal rights. A few of these, such as stability in financial policy and the sustainable stewardship of the environment, are simultaneously conditions for the long-term self-preservation of the global market itself. The concept of *global public goods*, elaborated in the context of UN Development Programme projects, has direct relevance for politics.[49] It lists a set of goods, such as international security, ecological sustainability, stability in financial markets, etc., that obviously benefit all of humanity and in the provision of which, therefore, all of us should take an interest. But it also enumerates some elementary collective goods, such as access to health care, education, social security, and employment opportunities, that should be available to every person as a way to satisfy the minimum conditions of a life with dignity. The approach is tied to cooperative development and is thus conceived as a *project of global cooperation*.

There are several attractive aspects of this idea: its direct connection to the United Nations and collaborative international development work; its enlightened suggestion that everyone has an interest in helping to provide collective goods; and its Third World orientation. It shows how to lay the foundations for a life with dignity in the disadvantaged parts of the world as well as to cultivate responsible cooperative relationships between the haves and have-nots. Finally, it would make the rich – and therefore most politically capable – countries shoulder a lion's share of the responsibility for providing global public goods.

Economic and financial policy

A globe-spanning regulatory policy committed to liberal and social rights must extend into every sphere where free markets generate externalities that infringe on universal rights. This holds true not only for social and labor rights in the narrow sense, but also in cases such as taxes, finances, migration, the environment, crime, trade, investment policy, intellectual property rights, competition, biotechnology, and e-commerce. In particular, the global financial architecture needs a new system of fair, effective regulation.[50] In accord with its original enabling law, the International Monetary Fund should grant limited credits for financial restructuring in response to crises. But above all it should try to prevent crises in the first place, and put its proposals to the governments of borrower nations on the public record for the sake of transparency.

Hitherto, the Fund's internal power structure has reflected the size of the deposits of its chief investors. But to treat the interests and needs of the poor countries dependent on its aid with greater fairness, the IMF requires thoroughgoing democratization. The de facto veto power of the United States, a function of its large stake in the Fund, should be removed. Since most IMF donor countries belong to the rich world, while most of the borrowers are Third World nations, the system of weighted voting should be revisited. Furthermore, one important contribution to greater fairness and the inclusion of the recipient nations' voices would involve the regionalization of the global banking system. The IMF should include universal fundamental rights in its borrowing terms, and its decisions should accommodate the interests and opinions of the recipient countries during the consultation phase.

The responsibilities of the IMF must be separated from those of the World Bank. The Bretton Woods Agreement assigns to the latter the task of alleviating poverty. The IMF is supposed to confine itself to easing financial crises by granting short-term credits, while the World Bank and regional development banks are charged with providing long-term financing of structural development programs. We need to distinguish clearly between aid for the purpose of debt relief and the financing of development projects. In order to coordinate the flow of global finance, it seems advisable to expand the Financial Stability Forum, founded in 1999, into a world financial authority. The World Financial Authority must be endowed with the power to regulate transnational financial flows and risk-management. It should therefore be authorized to monitor global finance and intervene whenever necessary.

Another popular plan would entrust the coordination of activities in this domain to a proposed UN Security Council for Economic and Social Affairs. It would outrank all other comparable organizations and institutions, while directing them to give priority to fundamental rights.[51]

All of these institutions should cooperate under the aegis of the United Nations and the principle of cosmopolitan citizenship to insure that, in any balancing of interests, universal rights will have the last word. A World Economic and Social Council that would coordinate all of these activities is the proper institution to impose binding rules on the activities of transnational corporations in developing countries.

5.5 Globalization and political contingency

The limits of negative and positive globalization

Neither the march of negative globalization nor advances in positive globalization can be interpreted as teleological developments embodying irreversible trends. Rieger and Leibfried have explained why protectionism in the United States has become a stand-in for the income security policies the government has failed to enact.[52] To support the "conservative welfare function," that is, guaranteeing an already attained level of social welfare, welfare state policies are nearly interchangeable with those of protectionism. There is always a temptation to prefer protectionism in welfare state democracies because of pressure from interests hoping to shore up the status quo. Advances in positive globalization are never secure, even when they are eminently justifiable from the standpoint of democratic theory and steering policy. Indeed, the entire field of globalization policy has become a highly contingent project, because of the political calculations and perceived self-interest of influential political actors. A realistic theory of social democracy must accept such contingency as a given.

Even in the best-case scenario, in which positive globalization succeeded brilliantly, it would scarcely be able to restore the socio-political *status quo ante* in the global arena, since it had already been disrupted at the nation-state level. The methods of comparative policy studies, developed to show what conditions favored social democratic policies, worked only on the assumption that nation-state actors would still have effective sovereign control over the external boundaries of their political-economic systems. The creation of global open markets in the 1970s dramatically changed the conditions for social democracy and cast doubt on the usefulness of its once promising instruments in crucial areas of politics.

All of the countries whose governments were committed to social democratic norms of legitimation reacted to globalization by revising their economic policies. There were two important changes that were clearly precipitated by the rise of open markets. *First*, some industrial and service sectors were exposed to intensified global competition. *Second*, flows of speculative cash attained unprecedented mobility; their impact became a matter of great significance for any economy, and a matter of life and death for small economies.

If one inquires into the chances for shaping globalization in accord with the normatively established standards of social democracy, the decisive question is: which of the already examined effects of globalization can be regulated or even reversed? Is it possible for political actors in a broader political arena approximately to re-create the conditions that prevailed before globalization?[53]

Best-case scenarios

We may try to imagine how a best-case scenario of positive globalization might play out. It would occur if a global order emerged in which all the familiar, feasible proposals for the positive shaping of global socio-economic regulation were put into practice and supported by the best imaginable coalition of actors in the global arena. The result might look something like the following.

First, the flow of financial capital: it seems conceivable that a global financial monitoring office could be placed under UN authority. Likewise, some form of control over short-term transnational financial flows could be instituted, perhaps along the lines of the Tobin tax. In those ways, it should be possible to impose some checks on short-term speculative capital flows, in respect to both their magnitude and their tempo. Nevertheless, even a global control institution with far-reaching powers could not reverse the stubborn trend that large amounts of speculative capital move into and out of economies depending on anticipated returns on investment. Even under the best-case scenario of positive globalization, national and regional actors will have to take transnational speculation as a given.

Second, social and ecological standards: the most effective possible implementation of social and ecological standards worldwide, perhaps in line with ILO criteria or a consistent application of the Rio/Kyoto process, would make the world as a whole socially and ecologically more secure. It would help insure sustainability while reducing the unjustified advantages enjoyed by some business locations over others. Of course intensified competition in exposed sectors would continue. It would not likely yield a unified world welfare state with homogeneous standards of social security and services, one that would relieve the economies that now compete on the world market from the necessity of debating the cost-effectiveness of different forms of financing for their social welfare states. Instead, the differentials in welfare state coverage would help some countries establish competitive advantages of location, which in turn influence their competitiveness and long-term economic prospects. Even in a fairly regulated world economy, the more productive countries could not escape the rigors of global competition any more than they could avoid intensified competition with each other.

Third, competition in the high productivity sector: fairer world trade rules and better controls on the behavior of transnational firms would sharpen competition in the internationally exposed sectors of highly productive goods and service industries. Those measures would bring about still more open markets, easier access to them for products from low-wage countries, and improved control of monopolies in world markets.

Is globalization sustainable?

From the perspective of social democracy, all the aforementioned regulatory policies are theoretically defensible and desirable as democratic policy. Yet they would do little to mitigate many of the most severe impacts of free markets on national and regional political economies. Indeed, they might even intensify those impacts. Consequently, there is nothing to indicate that the global reimbedding of markets would ease the pressures to adapt exerted by globalization. Nor is it likely that conditions in the global arena could be restored to anything like what they were in the golden age of social democracy on the nation-state level. Thus, even though it is a highly contingent matter whether globalization can be "shaped" in a political-economic sense, one can still identify a set of factors that will continue to operate under all circumstances and time-frames. Thus, social democracy should adopt a normatively and empirically defensible two-track strategy. It should elaborate a political vision – and rally actors behind it – that would lead to a gradual triumph of social globalization. It should likewise promote the transformation of political-economic structures and instruments in particular countries to insure the success of social democracy under what now appear to be permanent conditions.

The dual nature of social democracy

The characteristic dual nature of social democracy is again becoming apparent under the radically changed conditions of the contemporary globalized world. It draws strength from normatively exalted principles: the universal rights to secure negative liberty and create positive liberty. Yet it also must acknowledge the realistic assessments suggested by actor theory in complex contemporary societies. It accepts these as a point of departure, not as the final goal of political action. Aware of the tension between its two goals, it tries to make democracy more social and thus more real, while simultaneously allowing it to contribute to economic efficiency, social integration, and stability.

Democratic theorists doing research on stability have proven amply that waiving the normative aspirations of universal rights, supposedly in the interests of realism and efficiency, actually undermines both values.[54] It thereby calls into question the very rationale for the sake of which it was acting. A one-dimensional attachment to norms that ignores the reality principle in turn undermines the legitimation of its own theoretical claim by making it appear inherently unrealistic. Defective democracies that only partially honor their democratic values live with the Achilles heel of weakened legitimation and perpetual vulnerability.[55]

5.6 Shaping and coping

Theoretical foundations

Actor theory highlights a dilemma that inevitably confronts any grand political project: the tension between people's aspirations to shape events and the constraining force of circumstances to which they must adjust.[56] The structures and logic of systems and constellations of actors always reduce the actor's political maneuvering room. System structures are reproduced in what the actors do and are thus themselves dependent on the actors' ideas of how to shape their environment.[57] Depending on how one looks at them, the prospects for shaping events appear more or less bright. From the systems perspective they certainly look dim, but from the actors' perspective they tend to seem more promising. In fact, for actors it sometimes seems feasible to transform the logic of the system itself. The polar extremes of the model, between which these variable relationships move, envision everything from an almost unlimited power of actors to shape events to a thoroughgoing determinism dictated by the logic of social systems.

One of the principal lessons learned from the collapse of Soviet-style planned economies was that economic functional logic sets narrow limits to the power of politics to shape events. When these limits are ignored, economic logic loses its effectiveness as a steering function. It is replaced by the logic of the political system, with the result that the society as a whole fails to reach its full economic potential, albeit contrary to the responsible actors' intentions.[58] The power of politics to shape its environment is thus limited. Whatever potential politics does have to refashion the economy can best be exploited when actors understand the economy's functional laws and know how to apply them in practice. The economic system may be shaped either by creating a framework of laws and rules or by direct intervention. In either case it is the economic subsystem itself that sets the outer limits of political manipulation. To transgress those limits invites "retaliation" by the economic system, either via functional breakdowns or through undesirable side effects brought on by intervention.

Contingency and openness

A crucial unresolved issue for the theory of social democracy is whether the free market global economy will impose rigid system requirements. That is, must our strategies merely adapt to global conditions in order to achieve social democratic goals, or can they call into question the economic framework itself and thus the rules under which those goals are pursued? There are two uncertainties here. First, it is not clear whether one can still influence the economic framework by political techniques, since it has been so strongly internationalized. Second, no one is sure whether political influence can be successfully applied to the functional logic of the international economy at all. For reasons of principle, neither question can be answered *ex ante*. Let us suppose that social science had reached consensus about the extent of our political latitude in transnational affairs and that its projections were accepted by numerous actors at the nation-state level. Still, there would also have to be a reliable, long-term consensus among global political veto-holders to allow the models to be put into effect. As long as the United States, for example, clings to its libertarian strategies, even the most plausible proposals for shaping the international environment will be unattainable. In this case the global free market starts to seem like a "fact of life," even though, as a *social* fact, it really is not.

But the proponents of social democratic policy certainly cannot afford to wait until all the relevant global veto-holders have been brought into the consensus, since the latter is an unlikely outcome anyway. Instead, they will likely have to seek a second-best, but realistic, solution by pursuing a *two-track strategy*. On one level they should do their best to improve the outlook for actively shaping the transnational economic environment. But they will also have to devise and carry out a suitable adaptive strategy that offers good prospects for achieving political goals in either the national or, as with the EU, the regional arena. This is a crossroads for the theory of social democracy. Some have assumed that the current situation, in which there is very little transnational political coordination, is one to which a realistic theory or policy simply must defer.[59] That would mean accepting the existence of a reality-threshold that could never be crossed and giving up any hope of implementing the normatively preferred strategies of democratization, imbedding of the economy, and regulation on a world scale. But in fact neither empirical evidence nor theoretical reasoning supports such an assumption. The pseudo-realist view actually conceals normative convictions similar to the premises of libertarian democracy, which of course social democracy rejects. There is a more optimistic scenario in which a normatively desirable degree of transnational political coordination could be achieved in a reasonable time, merely because it is practically necessary. Social democracy could then concentrate on shaping global society by political means. Unfortunately, that scenario has no more solid empirical and theoretical grounding than its opposite number.[60] For it to appear in the least plausible, there would have to be a solid phalanx of transnational actors behind it, but currently that is not the case.

Thus, in weighing policy instruments, a realistic theory of social democracy must stick with empirically defensible strategies. In terms of their modalities and eventual success, those will hinge on the question of whether the world market is, *for the time being*, a "fact of life" and/or whether it might become amenable to political shaping. By comparing data from countries that have tried such strategies, a theory of social democracy can choose the ones that are most likely to achieve some of its agenda, even on the gloomy assumption that actors can only cope with and not shape the global environment.[61] Still, it must at least discuss strategies that do envision the political shaping of world markets, even though it is at present hard to imagine a constellation of actors that would sponsor them.

Social democratic policy-making, present and future

In a social democracy, actors confront historically contingent conditions. They must deal with constellations of actors and systemic conditions that they can indeed reshape to some degree, but which they can neither ignore nor rearrange. That is one of the main reasons why the instruments they hope to use, from political programs to state intervention, exhibit such a range of variation, even though their ultimate ends and underlying political values do not necessarily change. Thus, to evaluate the ways and means by which social democracy might be achieved, especially in the core areas of economic and social policy, we must take account of the *context*, since it always affects the relative utility of those means. It makes a great deal of difference whether actors are pursuing the goals of social democracy as structural minority parties, as potential majority parties, or as structural majority parties. Likewise, it affects the options available to social democratic actors when they are seeking majority support in a libertarian-influenced political culture or in one in which the basic values of social democracy predominate.

As the overview presented here suggests, a theory of social democracy can certainly get along without an elaborate historical narrative; it may choose instead to focus on a systematic design for the present and near future. But even then it needs to elucidate the different contexts in which political action has taken place – and will take place – over time. Here we must distinguish three dimensions of the temporal sequence:

1 the phase *prior to* the present integration of world markets and of large portions of global society (the beginning of the 1970s)

2 the phase *since* the onset of globalization and continuing into the near future
3 a *future situation* in which it might be possible to shape global conditions in line with the desiderata of social democracy.

The first two phases partially overlap, since countries have been exposed in different degrees to the effects of integrated markets or have responded to them in different ways. There are several reasons for the time lag.

- Particular countries have been hit by global integration at different times and in varying degrees.
- Countries exhibit greater or lesser dependence on the world market and have managed its political effects in quite distinct ways.
- Political actors have shown a varying propensity to exploit the perceived constraints of the world market to reform their political instruments such as the social welfare state.
- Actors in different countries have been more or less willing to back strategies to redesign the global market.
- Numerous instruments of social democratic policy-making are still useful despite economic globalization.
- The reaction of individual countries to pressure from open markets depends markedly on the type of capitalist regime in each case.

In the post-global-integration phase, countries have tried to adapt to the new situation by innovative policy-making or revisions of traditional strategies.[62] Those adaptive strategies will continue to play a constitutive role in social democratic policy until some effective way to shape the global environment has emerged.

A long-term global policy of imbedding capitalism that would be functionally equivalent to what is done in European social democracies today might be successfully pursued. In that case many of the defensive adjustment policies that were necessary during the transitional phase might gradually lose their *raison d'être*.[63] One can sketch the contours of a desirable form of globalization, while describing the policies that are presently being practiced to adapt to the conditions of integrated markets. Still, it is difficult to foresee how the two strategies – national and global – might mesh with one another, especially since they would likely be asynchronous.

In short, there are many contingent factors affecting social democratic policy-making: the constellation of actors, the leeway that the system allows for effecting changes, and the extent to which reflection on already adopted political strategies may lead to their revision. That is why we must leave unanswered the deeper questions concerning coping and shaping. In any case, globally integrated markets generate unprecedented pressures to adapt, and that will continue to be true even if social democracy's most extravagant hopes for reshaping the world through imbedding and regulation were to be fulfilled.

The limits of negative and positive globalization

Neither the march of negative globalization nor the recent progress made in positive globalization can be interpreted as an irreversible trend. Rieger and Leibfried have demonstrated that protectionism can even become a functional substitute for the lack of income security that social policy ordinarily would provide.[64]

Progress in positive globalization must also be considered a contingent process. We cannot be certain that even regulatory policies that create public goods seemingly in everyone's interest will always be implemented or, if so, that they will continue in effect. Policy gains can never be understood as irreversible developmental benchmarks. Social conditions of globalization and the political schemes and interests of leading political actors transform globalization policy into an extremely *contingent project*. Social democracy must therefore opt for a sophisticated dual strategy: a short- and mid-range policy of adaptation coupled with a long-range policy of reshaping global conditions, in full awareness that the results will always be highly uncertain.

Part IV

Cultural Foundations

6

The Universalism of Social Democracy

The question concerning social democracy's claim to universality has to be resolved mainly on the level of political culture rather than in terms of formal institutions and organizational forms.[1] Research has shown that formal democratic institutions not deeply imbedded in a receptive political culture of democracy will neither work well nor endure.[2] In this sense democracy is not culturally neutral. Nevertheless, the identification of "Western" culture with democracy, whether proclaimed by advocates of "Western" values or their "anti-Western" adversaries, is factually incorrect. The kind of culture that liberal democracy needs to function well and remain stable has nothing to do with specific, religiously defined traditions, forms of life, or beliefs, in the way that Samuel Huntington, for one, argues.[3] Rather, it requires that a set of basic norms in modern civilization be socially anchored and serve as guidelines for political action.

In this context too it is appropriate to point out that the Western tradition itself, as it had taken shape in Europe since the ninth century, did not give birth to democracy. It was only a sharp break with that tradition, part of the transition to modernity that took place in the Enlightenment and then the proto-democratic revolutions of the eighteenth century in France and the United States, that laid the cultural groundwork for democracy in theory and practice.[4] Human rights and democracy, key principles of liberalism, both emerged around the same time from the modern postulate of autonomy rooted in the Enlightenment.[5] Once the traditional, substantial ethical life of a pre-modern culture passes away, regardless of which cultural or religious tradition originally gave it its content, the old ways of resolving conflict no longer work. Differences over ways of life, claims to religious truth, and disagreements about social and political order can no longer be settled, as they once were, by referring the competing claims to some privileged, allegedly absolute source of truth endowed with a generally accepted claim to legitimacy. Empirical analysis shows that a liberal current of thought begins to develop in *all* religious and cultural traditions of the world that take their bearings from the basic cultural and political values of modernity. But of course nascent liberalism still must compete with a traditionalism rooted in specific social milieus as well as the fundamentalist reaction to nascent modernization. Eventually, the individual – or, better, the spheres of private and public autonomy – must take responsibility for interpreting the claims of tradition. Democracy and human rights are the only cultural norms left standing, and the only techniques for handling differences in a shared order. Still, at no time did the liberal culture of modernity ever hold sway unchallenged, even within the "Western" tradition. By the same token, liberalizing trends always face a struggle to assert themselves against other manifestations of religious and cultural traditions. All cultures in modern times have been marked by the divergences among liberal, traditionalist, and fundamentalist cultural styles.[6]

As a normative claim to equality of rights in the uses of private and public autonomy, liberal democracy is thus universal for the same reasons as is the process of pluralistic differentiation. The latter gives rise to a multiplicity of divergent ways of life and interpretations of values flowing from cultural traditions that were once uniform and homogeneous. It is then unsurprising that fundamentalists should reject the very foundations of democracy and human rights, for opposition to both is in fact their constitutive principle. However, we should not imagine that we are dealing here with the expression of a difference between "Western" culture and the rest of the world. This is obvious when we recall that fundamentalists in the West also often oppose human rights and democracy.

Recent studies have made it apparent that all cultures have permitted certain principles to take root in the center of their value-systems: the reciprocity of rights and duties among all human beings and thus the implicit recognition of their equal worth. However, not unexpectedly, those principles have become imbedded in very different symbolic worlds and conceptual systems. The same holds true for the core content of another basic socio-political value: solidarity, or the obligation of all human beings to render mutual aid beyond what is due according to the requirements of justice.[7] Thus, one way or another, those values are eventually going to emerge and develop out of the cultural potentialities latent in every society. The only question is how they will intersect with the pace of social change in those societies, their political experiences, and their dealings with other cultures of the world. At least since the twentieth century, there have been groups active in civil society, politics, and intellectual circles within every culture that advocate the full practical realization of its latent democratic potential. They have claimed to speak for that potential even against those who despise it and who choose to interpret in anti-democratic ways the cultural sources they share in common with the democratizing factions.[8] The confrontations between government officials and representatives of democratizing civil society often observed at human rights conferences or UN conventions offer convincing testimony about those tensions. But they have also cropped up in the history and political practice of societies belonging to all the great world cultures.

In many ways India is the paradigm case of these trends. In 1948 Gandhi and Nehru introduced liberal democracy in a country with a population three-quarters Hindu but also including 140 million Muslims. Only one other country on earth contains more Muslim citizens than India. In the sense pioneered by Wolfgang Merkel, India is a defective democracy, yet it has functioned tolerably well for more than half a century, having demonstrated remarkable stability with the exception of one brief interlude.[9] India is also an excellent place to study both the conditions favoring mutual recognition and cooperation between cultural and religious groups and those that lead to the denial of that recognition, usually under the influence of fundamentalist agitation. From time to time, fundamentalists have also provoked the radical factions of both groups to quarrel about details concerning the legal status of the country's Muslims and the symbolic significance of Hinduism for India's national identity. Yet they have never questioned liberal democracy itself.[10] India shows not only that Hinduism and Islam can bring democracy as a form of life into existence and sustain it, but also that they can co-exist more or less peacefully in a shared democracy. Furthermore, India has produced an impressive tradition of social democracy in scholarship, political and intellectual history, and political practice that evinces remarkable parallels to European traditions but has scarcely been noticed outside of India.[11]

For over a century and a half, there have been intra-Islamic discussions going on in the Arab world as well as attempts to assert the value of democracy, human rights, and enlightenment against the prevailing traditionalist and fundamentalist forces.[12] Mohammed Arkoun, an Islamic scholar from Algeria, insists on the heuristic value of the Turkish example. In the 1920s Mustafa Kemal (Ataturk) managed to carry out successfully a secularizing, republican revolution in Turkey, at the time a highly traditional Islamic state. Initially, the revolution was a sort of voluntarist anticipation of future possibilities, since it was not preceded by any far-reaching transformation of the country's culture.[13] Nevertheless, the secularization of the public sphere did succeed, and has by now become part of the country's dominant culture. Although democracy in Turkey has exhibited obvious defects in the area of human rights and even been suspended several times, it still seems to have gained majority acceptance as the only legitimate form of government. Turkey proves that the secular state and liberal democracy can become

part of the majority culture in an Islamic society given favorable conditions, while still remaining rooted in a version of Islam reconstructed to
suit modern conditions.[14]

Recently, aspirations toward universal democracy and human rights
have been attacked by Asian politicians, too. They argue that those principles are inconsistent with genuine "Asian values" and represent a concealed form of renewed Western dominance. During the 1990s two
authoritarian leaders, Mohamad Mahathir of Malaysia and Lee Kuan
Yew of Singapore, were especially fond of this argument, while putting
it into effect with an iron hand in their own governing behavior. They
claimed that genuine Asiatic traditions, with their respect for authority,
conflicted with Western democracy; hence, they tolerated only a trun-
cated catalogue of human rights and practiced a version of culturally
adjusted democracy with the accent on authoritarian guidance.[15] Such
claims have been unambiguously rejected by political, intellectual, and
scientific representatives of their own Asian culture, as well as figures
from civil society.[16] The intra-Asian pro-democracy and pro-human
rights alternative has drawn support from representative voices all over
the continent, many of whom speak for larger groups of actors in (civil)
society. These advocates generally advance four arguments. *First*, in all
of the religious and cultural traditions of Asia there have been moves
toward democratic self-determination, some dating far back into the
past, that focused especially on local affairs. All of them sought justification in their own familiar cultural and religious values. *Second*, there
is no empirical basis for talking about a homogeneous Asiatic culture in
any of these societies. For one thing, virtually every major religion and
culture is represented in the region in significant numbers, and has
developed in ways specific to the society that surrounds it. For another,
all of those traditions have been polyvalent in a historical and social
sense, and all have been subject to quite different interpretations. *Third*,
no social consensus about the present-day meaning of "Asian values"
or the need to restrict human rights and democracy in their name underlies the political uses to which those values have been put. Rather, it is
only the interests of the authoritarian ruling groups in suppressing
opposition movements in their own societies that motivates such
claims. *Fourth*, even if Asian values such as spirituality, the pre-
eminence of the common interest, and respect for public authorities
actually did enter into the cultural mainstream in some societies, that
would not be a reason to restrict liberal democracy per se, but only to
enrich it through political, social, and civic culture. Accordingly, even if
one did encounter more pervasive community values in Asian societal
cultures than in "Western" democracies, that should properly only
show up in the way that liberal democratic institutions would be imbedded culturally and socially or supplemented, broadened, and enriched
by such traditions.

A highly respected Philippine social scientist and civic activist, Walden Bello, has trenchantly captured the relationship between "Western" democracy and democratization in other cultures. He probably speaks for many members of his own and other Asian cultures when he insists that what Asia needs is not the Western variant of a merely elite-dominated liberal democracy, but rather

> a substantive or social democracy, where citizens are genuinely equal because there are no sharp disparities in the access to wealth and income that allow the rich to purchase political decisions at the expense of the poor, whether this is done through illegal bribery in Thailand and the Philippines, or, as in the United States, through legal bribery via massive corporate campaign contributions.[17]

The Asian democracy movement is demanding the construction and expansion of a social democracy founded on basic rights, the rejection of rule by elites, support for an ethic of official conduct based on Asian traditions, the reinforcement of civil society, the democratization of political parties, and the revival of the traditional communal ethos in public life. Reflection on the relationship between Asian values and democracy in the post-1997 crisis period has tended to assume the form of a shift of emphasis to democratization via recovery of Asiatic traditions.[18] Thus, neither liberal nor social democracy is a specialty of the local culture of the "West," and certainly not in the sense that the form it took there could serve as a model everywhere else in the world. As democracy movements everywhere testify, both flow from a universal political culture in their core institutions and basic values. Genuine cultural traditions all over the world can develop and flourish best in an environment of democratic institutions and values. That insight is most clearly manifest in the case of so-called Asian values and their relationship to the cultural underpinnings of social democracy.

7

Cultural Divergence and Social Citizenship

7.1 Multiculturalism and political rights

The theory of social democracy and the politics of recognition

Social democratic theory has not had an easy time dealing with ethnic, religious, and linguistic differences, as distinct from those that arise from market-generated economic inequalities. On one hand, its defenders recognize that citizens are concretely situated in ways other than by social class. If this recognition had been developed theoretically by social democrats, it might have led to an expanded conception of social rights. After all, if there can be social rights for the economically precarious or disadvantaged, then why not for members of minority ethnic or language groups, aboriginal peoples, or non-mainstream sects? But as yet few prominent theorists of social democracy have favored expanded social rights, exemptions, or special arrangements for non-economic groups. There are several reasons for this reluctance to stretch social rights to include the claims of culture.

First, social democracy draws on two traditions of political theory, neither especially receptive to such claims: liberal democracy and orthodox socialism. Liberal democracy does have a romantic current, associated with figures such as Rousseau and Herder who championed self-determination for national minorities and/or urged language groups to unite within nation-states and develop the "individuality" of their cultures.[1] But on the whole liberal theorists have depicted the formation of civil society as an act of self-interest on the part of pre-political individuals seeking to preserve and enhance rights and opportunities that each holds singly, not as an act of collective self-determination undertaken by a cohesive community. Indeed, libertarian theorists, especially, have never satisfactorily accounted for why the boundaries of political communities should be drawn along ethnic, religious, or linguistic lines at all.[2] The liberal state is supposed to be neutral toward the religious and ethnic groups that presumably aspire to take advantage of public law and resources to enhance their own conceptions of the good.[3]

On the socialist side, ethnic, linguistic, and religious attachments have been even more vexing. For Marx, they were relics of an earlier age, which modern capitalism had already begun to extinguish.[4] Communism would finish the job that bourgeois society had long since undertaken of creating a world society without national boundaries or religious affiliations. So why worry about whether social rights should respect the claims of culture if cultural roots are being pulled up by global economic and political forces anyhow? Moreover, linguistic and cultural attachments have appeared to some socialist writers as unfortunate barriers to uniting the working class around purely economic demands.

Even theorists we have identified as the architects of social democratic thought, such as Heller and Marshall, have not been especially receptive to cultural claims within nation-states. Both writers were too preoccupied with the task of overcoming the alienation and marginalization of the working class to worry much about the rights or claims of cultural minorities. Of course, their views partly reflect their times, well before the demands for cultural recognition became intensely felt and politically potent. A contemporary theory of social democracy must confront the claims of culture anew and invent its own solutions.

In some ways, the claims of culture resemble demands for liberal and social rights in being universal: no one is supposed to be disqualified, in principle, from the opportunity to raise cultural claims, since everyone is equal. Yet the claims of culture ask public policy-makers to recognize and often accord special treatment to features of personal identity that bind persons to cultural, ethnic, linguistic, or religious groupings. The specific demands made on behalf of cultural difference range widely to include exemptions from laws or rules on the grounds that they violate religious obligations; "affirmative action" to achieve diversity and redress past discrimination; subsidies for speakers of minority languages; changes in mainstream educational curricula to reflect the experiences of minorities in a nation's history; requests for proportional representation for minorities; and greater political autonomy and even full self-determination for nations that lack their own state.

Following Nancy Fraser we may refer to all such claims as expressions of the politics of *recognition* as distinct from the traditional politics of *redistribution*.[5] She argues that our "postsocialist" condition has muted the older redistributive claims and increased the salience of demands that "difference" be given official recognition. The term "politics of recognition" emphasizes that today identity is something people must work out for themselves, partly by way of the quest for individual authenticity.[6] Moreover, a nation or ethnic group may also be seen as embarked on the historical task of defining itself, giving expression to its unique contributions.[7] The politics of recognition begins at the intersection of these quests. Individuals may become convinced that their identities are entwined with the cultural group to which they belong. In that case being ashamed of one's ethnic background, speaking the majority language instead of one's own, attempting to "fit into" the mainstream culture can seem like self-betrayal.

Recalling the often disastrous political consequences that have followed from the fusion of personal and group identity, we might conclude that liberalism and social democracy should not endorse the politics of recognition. Better, one might imagine, to encourage people to focus on common problems that cut across ethnic, religious, and racial lines, especially economic grievances. But that will not do. When the members of a minority group find their language proscribed, their traditions belittled, their racial features stigmatized, their sacred sites turned into strip mines, they suffer real hurt and disadvantage. Merely offering them the consolation of economic advancement, social support, or better jobs will not undo the harm wrought by the denial of recognition. In short, we should treat issues subsumed under "difference" and "recognition" as distinct from the traditional questions surrounding economic inequality and redistribution, since each involves a separate "paradigm of justice."[8] The theory of social democracy must show why and under what circumstances demands for recognition should be granted, while also indicating the *limitations* of such policies, given their potential to foster or intensify ethnic and religious hatreds. This section focuses on the first issue, while the next one addresses the second.

There are good reasons why social democracy should support differential treatment of minorities. The first concerns national minorities: cohesive groups whose members usually dwell in a compact, well-defined territory and identify with a shared history, often bound up with a common language and religious heritage. They have preserved a "societal culture," i.e., one that offers its members an integrated, coherent way of life across a spectrum of daily activities.[9] Basques in Spain, Francophones in Québec, and many Aboriginal peoples in Australia have maintained societal cultures. Most of these national minorities exercised some degree of autonomy before being incorporated into modern nation-states; most were involuntarily subordinated by their more powerful neighbors. England's conquest of Ireland, the United States' wars against the "first nations" of North America, and Spain's conquest of the Aztecs and Maya in Mexico all exemplify the injustices of "nation-building."[10]

These peoples' histories as once autonomous societies have profound implications for contemporary social democratic policy. We cannot simply assume that a *single*, homogeneous society exists within the boundaries of a nation-state. We must instead ask: how did this particular society come into being in the first place? Were some of its citizens forced to join it? Did they join as the result of guarantees of semi-sovereignty and exemption from laws that abridged their autonomy, or as a result of decisions made by rulers over whose actions they had no control? If any of those conditions obtains, we should not treat their claims simply as requests for *special exemptions* from laws or principles that apply to other citizens. Rather, recognizing the cultural differences of minority nationalities and religious confessions – and granting them a degree of self-determination – may be necessary to redress longstanding grievances, correct wrongs committed in the past, and achieve justice.

In fact, if a society is so fractured by cultural or ethnic cleavages that a "neutral" state cannot even be imagined, it may be necessary to build recognition of those cleavages into its institutions. Otherwise, the supposedly neutral state may end up either provoking social dissolution or becoming an engine of repression and exploitation. In such cases arrangements must be made to provide "group representation" for the constituent ethnic groups and/or to guarantee one or both certain economic advantages. Such arrangements will be distasteful to egalitarians, but without them it is doubtful that these societies would survive intact. In short, the theory of social democracy cannot simply assume that a homogeneous nation-state exists with an automatic right to govern all inhabitants of its territory. To be relevant to the many multinational states around the globe, social democratic theory must take into account the processes of nation-building, and the ethnic or cultural compromises that it may have required.

A second reason to put the politics of recognition on the agenda of social democracy flows from the notion of self-respect as developed by Walzer and Rawls. Both link it to citizenship and social rights. Rawls argues that the participants in a social contract will want to maximize primary goods while minimizing the risks of losing them. Therefore, they will choose the two principles of justice: equal liberty for all, plus economic arrangements designed to allow inequalities only to the extent that they benefit the least advantaged representative persons. But, Rawls adds, among the primary goods we must include "self-respect," the "most important" of them, since without it nothing we do seems worthwhile.[11] Walzer sharpens the argument by insisting that self-respect is a "function of membership" in a larger group, and that "prolonged unemployment and poverty . . . represent a kind of economic exile" that undermines self-respect. It follows that "the welfare state is an effort to . . . gather in economic exiles, to guarantee effective membership."[12]

But why should we treat self-respect exclusively as a function of socio-economic status? If our identities have been "malformed," as the result of the stigmatization of our culture, language, or color, it will be difficult for us to respect ourselves even if there are no legal barriers or economic deprivations that stamp us as second-class citizens.[13] A minority group cannot receive equal justice if the mainstream society holds in contempt its forms of cultural self-expression, since its members may lack the primary good of self-respect that most other citizens assume as a matter of course. They would still be exiles even if they were materially comfortable.

Multiculturalism versus universalism

To establish the limits of the politics of recognition, especially when it conflicts with the politics of redistribution or with fundamental human and civic rights, we must distinguish between national minorities and immigrant groups.[14] The former typically possess a "societal culture" developed when they were still self-governing, i.e., before they were incorporated into the nation-state against which they now claim certain rights and immunities. Their formerly autonomous status and coerced or quasi-contractual incorporation into the nation-state usually justifies the "special" treatment they ask to receive. For example, it would be unjust to deprive Native Americans of the treaty rights they acquired at such a high cost to their land base. Immigrant groups, by contrast, have an essentially different status within the nation-state, since they "come as individuals or families, rather than as entire communities, and settle throughout the country, rather than forming 'homelands.' "[15] Because they typically lack a societal culture or a history of self-government as a cohesive group, it is reasonable to expect that they will eventually integrate into the mainstream societal culture by learning the most widely used language(s), respecting the laws and norms of their adopted society, attending its schools, and participating in its political system.

Theoretical difficulties arise when immigrant groups claim special rights and immunities similar to those granted to national minorities, or when there are groups in society (say African Americans) whose history distinguishes them from both national minorities and immigrants. First, a group may argue that it should have a right to treat its own members – often women and children – in ways that violate universal basic rights. Or some groups may demand special treatment as redress of past injustices, as in the case of affirmative action programs and quotas for minorities.

The first case is perhaps the clearest. Social democracy assumes the primacy of civil and human rights. Violations of such fundamental rights in the name of cultural difference cannot be tolerated. Social democracy cannot abide "internal restrictions" (Kymlicka's term) placed on members of a cultural minority, designed to "keep them in line" or prevent them from leaving or acquiring knowledge forbidden by the group.[16] There must always be a "right of exit" that permits members to defect, exercise their autonomous judgment, educate themselves, or simply dissent from the group's values. As Benhabib has argued, cultures only look monolithic and seamless from the outside; internally they are always contested.[17] Social democratic theory should not unwittingly abet the more fundamentalist elements of a cultural community by awarding them legal authority to discipline their members, stifle dissent, and punish apostates. The requirements of deliberative democracy ought to apply to the internal debates within cultural groups, which should be as open and uncoerced as possible.

The second, more complex case concerns political demands to redress past injustices. A bewildering range of policies fit into this category: reserving places in universities for disadvantaged minority groups; factoring minority status into admissions decisions by adding extra "points" for minority candidates; asking employers to hire a specified quota of minority applicants; or requiring that minority contractors obtain a certain percentage of the contracts for government-funded construction projects. In principle social democratic theory should support policies that rectify the deleterious effects of past discrimination. But social democratic theory must meet "egalitarian" objections to such programs that would not deter a classical liberal.

To begin we must revisit the distinction between national minorities and immigrant groups. In some instances quotas may be required not so much to redress past discrimination, but simply as a political solution to ethnic, linguistic, or religious fissures that threaten the integrity of a multinational state. For example, under Belgian law there must be an equal number of ministers from the Flemish and French language groups, and in Fiji the native Fijians enjoy an automatic majority in the national legislature, since they are assigned thirty-seven seats to the Indians' twenty-seven. The point of such arrangements is not simply to rectify discrimination and improve the economic prospects of the groups involved, but to give official recognition to the implicit or explicit "social contract" that holds these multinational states together, preventing secession or civil war. As noted, the theory of social democracy should endorse such arrangements in principle, since they reflect attempts to transcend the violence and injustice that have so often accompanied nation-building.

Affirmative action plans and quotas for groups that do not count as national minorities must be justified in other ways. One compelling argument would adapt Rawls's difference principle (inequalities are permitted only if they improve the prospects of the least advantaged) to incorporate ethnic, religious, or cultural membership as well as social classes. This adjustment to Rawls's theory makes sense, because theoretically it might be possible to improve, let us say, the prospects of the

bottom 20 percent of income earners in the USA, but with all the benefits going to whites, while the incomes of disadvantaged racial minorities in that quintile stagnated. That obvious injustice becomes visible
only if one takes race into account.

However, we cannot ignore the potential of group-differentiated
rights to jeopardize the egalitarianism and universalism that underlies
social democratic policies. Brian Barry has criticized multiculturalism
along just such lines. He points out that group differentiation tends to
foment hostility and competition among the groups locked into zero-
sum contests for a share of the money made available to promote
cultural self-expression. As a result of such competition, "efforts that
might have been devoted to more broad-based causes are dissipated on
turf wars."[18]

In sum, social democratic theory has a bedrock commitment to universal rights, egalitarianism, and the decommodification of labor. But in
most instances that commitment should not imply disapproval or rejection of measures designed to improve the prospects of disadvantaged
or marginalized national, ethnic, and cultural groups. The two types of
policies have different rationales, clienteles, and goals. Nevertheless,
social democratic policy cannot ignore the potential of ethnic, religious,
and cultural strife to polarize society, foment violence, and weaken
the bonds of solidarity on which social citizenship depends. To that we
now turn.

7.2 Cultural difference and social citizenship

Political civic culture

To achieve lasting political integration, democratic commonwealths
must have a political culture that adequately supports a common orientation to political citizenship throughout all of its divergent subcultures, in other words a real societal culture. What structural, political,
and legal conditions must be met to establish a political culture of
this kind in pluralistic societies with immigrants from many different
cultures?

The two necessary conditions for civic integration are *first*, the equal
right of every person to participate in political and social institutions,
and, *second*, equal access and an equal share for everyone in the social,
economic, and political rights and opportunities of society. The latter
run the gamut from participation in the political system and civil
society, to the educational system, employment, and social security. At
stake here are the rights, duties, and opportunities that the theory of
social democracy regards as the justified entitlements of every citizen.
Among the necessary factors of social integration we should also

include – and insure – a common political culture in practical civic action, notably in the state, civil society, and the life-world. Empirical research has identified a number of factors that may either encourage or impede such integration.

In principle, five kinds of relationships between majority and minority cultures can be distinguished:

1 *assimilation*: participation in which the values of the host society are largely adopted
2 *inclusion*: participation in which the values of the society of origin are preserved
3 *exclusion*: lack of participation despite abandonment of the values of the society of origin
4 *segregation*: lack of participation in which the values of the country of origin are retained, and in which an infrastructure of the minority's own ethnic group is sometimes created[19]
5 *integration*: participation in which the basic political values of the host society are adopted, while the cultural values related to the life style of the country of origin are kept.

The role of civil society

The emergence of a political culture that forms bonds among its members rests on shared experiences. Besides the educational system, it is civil society that does the most to act as an ad hoc enabling structure to provide those experiences.[20] It is evident that such a bond-forming political culture presupposes a common language or at least opportunities for ongoing translation as the minimal condition for the possibility of public consensus. Beyond that there must be a certain measure of shared cultural background and historical knowledge from which the collective identity of a commonwealth's political culture can be forged, since part of the political culture of any collectivity involves a scheme for political life and action both internally and externally. It is the educational system (for recent immigrants especially adult education) which is primarily charged with fulfilling these two prerequisites. Obviously the educational system can only carry out this phase of political-cultural assimilation if it has remained culturally intact itself.

The desideratum, then, is to create life-worlds and spheres of social action in civil society that can in principle be shared by all social strata. This is an ambitious yet indispensable condition for carrying out democratic political integration. Trust plus a reasonable measure of bond-forming social capital are the foundations of political culture in a democracy. Therefore, to the extent that ethno-cultural or cultural-religious *parallel societies* begin to form in democratic nation-states, we may expect that they will hinder the emergence of a solidly bonded political culture and retard the process of social and political integration. The more all-pervasive and closed they are, the more they tend to generate a form of exclusive internal solidarity that alienates ethno-cultural and ethno-religious groups from one another.

Integration must be understood as a longer-term, deliberate process that reshapes the identity of participants. Unless certain preconditions are met, it is unlikely to succeed. The first is simply to realize that integration involves a kind of reciprocity. It is a multidimensional process in which forms of mutual recognition and self-transformation are consciously linked. The very fact that people quite different from one another still have to grant mutual recognition requires of each person a degree of self-transformation. During the process of successful integration something new is born that transcends mere co-existence based on the grudging toleration of those who appear different almost by their very nature, as though, to cite Jürgen Habermas's analogy, integration meant something like obeying the Endangered Species Act.[21]

Mutual influence reaches into deeper layers, touching even the contents of political culture itself. The host society is unquestionably entitled to impose conditions of entry on immigrants, notably that they adopt the political culture of the democratic constitutional state. But in this context, when people with a different cultural identity enter a society, they change the "foundational totality" of the nation-state in question, which, in this new form, will henceforth have a legitimate right to make decisions concerning collective political identity. They will likely alter the concrete content of the political culture itself.[22]

In this respect too it is not the fiction of homogeneous identity, but rather the conception of trans-culturality, that is best suited to describe the complex interactions involved in the process of integration. Integration into a political culture requires a certain degree of assimilation, but in both directions. All immigrants are expected to adopt the basic norms of the original mainstream culture as well as the democratic rule of law and its associated dispositions. But the cultural pluralism that arises out of political integration also obliges the host society to define the shared political identity of the nation-state together with the immigrants who have become citizens and thus have equal rights to participate in that (re)definition. Though always limited by the rule of law, this process will presumably always lead to a new collective identity, in which all citizens can find a reflection of themselves.

A complex politics of recognition

As noted, equal citizenship demands that five categories of universal basic rights (civil, political, social, economic, and cultural) be respected. Only a policy of integration through recognition can manage to satisfy the conditions for such equality of rights, specifically:[23]

1. recognition of diverse cultural identities
2. recognition of juridical democracy as a binding legal framework and universal rights by all cultural collectivities; in short, the emergence of a common political culture and the equal right of all to share in the social and economic resources and opportunities that society offers.

Part V

Theory and Practice

8

Libertarian and Social Democracies Compared

The theory developed here has generated certain reliable criteria for distinguishing social democracy from other varieties of democracy. But, in applying them to the dichotomy between social and libertarian democracy, we should be aware that they yield ideal types that do not exactly fit real-world commonwealths. At first glance, the cognitive interest of the theory asks no more than this: a convenient way of distinguishing actually existing democracies as one or the other basic type. Theoretically speaking, model variations *within* each type are of secondary importance, although they may be significant in practice. As in the case of the distinction between autocratic and democratic political systems, so too in this one, between libertarian and social democracy, a fairly sharp dividing line runs between the types, even though empirical indicators reveal only shadings and gradual transitions. What divides the two is the scope of recognition extended to basic rights under public law. Social democracy recognizes all categories of basic rights, in accord with the 1966 UN Declaration, whereas libertarian democracy recognizes only its civil and political components.

When liberal democracies acknowledge only political and cultural rights as obligations of government policy, they qualify as libertarian democracies even though they may rank high in solidarity and charitable giving in the private sphere. Despite their private generosity they fail to meet the standard of legally guaranteed social citizenship that constitutes social democracy's core meaning. The status of social citizenship finds expression in state-backed services that fulfill the legal entitlement to social inclusion and create a basis for social recognition, especially in the face of social risks. In the quantitative comparison of twenty OECD countries presented here, only the United States qualifies as a fully libertarian democracy. However, Ireland is a borderline case that should also be classified as a weakly libertarian democracy, for reasons to be explicated presently.

In measuring social democracy we need to consider the extent to which entitlements are actually honored in practice by the provision of state-backed services. Unless there is empirical confirmation that actual outcomes meet the relevant standards across the board, a country does not deserve to be called fully social democratic. Only the interplay between real-world service provision and legal entitlements will be considered in assigning values to the various factors in quantitative comparisons.[1] To put it differently, empirical studies reveal the extent to which governments actually honor in practice the legal obligations they profess to uphold. For example, Ireland receives such low scores in empirical comparisons that there is reason to doubt whether it should count as a social democracy at all. Indeed, its low marks for social inclusion justify classifying it as a weakly libertarian democracy. From a theoretical point of view, the criterion that really matters is whether the entitlement to social inclusion implicit in social citizenship has actually been honored.[2]

The theory of social democracy has suggested two reasons why social and economic rights play a constitutive role. First, they are a vital aspect of the "politics of recognition." Second, they provide a means of protecting a person's private, social, and political autonomy when social risks occur. All of these three dimensions of personal autonomy, as protected by basic rights, are epitomized in the sociological category of *inclusiveness*. If they do nothing else, social democracies must therefore guarantee social inclusiveness. It may accordingly be defined as the maintenance of adequate conditions for the enjoyment of private, social, and political autonomy against the occurrence of social risks. It gauges the extent to which a person's freedoms to act and participate in public life as a citizen have been maintained and supported even in the face of social risk. In light of the theory of social democracy, inclusiveness assumes concrete form in certain key areas that can be compared and measured by the following indicators.

The foundations of the theory of social democracy together with available welfare state data suggest that inclusiveness can be measured by five structures of institutionalization (1–5) and four factual outcomes related to inclusiveness (6–9).[3]

1 In addition to civil and political rights, *social and economic rights must be institutionalized* so that the status of social citizenship can make social inclusion into an achievable civil right. Because this is such a crucial indicator, it would exclude non-qualifying countries from being considered social democratic, unless empirical outcomes in the aforementioned key areas prove it to be inconsequential.

2 The *social welfare state duly supported by fundamental rights* is the most critical mainstay underwriting the social and economic rights that follow from guarantees of inclusiveness. Assuming they are all committed to fundamental rights, the social welfare states examined here are distinguished primarily by the degree of universality and generosity of the entitlements they grant in specific areas. This criterion is used to determine their respective scores.[4]

3 *Social expenditure as a percentage of GDP (the "social welfare state score")* roughly gauges the extent of a welfare state's commitment to secure the real-world efficacy of social rights.[5]

4 According to social democratic theory, an effective form of *coordinated market economy*, as distinct from a liberal market system, should be deemed a decisive political-economic structure for striking a suitable balance between socio-economic and civil or political rights.

5 *Co-determination* on the shop floor and in the firm is a crucial institutional form for guaranteeing the social autonomy of blue- and white-collar employees.

6 The *relative poverty rate* offers insight into the proportion of a population that is either partly or wholly excluded from a share in essential aspects of social, economic, and political life on account of their low income.

7 *Social stratification in the educational system* indicates the extent to which parents' social status affects the educational prospects and attainments of the next generation. The educational system has enormous influence in distributing opportunities over a lifetime, both in life generally and for specific opportunities to participate in the affairs of society. High rates of stratification in the educational system translate into high levels of exclusiveness in society.

8 The *workforce participation rate* is a measure of inclusion in the world of work. It is simultaneously an indicator of several crucial dimensions of social participation: social recognition and self-respect, a sense of personal efficacy, and inclusion via income-earning.

9 *Income equality* offers insight into a key factor affecting the distribution of opportunities for personal autonomy, participation in politics, and the life of society.

By combining these nine indicators, we arrive at a melange of institutional characteristics drawn from the liberal democracies under investigation and outcome factors resulting from their institutional arrangements. By mixing indicators measuring institutional patterns and contingent matters of fact, we avoid any narrow preoccupation with institutional structures alone. The measurements contained in the empirical outcome indicators furnish tests for ascertaining whether institutional systems actually accomplish what they are theoretically supposed to. In this respect the particular indicators allow for cross-cutting interpretation and correction.

There is good reason to think that some of the correlations uncovered by these indicators confirm the theoretical conclusions already outlined in this book.[6] The institutional indicators of economic rights, a universal social welfare state, and a coordinated market economy exhibit high positive correlations with two outcome indicators, a low poverty rate and relatively low income inequality, both of which are crucial to inclusion. The coordinated market economy measure correlates positively with a low poverty rate and low level of income inequality, but not with a high labor-force participation rate. This is because labor-force participation rates may be very high in some uncoordinated market economies as well, albeit at a price: high income inequality and a markedly greater poverty rate. Only when the scores for labor-force participation, poverty, and income are aggregated – a move well supported in theory – do we get a positive correlation with the institutional characteristic of a coordinated market economy.

By adding together the scores from the tables comparing specific dimensions of social inclusion, we arrive at a ranking of the countries under comparison in regard to the overarching value of social inclusiveness. The demarcation between social and libertarian democracy evidently reflects not just social citizenship, our distinguishing criterion, but likewise the empirical scores in the individual dimensions of inclusiveness. Indeed, the latter determine entirely on which side of the boundary Ireland falls.[7] The clear differences in the aggregate scores achieved, together with the rank-ordering derived from them, suggests a tripartite division into social democracies of high, moderate, and low inclusiveness.

The theory would lead us to expect that certain countries – notably those in Scandinavia and some in continental Europe with high scores for the social and political-economic institutions associated with social democracy – would also receive high marks for outcomes of social inclusiveness, especially for poverty-prevention and social equality. Interestingly, there appears to be a rough proportionality in evidence. Although uncoordinated markets may display comparable scores for the efficacy of their institutions, their service delivery is so precarious that it is accompanied by high poverty rates.

The great majority of the countries studied here turn out to be social democracies, although the extent of their inclusiveness varies dramatically. Indeed, that variation suggests a further subdivision within the social democratic regime type according to the degree of inclusiveness. But since the scale exhibits no obvious gaps, there will be an element of arbitrariness in drawing the boundary lines between these internal groupings. Despite those reservations, the data presented here support

Table 8.1 Ranking: Social Democracy (based on scores from 1996 to 2003)[8]

Highly inclusive social democracies

1	Sweden	25
2	Denmark	24
3	Finland	23
4	Norway	23
5	Netherlands	20
6	Austria	20

Moderately inclusive social democracies

7	Switzerland	17
8	Germany	17
9	Japan	17
10	France	16
11	Belgium	16

Less inclusive social democracies

12	Italy	13
13	New Zealand	13
14	Canada	13
15	Portugal	11
16	Australia	11
17	Spain	11
18	United Kingdom	10

Exclusive democracies (libertarian democracies)

19	Ireland	8
20	The United States	3

a further refinement and classification. Because of the breadth of the differences exhibited, the ranking is both theoretically relevant and empirically informative.

Another criterion that could be used to draw clear distinctions within the social democracies studied here is equality of opportunity. From a theoretical point of view, great weight should be assigned to inequality in the educational system, since it has so powerful an influence on a person's opportunities in every other sphere of society. This is especially so in our era, when people without a good education have many fewer opportunities than they once did to get ahead by dint of their own efforts. In short, low scores on this scale entail enduring limitations on social democracy. But the same can be said for the poverty rate in a society, since poverty severely limits the private, social, and political autonomy of its victims, and thus represents a tenacious form of exclusion.

One independent institutional factor of great importance for the social quality of liberal democracies turns out to be the way in which the educational system is institutionalized. That factor is not entirely independent of the political system's willingness to protect social and economic rights, but neither can it be inferred directly from the guidelines assembled here. It is certainly no coincidence that the Scandinavian countries, with their universalistic social welfare states, tally the highest scores for the socially leveling effects of their educational systems. But there is no reason to believe that continental European or Anglo-Saxon social welfare state regimes might not approach the Scandinavian standards as they respond to the pressures of a knowledge society. One could of course ascribe their shortcomings in meeting high equalization standards to the resistance of entrenched political cultures. Yet other factors – the shock of poor PISA study results,[9] the imperatives of the knowledge economy, and the findings of the theory of social democracy itself – might eventually help to overcome such resistance in some countries without requiring any massive systemic transformations.

Appendix

The index employs a scale from 0 to 25 points, in which 0 indicates the absence of any social democratic characteristics, while 25 depicts a fully developed social democracy.

Nine different aspects of social democracy are considered:

1 institutionalized social and economic rights (maximum 2)
2 a universalistic social welfare state committed to upholding basic rights (maximum 3)
3 social expenditure as a percentage of GDP (maximum 3)
4 coordinated market economy (maximum 3)
5 co-determination (maximum 2)
6 relative poverty rate (maximum 3)
7 social stratification in the educational system (maximum 3)
8 labor-force participation rate (maximum 3)
9 income equality (maximum 3).

1 Are basic social and economic rights institutionalized?

Has each country in question signed and ratified the 1966 United Nations Covenant on economic, social, and cultural rights?
Yes = **(2)**; No = **(0)** points

1	Australia	18 Dec. 1972	10 Dec. 1975	**(2)**
2	Austria	10 Dec. 1973	10 Sept. 1978	**(2)**
3	Belgium	10 Dec. 1968	21 Apr. 1983	**(2)**
4	Canada		19 May 1976[a]	**(2)**
5	Denmark	20 Mar. 1968	6 Jan. 1972	**(2)**
6	Finland	11 Oct. 1967	19 Aug. 1975	**(2)**
7	France		4 Nov. 1980[a]	**(2)**
8	Germany	9 Oct. 1968	17 Dec. 1973	**(2)**
9	Ireland	1 Oct. 1968	8 Dec. 1989	**(2)**
10	Italy	18 Jan. 1967	15 Sept. 1978	**(2)**
11	Japan	30 May 1978	21 June 1979	**(2)**
12	Netherlands	25 June 1969	11 Dec. 1978	**(2)**
13	New Zealand	12 Nov. 1968	28 Dec. 1978	**(2)**
14	Norway	20 Mar. 1968	13 Sept. 1972	**(2)**
15	Portugal	7 Oct. 1976	31 July 1978	**(2)**
16	Spain	28 Sept. 1976	27 Apr. 1977	**(2)**
17	Sweden	29 Sept. 1967	6 Dec. 1971	**(2)**
18	Switzerland		18 June 1992[a]	**(2)**
19	United Kingdom	16 Sept. 1968	20 May 1976	**(2)**
20	United States	5 Oct. 1977		**(0)**

(a) Indicates either accession to or ratification of the treaty

2 A universal social welfare state supported by basic rights

Generosity and universality **(3)**, generosity and limited universality **(2)**, limited services and universality **(1)**, limited services and limited universality **(0)**

1	Australia	**(1)**
2	Austria	**(2)**
3	Belgium	**(2)**
4	Canada	**(0)**
5	Denmark	**(3)**
6	Finland	**(3)**
7	France	**(2)**
8	Germany	**(2)**
9	Ireland	**(1)**
10	Italy	**(2)**
11	Japan	**(1)**
12	Netherlands	**(2)**
13	New Zealand	**(1)**
14	Norway	**(3)**
15	Portugal	**(1)**
16	Spain	**(1)**
17	Sweden	**(3)**
18	Switzerland	**(2)**

| 19 | United Kingdom | **(1)** |
| 20 | United States | **(0)** |

3 Social expenditures as a percentage of GDP (social welfare state score)

0–14.9% = **(0)**, 15–19.9% = **(1)**, 20–25.9% = **(2)**, over 26% = **(3)**[10]

1	Australia	18.0	**(1)**
2	Austria	26.0	**(3)**
3	Belgium	27.2	**(3)**
4	Canada	17.8	**(1)**
5	Denmark	29.2	**(3)**
6	Finland	24.8	**(2)**
7	France	28.5	**(3)**
8	Germany	27.4	**(3)**
9	Ireland	13.8	**(0)**
10	Italy	24.4	**(2)**
11	Japan	16.9	**(1)**
12	Netherlands	21.8	**(2)**
13	New Zealand	18.5	**(1)**
14	Norway	23.9	**(2)**
15	Portugal	21.1	**(2)**
16	Spain	19.6	**(1)**
17	Sweden	28.9	**(3)**
18	Switzerland	26.4	**(3)**
19	United Kingdom	21.8	**(2)**
20	United States	14.8	**(0)**

4 Coordinated market economy

Coordination index according to Hall and Gingerich (2001), calculated on the basis of (a) shareholders' power, (b) diffusion of management's decision-making power, (c) size of the securities market, (d) level of wage negotiations, (e) frequency of job-changing, (f) extent of wage coordination. The field for evaluation extends from 1 (strong coordination) to 0 (no coordination at all); scores in each area are added together.

1–0.67 = **(3)**, 0.66–0.34 = **(2)**, 0.33–0.01 = **(1)**, 0 = **(0)**

1	Australia	0.36	**(2)**
2	Austria	1.00	**(3)**
3	Belgium	0.74	**(3)**
4	Canada	0.13	**(1)**

5	Denmark	0.70	(3)
6	Finland	0.72	(2)
7	France	0.69	(3)
8	Germany	0.95	(3)
9	Ireland	0.29	(1)
10	Italy	0.87	(3)
11	Japan	0.74	(3)
12	Netherlands	0.66	(2)
13	New Zealand	0.21	(1)
14	Norway	0.76	(3)
15	Portugal	0.57	(2)
16	Spain	0.57	(2)
17	Sweden	0.69	(3)
18	Switzerland	0.51	(2)
19	United Kingdom	0.07	(1)
20	United States	0	(0)

5 Co-determination

Co-determination in business enterprises of the EU.[11] Extensive co-determination **(2)**, limited co-determination **(1)**, very limited or no co-determination **(0)**

1	Australia	(1)
2	Austria	(2)
3	Belgium	(0)
4	Canada	(0)
5	Denmark	(2)
6	Finland	(2)
7	France	(1)
8	Germany	(2)
9	Ireland	(1)
10	Italy	(0)
11	Japan	(2)
12	Netherlands	(2)
13	New Zealand	(1)
14	Norway	(2)
15	Portugal	(1)
16	Spain	(1)
17	Sweden	(2)
18	Switzerland	(0)
19	United Kingdom	(0)
20	United States	(0)

6 Relative poverty rate

Percentage of the population living on incomes under 50% of the median.[12] 0–7.9% = **(3)**, 8–10.9% = **(2)**, 11–13.9% = **(0)**

1	Australia	11.2	**(1)**
2	Austria	9.3	**(2)**
3	Belgium	–	–
4	Canada	10.3	**(2)**
5	Denmark	4.3	**(3)**
6	Finland	6.4	**(3)**
7	France	7.0	**(3)**
8	Germany	9.8	**(2)**
9	Ireland	15.4	**(0)**
10	Italy	12.9	**(1)**
11	Japan	15.3	**(0)**
12	Netherlands	6.0	**(3)**
13	New Zealand	10.4	**(2)**
14	Norway	6.3	**(3)**
15	Portugal	13.7	**(0)**
16	Spain	–	–
17	Sweden	5.3	**(3)**
18	Switzerland	6.7	**(3)**
19	United Kingdom	11.4	**(1)**
20	United States	17.1	**(0)**

7 Social stratification in the educational system

PISA-Test: correlation between students' achievement level and socio-economic background:[13] strength of the correlation between students' scores on the comprehensive scale of reading competence and the PISA index of economic, social, and cultural status. ESCS strength of correlation; OECD median: 20.

1	Australia	17	**(1)**
2	Austria	14	**(2)**
3	Belgium	21	**(0)**
4	Canada	11	**(3)**
5	Denmark	15	**(2)**
6	Finland	9	**(3)**
7	France	22	**(0)**
8	Germany	22	**(0)**
9	Ireland	13	**(2)**
10	Italy	11	**(3)**
11	Japan	6	**(3)**
12	Netherlands	15[a]	**(2)**
13	New Zealand	16	**(2)**
14	Norway	13	**(2)**
15	Portugal	20	**(1)**
16	Spain	16	**(2)**
17	Sweden	11	**(3)**
18	Switzerland	19	**(1)**

19	United Kingdom	19	**(1)**
20	United States	22	**(0)**

(a) Indicates rate of participation is too low to guarantee comparability.

8 Labor-force participation rate (employment/population ratio)[14]

0–60.9 = **(0)**, 61–65.9 = **(1)**, 66–69.9 = **(2)**, over 70 = **(3)**

1	Australia	69.5	**(2)**
2	Austria	66.5	**(2)**
3	Belgium	60.5	**(0)**
4	Canada	72.6	**(3)**
5	Denmark	76.0	**(3)**
6	Finland	67.2	**(2)**
7	France	62.8	**(1)**
8	Germany	65.5	**(1)**
9	Ireland	65.5	**(1)**
10	Italy	57.4	**(0)**
11	Japan	68.7	**(2)**
12	Netherlands	73.1	**(3)**
13	New Zealand	73.5	**(3)**
14	Norway	75.6	**(3)**
15	Portugal	67.8	**(2)**
16	Spain	62.0	**(1)**
17	Sweden	73.5	**(3)**
18	Switzerland	77.4	**(3)**
19	United Kingdom	72.7	**(3)**
20	United States	71.2	**(3)**

9 Income inequality

(GINI Index): 0–26.9 (slight inequality) = **(3)**, 27–31.9 = **(2)**, 32–34.9 = **(1)**, 35–100 (great inequality) = **(0)**[15]

1	Australia	**35.2**	**(0)**
2	Austria	**30.0**	**(2)**
3	Belgium	**25.0**	**(3)**
4	Canada	**33.1**	**(1)**
5	Denmark	**24.7**	**(3)**
6	Finland	**26.9**	**(3)**
7	France	**32.7**	**(1)**
8	Germany	**28.3**	**(2)**
9	Ireland	**35.9**	**(0)**
10	Italy	**36.0**	**(0)**

11	Japan	24.9	(3)
12	Netherlands	30.9	(2)
13	New Zealand	36.2	(0)
14	Norway	25.8	(3)
15	Portugal	38.5	(0)
16	Spain	32.5	(1)
17	Sweden	25.0	(3)
18	Switzerland	33.1	(1)
19	United Kingdom	36.0	(0)
20	United States	40.8	(0)

9

Defective and Consolidated Democracy

Empirical research on democracy has long been preoccupied with the conditions of democratic stability.[1] Robert Dahl summarizes the results in drawing a distinction between *necessary* and *enabling* conditions for the stability of democracies.[2] The *necessary* conditions include control of the police and military by elected officials, the presence of a democratic political culture, and the absence of foreign control hostile to democracy. Among the *enabling* conditions are a modern market economy and society as well as a weakly developed subcultural pluralism. Dahl's classification relates only to the stability of the institutional system of a constitutional democracy, not to its quality. As he sees it, there is an ineluctable ambivalence in the relationship between market capitalism and democracy.[3] On one hand, the free market enhances the stability and smooth functioning of democratic institutions. On the other, many functional conditions and effects of market capitalist systems jeopardize both the quality and the stability of democracy.

In discussing the stability and functional requirements of democratic institutions, Dahl shows that a market capitalist system is only workable and compatible with democratic institutions when it is stabilized and tamed by extensive intervention and regulations.[4] Furthermore, market capitalist systems systematically lower the quality of democracy by generating extreme inequalities in the distribution of political resources and thereby predetermining the degree of real influence citizens will be able to exert. These inequalities are not trivial; they are serious limitations, since they undermine one of democracy's moral underpinnings, the right to have an equal chance to participate in public life.[5] The distributional effects of market capitalism may even render citizens' opportunities to influence democratic decision-making so grossly unequal that they violate one of democracy's constitutive principles, equal rights for all. That would be highly relevant to the stability issue, since most scholars of democracy agree that citizens' *perception* of the legitimacy of an institutionalized democracy is the decisive factor affecting its stability.[6] To be sure, some studies on democracy, especially those of Seymour Martin Lipset, attribute democracy's durability to such factors as GDP and educational levels.[7] But other studies draw attention to the fact that the social distribution of education and affluence – the dimension of social justice – also has a significant causal link to democratic stability.[8]

Prior to the introduction of democratic institutions, market capitalist systems fulfill a pro-democratic function by undermining the social foundations of autocratic rule and reinforcing the position of the lower social strata with a special interest in democratization.[9] But their democratic valence shifts once constitutional democracy has been successfully established. As Dahl remarks, "once politics and society are transformed by market-capitalism and democratic institutions are in place, the outlook fundamentally changes. Now the inequalities in resources that market-capitalism churns out produce serious inequalities among citizens."[10]

Recent research on the relationships between quality and stability in democratic systems has turned to the problem of "defective democracy." Situated between completely undemocratic regimes, *autocracies*, and fully developed *constitutional* or *juridical* democracies, there are some transitional forms that emerge either on the road to democracy or as products of its decay.[11] Defective democracies have generally prepared the way for democracy by ushering in universal suffrage, but in other respects they may fail to live up to democratic norms. In the contemporary world defective democracies are in fact quite numerous and thus particularly significant.[12] They may contain the germ of complete democratization when their flaws are merely the expression of an early phase in the development toward full democracy. But they can also presage the end of an existing democracy when they arise as a result of the dismantling of established democratic elements of governance.

Wolfgang Merkel has singled out the following five defects in governmental practices.[13]

First, there are defects in *access to political power*. Regimes may constitutionally guarantee universal suffrage, and many citizens may actually use it. However, others may experience nearly insuperable obstacles to full participation in elections and other aspects of the political process. This may happen when residents of remote districts have difficulty reaching polling places, or when some people are intimidated or blocked from registering to vote, when women are deterred from electoral participation by pressure or threats, or when ballot secrecy is compromised.

Second, defects in *claims to legitimate political authority* may occur. Although the constitution and public political pronouncements of the authorities may acknowledge legal limits to the exercise of political power, those authorities may simply ignore the limits upon the exercise of their power. That may be the case, for example, when threats and reprisals deter some groups from taking advantage of their rights of assembly, freedom of opinion and association, and joint action, or when the media or journalists trying to insure the free flow of information are threatened with sanctions. And it is even more clearly the case when opposition parties are harassed or prevented from exercising their rights.

Third, there may be defects in the *monopoly of legitimate authority*. In a fully fledged democracy all political matters are supposed to be decided exclusively by democratically legitimated authorities. It is a breach of democratic legitimacy when powerful veto groups act in defiance of duly constituted authority and sometimes even become the supreme ruling power themselves. This is true regardless of whether military or economic power-brokers or influential clans beyond the reach of democratic authorities are the refractory elements.

Fourth, flaws may arise in the *structure of political authority*. Democratic authority must be pluralistic. Restrictions on pluralism not intended to preserve the rule of law therefore undermine democratic legitimacy. It is undemocratic to exclude any interest from the decision-making process unless it has itself violated democratic norms.

Fifth, there may be defects in the *form of rule*. Political authority in a democracy must obey the rule of law. Violations of human rights, legal authority, and the courts' monopoly on the interpretation of law thus interfere with democracy's fundamental values.

Interactions among these defects can have far-reaching consequences, ultimately eroding the substance of democracy despite the maintenance of equal, universal suffrage. At first glance all of these defects involve restrictions of democratic functioning in the liberal democratic institutional system itself. They display the characteristics of *illiberal democracy*.[14] But it is evident that some defects, such as those related to access to power, or the monopoly and structure of political authority, can be traced back to social-structural causes. That is the connection that Guillermo O'Donnell wishes to capture in his category of a merely *delegative democracy*. Here democracy is practiced, but the lower social strata, i.e., the groups most often victimized by social-structural risks,[15] are largely excluded from it.

According to Dahl, democratic legitimation is acquired partly by adherence to political equality; yet formal political equality is contradicted by a market capitalist system that inherently generates political inequality by distributing social resources inequitably. Thus, democratic theorists must ask whether the existence of a democratic system of institutions alone, absent a reasonably equal distribution of political resources to all citizens, should count as a *consolidated democracy* at all, or whether such a system should be regarded as a *defective democracy*.

Besides the *necessary* and *enabling* conditions, which relate only to the stability of the system of democratic institutions, we should include the idea of the *fulfilling* conditions, without which the institutional system by itself cannot redeem the promise of equality. Formal democracies that fail to meet those fulfilling conditions resemble defective democracies.[16] While they provide many of the prerequisites of democracy, in practice they exclude large groups of citizens from the opportunity to share equally in decision-making, thereby failing to meet the standards of full democratic legitimation.

Orthodox socialists have sometimes even argued that, judging by the substantive norms of political equality, formal democracies are nothing but dictatorships or autocracies in disguise, since they practice class domination. But that characterization is mistaken for two reasons. For one, the maldistribution of socio-economic goods initially skews only a portion of possible political resources; its outcome does not entirely block participation in the political process. For another, formal democratic institutions offer an opening for an opportunistic politics that would accumulate political resources by using democratic pressures to impose redistributive policies on the state. In short, institutionalized democracies often lack full civic equality, but they are not autocracies.

Wolfgang Merkel proposed a matrix of possible democratic defects in studying the processes of transformation in Eastern Europe and Southeast Asia. Judging by his criteria, a strictly *libertarian* democracy is not really a consolidated democracy at all, falling short in at least two respects.

1 *Social security* Libertarian democracies may fail to respect two of the constitutive elements of juridical democracy, the *rule of law* and *democracy* itself. There may be some point at which the denial of a legal entitlement to social security inherently violates the universal validity claim that fundamental rights enjoy in any democracy. Failure to honor that claim certainly implies an unwillingness to respect the standards of juridical democracy itself. Refusal to grant any rights to social protection at all would violate the norms of the rule of law, even if a culture of voluntary, private charity had taken root in the society in question. That is a defect of the *form of rule* in that putative democracy.
2 *Social democratization* It is debatable whether the lack of any opportunities for democratic participation in the subsystems of society should count as a defect of liberal democracy itself. Good reasons can certainly be adduced for believing so, if the social issues to be debated can be characterized as inherently political, especially if they facilitate the accumulation of social and political influence on the democratic process. That produces the democratic defect Merkel calls the *monopoly of political authority*.

Regimes with these defects count as *unsocial* democracies (the term is modeled after Zacharia's notion of an *illiberal* democracy). They are the mirror image of *defective* democracies in failing to respect fundamental material rights.

There is a long tradition in the social sciences devoted to the issue of access to power. It examines what must occur if people are to take full advantage of their nominally equal citizen status to gain equal access to real power.[17] In part this tradition inquires into the issue of communicative competence as a prerequisite for the claims of democratic citizenship.[18] Previous discussion of these issues finds expression in four main strands of theory-formation:

1 the theory of socially universalized citizenship *rights* as the normative expression of the political, social, economic, and cultural aspirations of modern citizenship[19]
2 the theory of the social welfare state as the underwriter of rights to social protection and personal autonomy[20]
3 the theory of deliberative democracy as a practice awarding citizens ample opportunity to shape the decisions that affect their lives[21]
4 the theory of redistribution and economic regulation as means to guarantee that all individuals, both as human beings and as citizens, have the material prerequisites to defend their political and social interests.[22]

Comparative studies intending to measure the democratic quality of institutional democracies often neglect to inquire whether the formal political equality of citizens translates into de facto equality in the practice of their rights. That question touches on several contexts in which real-world equality matters: participation in political deliberations; decisions about political programs; which officeholders or officials are accountable for carrying out specific policies; how judicial decisions will be implemented; and who should monitor their implementation. The example of the United States, with its plutocratic barriers to political access, illustrates the limitations that plague the usual indicators of the state of democracy in a political system. They may rank an institutionalized democracy like the USA highly, even though closer empirical analysis reveals that structural patterns of exclusion prevent significant segments of the lower classes from having any effective share in power and decision-making.[23] Such defects have several types of implications for the quality of democracy in any society.

1 Systematic *distortions* may arise in the political process through which societal interests are articulated and put into effect.
2 Deficits of political equality on the input side will likely be replicated as deficits of equality on the output side, i.e., as unequal political outcomes.

3 The political *conditions affecting the legitimation* of civic equality may be contravened.

An index faithful to the standards of liberal democracy should be able to register the factors that most affect opportunities for democratic influence in the real world of politics. These might include the percentage share of legislative seats, government offices, or politically relevant judgeships that went to the lower quartile or half of the population as measured by income or wealth. The same approach could be taken to determine their voter participation rate and their share of the politically relevant activities in civil society.

In classifying defective democracies, Aurel Croissant has noted a conceptual lacuna in the literature. He points out an obvious link between high levels of social and economic inequality and *exclusive* or *delegative* democracy. Yet criteria derived from the socio-economic sphere have never been carried over into the distinctions between *consolidated* and *defective* democracies.[24] It makes sense that socio-economic indicators recognized as contributors to democratic stability – size of GDP, unequal distribution of income and wealth, the unemployment rate – should not be directly included in a list of the structural features of democracy. Otherwise, new democracies in the developing world would be downgraded through biased, scientifically irresponsible methodologies. But, in any such classification one should ask whether, in light of *their own self-selected* criteria of legitimation, adjustments have been made in the institutional scaffolding of democratic structures to insure that the latter work properly. The latter domain is the one in which most elements of social democracy belong: institutionalized rights of social citizenship; guarantees that basic requirements of societal democratization will be put in place; the securing of equal opportunities for education.

An institutionalized democracy should make sure all citizens have the means to take full advantage of the basic rights indispensable to equal participation in political decision-making. If it cannot do so, then it does not meet the minimum standards for a consolidated democracy. That conclusion is inescapable if one follows the logic of the theory of defective democracy, which uncovers deficits in the way that formal, institutionalized democracies actually operate under real-world conditions. Some of those are serious enough to weaken or refute the implicit claim to legitimation in institutionalized democracies. Failure to guarantee the social preconditions of equal political participation – assuming it is in the power of a political system to do so – must be classified as a radical defect of the democracy in question. In terms of the table presented by Merkel and Croissant (2000) displaying various defects of democracy, this would count as a defect in the *access to power*. For the sake of precision, a quantifiable minimum threshold has to be established such that liberal democracies with scores falling below it would be deemed socially defective. Theoretical considerations and comparative empirical research suggest a criterion combining the level of institutionalization of social and economic rights with comparatively low "outcomes" scores for empirical inclusiveness.[25] Based on these criteria, one may conclude that libertarian democracies that fail these tests – i.e., that show high rates of social exclusion – should count as socially defective. In other words, there are two somewhat independent reasons for classifying these democracies as "defective." They generally fail to secure fully valid, effective basic rights for their citizens. And, as empirical findings confirm, they exclude large groups of citizens by denying them equality of opportunity, a decent education, and adequate incomes.[26] The result is that such a democracy is only *delegative* (in O'Donnell's terminology), i.e., a commonwealth in which citizens must allow themselves to be represented in their role as citizens.[27]

Under those circumstances, injustices may be experienced subjectively as apathy or alienation. Both attitudes undermine the stability of democracy and deepen its legitimation deficits.[28] For many of the reasons cited here, we should endorse the thesis formulated by John Dryzek to recapitulate the state of research: a social democracy that combines the security typical of a social welfare state with social participation and a coordinated market economy is the best guarantor of stable democracy.[29] Conversely, in the vicinity of the ideal type of libertarian democracy one will undoubtedly encounter defective – that is, *unsocial* – democracies.[30]

Conclusion

The theory presented here understands social democracy on two levels. It is a political *obligation* imposed on every commonwealth as well as the global order as a whole, one that follows from the universal rights set forth in the UN Covenants of 1966, now a valid part of international law. But social democracy is also a *condition* for democratic stability. Foreseeable trends do not justify the pessimistic conclusion that open markets will inevitably undermine the political alignments favoring social democracy. Yet there is little reason to endorse the contrary notion that the arsenal of regulatory techniques developed by social democracy during the twentieth century could ever be replicated in the global arena. Even if we could put into effect all the projects of transnational democratization and imbedding of markets advocated in global regulatory programs such as the Rasmussen Report of 2002,[1] the opening of global markets would still confront states and regional alliances with an entirely new reality. Reforms that guarantee the survival and sustainability of social welfare states and their economic systems in a free market environment are indispensable means of securing the future of social democracy in the face of globalization.

From now on social democracy will require a complex new pattern that combines the regulatory *resources* of the state, the market economy, and civil society with national, regional, and global regulatory *structures*. Only those institutions and strategies can be seriously considered that might be implemented under given or foreseeable empirical conditions. Here we have surveyed the most promising aspects of social democracy, those both empirically well founded and normatively justified.

The radically new conditions of a globalized world reveal the characteristic dual nature of the idea of social democracy. On the one hand, it rests on a sophisticated normative foundation, notably the universal rights that facilitate and secure freedom. On the other hand, the harsh conditions imposed by the reality principle in complex, modern societies force social democracy to modify its aspirations. It must accept those conditions as a starting point and as limitations on its grand design, yet it should also use them as political resources that may harbor unexpected opportunities to shape events. Political action can change the world only by operating within the constraints imposed by the case-specific interactions of structures and actors.[2]

Inevitably social democracy must maintain a delicate balance between these two objectives: making democracy both social and effective. Democracy must perforce be given a social foundation, since without that there is no civic equality. It is what makes democracy democratic. Yet the social groundwork must assume forms that simultaneously contribute to economic efficiency, social integration, and democratic stability, for those too are prerequisites of sustainable democratization.

Thus all the projects of social democracy must *simultaneously* satisfy three conditions that allow of no substitutes. *First*, they should be justified by universalistic reasoning; *second*, they must be compatible with the functional logic of societal subsystems; *third*, they should have a reasonable chance of winning majority support.[3]

The normative ambitions of social democracy, especially in its exegesis of basic rights, will thus enter into permanent tension with a reality principle that must rely on the findings of autonomous social scientific research to determine how those normative claims might be applied. This tension is both an advantage and a weakness of the theory of social democracy. It is an advantage, since actors will be most likely to heed both aspects in the course of socially transformative processes when the tension between them is fully manifest. Thus, tension serves the cause of democratic legitimacy and the long-term stability of democratic arrangements on all levels. Yet it also appears to be a weakness, because social democracy must leave the details of its application somewhat open-ended, except for basic economic structures and regulatory principles. For good reasons, then, the array of possible social democratic policies remains as contingent as the evolving societal conditions in which they must operate. What from one perspective might seem to be a weakness in the theory proves to be one of its strengths in practice, since it obliges the practitioner to learn from real-world experience, and self-reflexively correct the theory as it collides with practice.

Theoretical research on democratic stability confirms that abandoning the normative aspirations of universal rights in the presumed interest of greater realism and efficiency actually undermines the stability of democracies. Democracy simply cannot be effective without a stable basis of legitimation. By the same token, an exaggerated, unempirical commitment to normativity may likewise vitiate the legitimacy of its theoretical standards by making them seem impractical. Yet defective democracies that only partially honor democratic standards live with the Achilles heel of weakened legitimation and perpetual vulnerability.

Even Hermann Heller, the first architect of a theory of social democracy, realized that the latter could fulfill its implicit claims of legitimation without meeting every normative requirement simultaneously. What matters is instead the *credibility* of the entire process as it operates under shifting conditions. The full enjoyment of universal civil and political rights is a promise that democracy must honor. It must do so in part by granting universal social and economic rights, for only thus can it insure that civil and political rights become real and meaningful for every person. That is the true meaning of social democracy everywhere, regardless of differences in cultural traditions and levels of socioeconomic development.

Briefly, there are four globally valid principles that may be justified on universal grounds.

First, the most basic normative elements of democracy are the validity of fundamental rights, economic regulation, minimal security provided by a social welfare state, especially in the areas of health care and education, and equality of opportunity. These are *obligations of result*. They can and must be achieved without delay everywhere.

Second, the level of social security provided by the welfare state, the criteria for distributing opportunities for social participation, and justice in the distribution of life chances in society are all *obligations of conduct* that concern the goals of political action. Citizens should always be able to see that everything possible is being done to achieve those goals.

Third, the duty of primary self-reliance is equivalent in order of rank to the basic rights themselves. As a society improves its ability to guarantee social and economic rights to its citizens, the significance of the self-reliance obligation grows, as does society's entitlement to impose sanctions for non-compliance.

Fourth, social democracy is a project for each individual society, for regional cooperative alliances, and for the world order generally.

In light of the theory presented here, the political projects of social democracy may be justified as contributing to the conditions under which democracy can flourish. Without those projects democracy would never be perceived as fully legitimate. That is the foundation of its long-term stability. Of course, social democracy is not an instant recipe that can be applied in the same way at all times and in all places. It is a perennial task, full of tensions and trade-offs, but, as many countries have impressively demonstrated in practice, it is also a promise that can be redeemed.

Notes

Introduction

1 Lipset 1959, 1992, 1994, 1998; Dahl 1989, 1998; Powell 1982.
2 See the informative overview of relevant research findings in M. G. Schmidt 2000.
3 O'Donnell 1979, 1994; Merkel 2003.
4 On this point and for the relevant literature, see chapter 5.
5 Sartori 1997.
6 For the context of democratic theory, see M. G. Schmidt 2000 and Przeworski 1985.
7 Scharpf 1999b.
8 Gray 1989, 1995; Sartori 1997; M. G. Schmidt 2000.
9 In contrast to the terminology proposed here, Gray speaks of "revisionist liberalism" in theoretical contexts that seem to suggest that he has social democracy in mind, while referring to theories such as that of Hayek as instances of libertarian theory (Gray 1995: 36).
10 This terminology, though employed by the primary author himself in previous writings, may give rise to misunderstandings, because it uses the same word for two quite distinct states of affairs.
11 Eide 1989; Alston and Quinn 1987.
12 Streeck 1999.
13 A detailed justification for this procedure is offered in chapter 3.

Chapter 1   Social Rights, Risks, and Obligations

1 Habermas 1987, 1996; Gray 1995.
2 Mommsen 1978; Schiller 1978; Vorländer 1987; Gray 1989, 1993; Habermas 1996.
3 Meyer 2002c.
4 This conclusion does not amount to an endorsement of Fukuyama's "end-of-history" thesis. Our claim is that the unresolved contradictions in liberal

political theory have led to a global rivalry between its libertarian and social wings that defines the historical agenda today. See Fukuyama 1992.

5 Schwan 1982; Seliger 1985.
6 Habermas 1996; Münch 1986.
7 Neumann 2000.
8 Sartori 1997.
9 Gray would concur, although he defines the basic issues differently than in the now dominant version of liberalism. For him the "libertarian" strand counts as "classical" liberalism, while the social democratic position is characterized as "revisionist liberalism" (Gray 1995: 35f.).
10 Here I shall follow Martin Seliger's interpretation (1985) of Locke rather than C. B. Macpherson's (1962).
11 See Locke 1970.
12 In the sections of his theory devoted to social policy Locke does take this into account, at least tangentially. See Seliger 1985: 393–400.
13 Locke 1970: ch. 5.
14 Locke 1970: chs. 4–5.
15 That situation is not fundamentally altered by the attempts of modern libertarians to retain a Locke-inspired notion of freedom as property-based, while extricating it completely from the original acquisition scenario and even envisaging compensation for past injustices committed during the acquisition of property. In the end even this scheme must treat current exchange as the only source of legitimation. Gray 1995: 61ff.
16 Hayek 1977, 1979, 1981; Nozick 1974.
17 Hutton 2002.
18 Nozick 1974; Gray 1995: 62ff.
19 Berlin 1958, 1969. See also Gray 1989, 1995.
20 Sen 1999a, 1999b.
21 Gray 1993: 64.
22 Ibid.
23 For this reason the link between the concept of freedom and the understanding of justice will be reviewed again later.
24 Dworkin 2000.
25 Meyer 2001a.
26 Faulks 2000; Castles and Davidson 2000; Holz 2000.
27 Marshall 1964.
28 Turner 1986; Barbalet 1988.
29 For a systematic overview, see Schmalz-Bruns 1994.
30 Marshall 1964: 70ff.
31 Ibid.: 88.
32 Ibid.: 92.
33 This is Nozick's main objection (Nozick 1974).
34 Faulks 2000: 59ff., 73ff.
35 Ibid.: 59.
36 Ibid.: 73.
37 Randzio-Plath 1983, 1999.
38 Rawls 1993.
39 See Eichler 1973.

40 As of November, 2003. Source: Office of the United Nations High Commissioner for Human Rights.
41 Simma 1995.
42 Heidelmeyer 1972: 254ff.
43 Ibid.
44 Kersting 2000.
45 Höffe 2001.
46 Kokott et al. 2003: 118.
47 Covenant A, II, Art. 2.
48 Engels 2000.
49 Kimminich and Hobe 2000: 344.
50 Arendt 1993.
51 Hinsch 1997.
52 Meyer 1991. See also Bobbio 1987.
53 Marshall 1965, 1964.
54 See especially Beck 1992; Luhmann 1989.
55 Beck 1992; Luhmann 1993: 244.
56 Baldwin and Cave 1999; De Swaan 1993.
57 Dworkin 2000: 73.
58 Ibid.: 74–8.
59 Birnbacher 1996.
60 Beck 1992.
61 Strasser and Traube 1984.
62 Beck 1992.
63 Nussbaum and Sen 1993; Nussbaum 1999; Sen 1999a, 1999b.
64 Rawls 1971, 1958.
65 Dworkin 1990, 2000.
66 Fishkin 1991; Habermas 1992.
67 Meyer 2002a.
68 Ibid.: 15ff.
69 Berger et al. 1973.
70 Nida-Rümelin 1996.
71 Giddens 1994.
72 Dworkin 2000.
73 See Merkel and Croissant 2000; Croissant 2002.
74 See for example, the reasoning of the German Constitutional Court in its 1976 decision on co-determination.
75 De Laurentis 1987; Butler 1990; Benhabib et al. 1995; Holland-Cruz 1999.
76 See chapter 7.
77 Strasser and Traube 1984.
78 Beck 1992; Berger et al. 1973.
79 Altvater and Mahnkopf 2002a, 2002b.
80 Strasser 1999, 2003.
81 Nida-Rümelin 1996.
82 General Declaration of Human Duties, proposed by the InterAction Council, 1997.
83 See chapter 2.
84 White 2000.
85 Dworkin 2000.

86 Hammar 1990; Cover 1983.
87 Etzioni 1997.
88 Hinsch 1997, 2002, 2004.
89 White 2000.
90 Dworkin 2000: 285.
91 Habermas 1996, 1998.
92 Berkes and Folke 1994: 23, 130; McDaniel and Gowdy 2000: 165; Czech 2000: 115; Daly 1996: 27.
93 WCED 1987: 8.
94 Eliot 1999: 16.
95 Polanyi 2001: 71.
96 Ibid.: 48.
97 Ibid.: 3.
98 Ibid.: 75–6.
99 Ibid.: 76.
100 Trainer 1995: 182.
101 Prugh et al. 2000: 18–24; Hawken et al. 1999: 151; Berkes and Folke 1994: 129–30.
102 Putnam 2000: 18–21.
103 Hawken et al. 1999: 2, 4; Berkes and Folke 1994: 129.
104 Turner et al. 1994: 275.
105 Harrington 1989: 21.
106 Daly 1996: 3.
107 Norgaard 1994: 34; Czech 2000: 114–15; McDaniel and Gowdy 2000: 165–6.
108 Prugh et al. 2000: 9.
109 Hawken et al. 1999: 2–4; Athanasiou 1996: 56–102; Trainer 1995: 62.
110 Daly 1996: 62.
111 Ibid.: 65; Prugh et al. 2000: 20.
112 McDaniel and Gowdy 2000: 142.
113 OECD 2001: 188–9.
114 Ibid.: 42–3.
115 DiZerega 2002: 49–54.
116 Jansson et al. 1994: 13.
117 Prugh et al. 2000: 17.
118 Hawken et al. 1999: 59–60; Redclift 1987: 16.
119 Hawken et al. 1999: 155.
120 National Research Council 1999: 24.
121 Hawken et al. 1999: 11–14.
122 McDaniel and Gowdy 2000: 145.
123 Dryzek 1987: 74–5.
124 Daly 1996: 36.
125 Tocqueville 2000: II, ii, 483.
126 Rawls 1971: 206.
127 Ibid.: 289.
128 Ibid.: 290.
129 Prugh et al. 2000: 8.
130 Meyer 1994: 264–6.
131 Eliot 1999: 21; Hinchman and Hinchman 1996: 361–2.
132 OECD 2001: 14.

133 WCED 1987: 3.
134 Barbier 1994: 310.
135 Eliot 1999: 45.
136 Hawken et al. 1999: 149.
137 WCED 1987: 49.
138 National Research Council 1999: 96.
139 Daly 1996: 70.
140 Jänicke et al. 1999: 90.
141 WCED 1987: 46.
142 Prugh et al. 2000: 10.
143 Barber 1984: 117–38.
144 Prugh et al. 2000: 74.
145 Daly 1996: 7; Prugh et al. 2000: 72.
146 Jänicke et al. 1999: 137.
147 Ibid.: 88.
148 WCED 1987: 46.
149 O'Connor 1998: 237.
150 Hawken et al. 1999: 11–14.
151 Prugh et al. 2000: 24.
152 Daly 1996: 146–65.
153 Ibid.: 34.
154 Daly 1994: 35.
155 Ehrlich 1994: 48–50.
156 Prugh et al. 2000: 161.
157 Heidelmeyer 1972: 40.
158 Höffe 2001.
159 Rawls 1958, 1993.
160 Gray likewise sees this as the culmination of the tradition of classical liberalism. Gray 1995: 56ff.
161 Eichler 1973.
162 Nagel 2002.
163 Rawls 1971, 1993.
164 Habermas 1996, 1998.
165 Nozick 1974.
166 Berlin 1958, 1969.
167 Berlin 1958: 7ff.
168 Macpherson 1977.
169 Ibid.
170 Höffe 1999: 75ff.
171 Ibid.: 76.
172 Ibid.: 77.
173 For a discussion, see Nida-Rümelin 1993. Murphy and Nagel have shown that even consequentialist positions can be made to yield arguments on political justice that dovetail with the essentially deontological theories considered here (Murphy and Nagel 2002: 42f.).
174 These theories have in fact frequently been invoked by the discourses on social democracy.
175 Walzer 1983.
176 Merkel 2002; Merkel et al. 2005.

177 See chapter 4.
178 See chapter 4.

Chapter 2   Regulation, Participation, and Actors

 1 Giddens 1994, 1998.
 2 See Johnson 1996.
 3 This conviction is still evident in Brandt 1986.
 4 Meyer 1977.
 5 Schimank 1996.
 6 On actor theory, see Giddens 1984; Mayntz et al. 1988; Scharpf 2000; Schimank 1988, 1996, 2000.
 7 Mayntz et al. 1988: 17–18.
 8 Schimank 1992: 175.
 9 Habermas 1984.
10 Merkel 1993; Merkel et al. 2005.
11 Blanke 1998: 175ff.
12 Ibid.: 174.
13 Panebianco 1988; Gabriel et al. 1997; von Alemann 2003.
14 Blanke 1998: 175.
15 Ibid.: 179.
16 Blanke (1988) distinguishes among the variants advocated, respectively, by Max Weber, Michel Foucault, Niklas Luhmann, and Jürgen Habermas. Ibid.: 180ff.
17 Ibid.
18 Rothstein 1996, 2002; Hemerijck 2002.
19 V. A. Schmidt 2000b.
20 Sassoon 1999.
21 Kremendahl 1983.
22 Przeworski and Sprague 1986; Sassoon 1999.
23 von Alemann 2003.
24 Michels 1970.
25 Weber 1979.
26 Klingemann et al. 1994.
27 von Alemann 2003.
28 M. G. Schmidt 2000: 381–9.
29 This table combines Manfred Schmidt's overview of government participation by parties (2000: 381) with the last column in his table showing the strength of social democracy in the countries under comparison (2000: 388).
30 Meyer 2002a.
31 See chapter 5.
32 Haller 2002.
33 Calleo 2002.
34 Evidence can be found, for example, in Czempiel 1990.
35 Of course there is a well-known contradiction between the foreign policy of the People's Republic, which proclaims adherence to the theme of "international democracy," and the fact that for now its internal socio-political life does not adhere to the norms of liberal democracy.

36 On this topic, see also the report *A Fair Globalization* (International Labour Organization 2004).
37 Czempiel 2002.
38 Telò 2003, 2006.
39 Telò 2001; Rodriguez 2002; Rasmussen 2003.
40 See M. G. Schmidt 2000; Scharpf 1970.
41 Jann 2003.
42 Offe 2000.
43 Barber 1984; Hirst 1994.
44 Offe 2000.
45 Scharpf 1989, 1998.
46 Meyer and Weil 2002.
47 Held 1995, 2000; Zürn 1998.
48 See M. G. Schmidt 2000.
49 Meyer 2002a: 289–93.
50 Guéhenno 1995.
51 Streeck 1999.
52 Scharpf 1998.
53 Weizsäcker 2000.
54 Meyer 2002b.
55 Willke 1993, 2003.
56 Beck 1998, 2000a.
57 Luhmann 1989.
58 Buchanan and Tullock 1962; Jänicke et al. 1999; Dettling 1980; Prisching 2003.
59 Scharpf and Schmidt 2000; Hall and Soskice 2001; Merkel et al. 2005.
60 Anheiner et al. 2000; Jann and Reichhard 2001; Jann 2003; Jann and Wegrich 2004; Giddens 1984, 1998.
61 Granados and Gurgdies 1999.
62 Horn et al. 1988; Fritsch et al. 2003.
63 Polanyi [1957] 2001.
64 See Roth 2004.
65 See Hennis 1977.
66 Vilmar 1973; Brandt 1986, 2001; Meyer 1980; Meyer et al. 1986.
67 This perspective might yield an alternative interpretation of the term *stakeholder society*. See Ackerman and Alstott 1999.
68 Adler-Karlsson 1969.
69 Offe 2000.
70 Roland Roth correctly points to the "dark sides" of civil society (Roth 2004). Referring to this, one might even speak of a "failure of civil society" alongside failure of market and state.
71 Dubiel 1994.
72 Anheier et al. 2000.
73 Putnam 2000.
74 Putnam 1996.
75 Deutscher Bundestag 2002b.
76 Evers et al. 2002.
77 Roth 2001.
78 Ibid.
79 Putnam 2000.

Chapter 3   The Social Market Economy

1 Shaw et al. 1962; Lassalle 1970; Bernstein 1999; on this point, see Meyer 1977; Heimann and Meyer 1982; Novy 1978.
2 Esping-Andersen 1990: 12.
3 Esping-Andersen 1990.
4 Polanyi [1957] 2001; Heimann 1954.
5 Polanyi [1957] 2001.
6 Ibid.
7 Luhmann 1989.
8 Milner 1989: 213.
9 See section 3.5.
10 Ostheim 2003.
11 Bator 1958; Horn et al. 1988; Krakowski 1988; Salanié 2000; Fritsch et al. 2003.
12 Esping-Andersen 1990: 38.
13 See also Kaul et al. 2002.
14 Matzner 1982.
15 Samuelson 1954.
16 Schweizer 1999.
17 Klein 2001; also see chapter 2.
18 Deutscher Bundestag 2002b.
19 This is the heart of Hayek's argument (1952, 1981), still presumed valid in this tradition.
20 Czada et al. 2003: 16.
21 Kay and Vickers 1988: 306–8.
22 Beck 1992.
23 Meier et al. 2003; Brunner 1997.
24 Meyer 1977.
25 Novy 1978; Sik 1973, 1979.
26 Heimann 1929.
27 Naphtali 1977; Novy 1978.
28 Adler-Karlsson 1969; Lemân 1969.
29 Hall and Soskice 2001.
30 Scharpf 1997.
31 Hall and Soskice 2001.
32 See Albert 1993; Streeck 1997.
33 To avoid any confusions with the terms "liberal" and "libertarian" as used in the political theory chapters of this book, only the expressions "coordinated" and "uncoordinated" will be employed in the following comments. However, the notion of an "uncoordinated market economy" is conceptually identical with that of a "liberal market economy" in the sense intended by Hall and Soskice.
34 Soskice 1999; Hall and Soskice 2001.
35 Hall and Soskice 2001; Hall and Gingerich 2001.
36 Rhodes 1997.
37 Lütz 2003: 15.
38 Streeck 1997.
39 Hall and Soskice 2001: 13.
40 Streeck 1991.

41 Hall and Soskice here refer to data collected by Knetter (1989).
42 Scharpf and Schmidt 2000: Statistical Appendix, Table A.4.
43 Esping-Andersen 2003.
44 Scharpf 1999a, 2000.
45 Scharpf and Schmidt 2000.
46 Scharpf 1999b.
47 Pontusson and Yong Kwon 2004.
48 Kitschelt et al. 1999.
49 Benner and Bundgaard Vad 2000.
50 Western and Beckett 1999.
51 Kitschelt et al. 1999.
52 Iversen and Pontusson 2000.
53 The model is named after the labor economists who originated it, Gøsta Rehn and Rudolf Meidner. Their steering strategy combines classical Keynesian anti-cyclical demand-side theory with the instrument of wage policies that are well suited to heterogeneous macro-economic structures. It relieves the most competitive firms and sectors of unnecessary wage burdens while exposing the less competitive ones to more intense wage pressures.
54 Whyman 2003.
55 Pontusson 1992.
56 Iversen and Pontusson 2000.
57 Traxler 1995.
58 Wallerstein and Golden 2000.
59 See Albert 1993. He distinguishes Rhenish from Atlantic capitalism.
60 Iversen and Pontusson 2000.
61 See Kittel 2003.
62 Crouch 1993.
63 See Crouch 1999; Esping-Andersen 1990.
64 Pierson 2000.
65 See chapter 4.
66 Czada et al. 2003: 6.
67 Majone 1997.
68 See chapter 5.
69 Scharpf and Schmidt 2000; Leibfried 2001; Hemerijck 2002.
70 Briggs 1961.
71 Powell and Hewitt 2002: 6.

Chapter 4   A Rights-Based Welfare State

1 Hemerijck 2002: 178.
2 Esping-Andersen 1990.
3 Hemerijck 2002: 173.
4 Streeck 1992, 1997.
5 Esping-Andersen 1990.
6 Scharpf and Schmidt 2002: 310–36.
7 Visser and Hemerijck 2000.
8 See the chapter on the United States by Hinchman in Meyer 2006.
9 See the chapter on Sweden by Gurgsdies in Meyer 2006.

10 Esping-Andersen 1990.
11 Scharpf and Schmidt 2000.
12 Esping-Andersen 1990: 49.
13 Habermas 1998.
14 On this point see the later discussion of the "unconditional basic income" proposed by Van Parijs 1992.
15 Visser and Hemerijck 2000; Hemerijck 2002.
16 See, for example, Visser and Hemerijck 1998; Gamillscheg 2004; Koch and Walwei 2003.
17 In this way the unemployed are integrated into the world of work, while people already employed are sent off for further training.
18 In 1998 the sabbatical model was abolished again.
19 The first refusal costs the unemployed person three weeks of benefits. A second refusal entails denial of benefits altogether.
20 Gamillscheg 2004: 2.
21 Van Parijs 1992, 1995.
22 Elster 1986; Kersting 2000: 268ff.
23 Hirst 1994; Johnson 1999; Pesthoff 1997.
24 The best examples of this school of thought are the series IEA Readings, produced by the Institute of Economic Affairs, and Seldon 1996.
25 Rein 1996, 2000, 2004.
26 Vilmar and Runge 1986.
27 Esping-Andersen 1990: 35ff.
28 Bosch 1998.
29 Beck 2000b.
30 Ibid.
31 Ibid.
32 The *locus classicus* for this is Jahoda et al. 2002.
33 Sen 1999b.
34 Honneth 1995; Margalit 1996.
35 See especially Scharpf and Schmidt 2000.
36 Bosch 1998.
37 Ibid.
38 Scharpf and Schmidt 2000.
39 Frenzel 2002.
40 Allmendinger and Leibfried 2002.
41 Schleicher 2003.
42 Ibid.
43 Deutsches PISA-Konsortium 2001, 2003.
44 Sachverständigenrat Bildung bei der Hans Böckler Stiftung 2002: 91.
45 Esping-Andersen 2002.
46 Esping-Andersen 2003.
47 Deutsches PISA-Konsortium 2003: 55–7.
48 Furthermore, comparative studies show that higher labor-force participation by women improves the overall employment outlook and strengthens the financial underpinnings of the social welfare state.
49 Sachverständigenrat Bildung bei der Hans Böckler Stiftung 2002: 85–7.
50 Scharpf 2000.

Chapter 5   Progressive Globalization

1 The theory presented leaves no room for ideologically motivated theories of imperialism after the manner of Hardt and Negri (Michael Hardt and Antonio Negri, *Empire*. Cambridge, MA: Harvard University Press, 2000) or for one-dimensional theories of American hegemony that lack realistic perspectives of action, such as the books by Ken Coates (*The New American Century?* Nottingham: Spokesman/Bertrand Russell Peace Foundation, 2002) and Benedict Anderson (*Under Three Flags: Anarchism and the Anti-Colonial Imagination*. London and New York: Verso, 2005).
2 Beck 1997; Held and McGrew 2000.
3 Archibugi et al. 1998; Offe 2003; Ruggie 1999; Scharpf 1999b; Streeck 1999; Held 1995; Held and McGrew 2000; Meyer 2001b, 2002b.
4 Ruggie 1999.
5 Leibfried 2001.
6 Streeck 1999.
7 Held 2000: 424.
8 Beck 1992, 2000a, 2005.
9 Tinbergen 1965.
10 Scharpf 1992.
11 Guéhenno 1995.
12 Meyer 2002b.
13 Blair 1998.
14 Höffe 1999.
15 See Dower and Williams 2002.
16 Wellmer 1993: 192f.
17 Höffe 1999; Held 1995; Held and McGrew 2000.
18 Seidelmann 1998.
19 See Höffe 1999; Hinsch 2002.
20 Dower and Williams 2002: 39.
21 Höffe 1999: 336ff.
22 Faulks 2000.
23 Van den Anker 2002.
24 Dower and Williams 2002; Hinsch 2002.
25 Falk 2002.
26 See chapter 1.
27 Barber 1995.
28 Weizsäcker 2000.
29 Höffe 1999.
30 Link 2001: 162ff.
31 Held 2000: 429; Beck 1998.
32 Weizsäcker 2000.
33 Giddens 1994.
34 Hauchler et al. 2003; Deutscher Bundestag 2002a.
35 See Deutscher Bundestag 2002a.
36 International Labour Organization 2004; Rasmussen 2003.
37 Stieglitz 2002.
38 Guéhenno 1995; Held 1995; Held and McGrew 2000; Czempiel 1990.

39 Rasmussen 2003; International Labour Organization 2004; Hauchler et al. 2003.
40 United Nations 2000.
41 That is the conclusion reached by the North–South Commission chaired by Willy Brandt.
42 Elsenhans 1995.
43 Kaul et al. 2002.
44 Independent Commission on International Development Issues 1980; WCED 1987; International Labour Organization 2004.
45 Altvater and Mahnkopf 2002b.
46 Bertelsmann Stiftung 2004.
47 Sen 2000; Merkel 2003.
48 International Labour Organization 2004.
49 Kaul et al. 2002.
50 Stieglitz 2002; Rasmussen 2003.
51 Held 2000; Held and McGrew 2000; Rasmussen 2003; Hauchler et al. 2003; International Labour Organization 2004.
52 Rieger and Leibfried 2001.
53 Altvater and Mahnkopf 2002a, 2002b.
54 Dahl 1989, 1994; M. G. Schmidt 2000: 489ff.
55 Merkel et al. 2003.
56 Schimank 1996, 2000; Mayntz et al. 1988; Scharpf 1997, 2000; See also chapter 2.
57 Giddens 1987.
58 Habermas 1990.
59 Tony Blair (1998) has advocated this view.
60 In effect, that is the view of Höffe (2001).
61 See chapter 8.
62 Scharpf and Schmidt 2000; Merkel et al. 2005.
63 That is especially true of regional or even global coordination of tax policy.
64 Rieger and Leibfried 2001.

Chapter 6   The Universalism of Social Democracy

1 Greven 1998: 22.
2 Almond and Verba 1963.
3 Huntington 1996.
4 Meyer 2002a.
5 Habermas 1996.
6 Marty and Appleby 1992; Meyer 2002a.
7 Kohlberg 1981, 1984; Küng 2002.
8 Bello 2002.
9 Merkel 1999; Kulke and Rothermund 1998.
10 Ashraf 1995.
11 The tradition founded by J. P. Narayan is especially noteworthy. Vivekanandan 1997, 2000.
12 Ende 1996; Adonis 1998; Arkoun 1998; Tibi 1993, 2003.
13 Arkoun 1998: 145ff.

14 Aydin 1998.
15 Mahathir 1998: 33ff.
16 Kim 1994; Anwar 1998; Bello 1999.
17 Bello 1999: 7.
18 Heberer and Derichs 2000; Heberer 2000.

Chapter 7   Cultural Divergence and Social Citizenship

1 Herder 1968: 190.
2 Nozick 1974: 12–17.
3 Sandel 1996: 7–8.
4 Marx 1988: 73.
5 Fraser 1997.
6 Taylor 1992.
7 Herder 1968: 191.
8 Fraser 1997: 13
9 Kymlicka 1995: 76–80.
10 Kymlicka 2001: 23–7.
11 Rawls 1971: 440.
12 Walzer 1983: 278.
13 Taylor 1992: 39.
14 Kymlicka 1995: 10.
15 Ibid.: 78.
16 Ibid.: 35–44.
17 Benhabib 2002: 102–3.
18 Barry 2001: 325.
19 Sen et al. 2001: 3.
20 Varshney 2002.
21 Habermas 1997.
22 Ibid.
23 Taylor 1992; Honneth 1995; Margalit 1996; Meyer 2002c.

Chapter 8   Libertarian and Social Democracies Compared

1 The procedures adopted here to determine whether a political system should count as a libertarian or social democracy, as well as those used to identify different degrees of inclusiveness in social democracy, begin from the premise that socio-economic basic rights impose obligations of conduct and therefore do not allow us to use an absolute scale of values. What we are measuring are not variables such as GDP or per capita income. Instead, the measures used here take certain institutional arrangements as given and quantify the probability of certain kinds of social relations within the society under consideration.
2 One must also ask whether states that ratified the UN Covenant on Social and Economic Rights have actually enforced its international law provisions in their own countries.

3 The index was developed together with Jan Turowski, University of Dortmund, Department of Political Science.

4 See the relevant explanations in each particular dimension.

5 This dimension raises a host of problems that somewhat limit its value as an indiator of social democracy. First, only gross scores are provided, which distorts the actual level of benefits provided by a social welfare state, because transfer payments are taxed at different rates in the countries being compared. In some, they are not taxed at all. Second, unemployment, which is generally a "negative" ingredient in social welfare, actually serves to raise a country's social welfare state score. Finally, scores in this dimension increase as a country's population ages. Nevertheless, we still consider it a useful indicator, as does much mainstream research, for the reasons adumbrated in the text above.

6 See the tables in the appendix to this chapter showing the results in each dimension.

7 Because those indices show that the formal recognition of social and economic rights there has meant almost nothing in practice.

8 Twenty OECD countries were selected on the basis of the following criteria: (1) the expectation that they would display the broadest possible range of data to be measured; (2) the most complete availability of relevant data; (3) the inclusion of all countries that were to be investigated in a complementary qualitative study (Meyer 2006). The point here is not to study countries all over the world, but simply to test the theory and the distinctions among types of democracy that it suggests.

9 PISA (Programme for International Student Assessment) is an internationally standardized assessment that was jointly developed by the participating countries and is administered to fifteen-year-olds in schools.

10 Public social expenditure by broad policy area of GDP; total public social expenditure (2001); "Selection of OECD Social Indicators: How Does Germany Compare?," www.oecd.org (March 8, 2005).

11 The European Company – Prospects for Board-level Representation, European Trade Union Institute, Hans Böckler Stiftung 2004, plus author's own evaluations for Australia, New Zealand, the United States, Canada, Switzerland, Norway, and Japan.

12 For the year 2000; "Selection of OECD Indicators: How Does Germany Compare?," www.oecd.org (March 8, 2005).

13 OECD 2001; "Learning for Life: Initial Results of the International School Achievement Study," PISA 2000, Table 8.1, p. 352.

14 For the year 2004. Source: OECD, *Employment Outlook* (2005).

15 For the years 2000 (Germany, Finland, Italy, Norway, Sweden, United States); 1999 (Netherlands, United Kingdom); 1998 (Canada); 1997 (Denmark, New Zealand, Austria, Portugal); 1996 (Belgium, Ireland); 1995 (France); 1994 (Australia); 1993 (Japan); 1992 (Switzerland); 1990 (Spain). Source: United Nations Development Program (2005), *Human Development Report 2005* (http://hdr.undp.org).

Because of differing statistical methods and data collection procedures, other studies have reached different conclusions. See Förster, Michael, and Mira d'Ercole, Marco: *Income Distribution and Poverty in OECD Countries in the Second Half of the 1990s* (OECD Social, Employment, and Migration

Working Paper No. 22) (http://www.oecd.org/els/workingpapers). Nevertheless, in view of the qualititative distinctions drawn in them, the findings of the GINI Index used here appear the most realistic.

Chapter 9   Defective and Consolidated Democracy

1 Rueschemeyer et al. 1992; Held 1996; Lijphart 1999; Burnell and Calvert 1999; M. G. Schmidt 2000; Dahl 2000.
2 Dahl 2000: 140.
3 Ibid.: 166ff.
4 Ibid.: 174.
5 Ibid.: 178.
6 See, for example, Burnell and Calvert 1999: 19.
7 Lipset 1959, 1960, 1992, 1993, 1994; Lipset and Marks 2000.
8 Rueschemeyer et al. 1992; Przeworski 1996; Burnell and Calvert 1999; Dahl 2000.
9 Rueschemeyer et al. 1992.
10 Dahl 2000: 178.
11 Merkel et al. 2003.
12 See Bertelsmann Stiftung 2004.
13 Merkel 1999; Merkel et al. 2003.
14 Zakaria 1997.
15 O'Donnell 1994.
16 Merkel 2003.
17 See especially the contributions of Lipset, Dahl, Marshall, and O'Donnell.
18 Elster 1986; G. A. Cohen 1989; Dworkin 1990; Habermas 1992, 1996; Hirst 1994; O'Donnell 1994; Offe 1997a, 1997b.
19 Turner 1986; Dworkin 1990; Habermas 1992, 1996; Offe 1996; Kymlicka 1997, 1999, 2001; Kymlicka and Wayne 2000; Cohen and Rodgers 1983.
20 Esping-Andersen 1990, 1999; Kersting 2000; Leibfried 2001.
21 Elster 1986; Cohen and Rodgers 1983; J. Cohen 1989; Fishkin 1991; Habermas 1996.
22 Heimann 1929, 1963; Adler and Karlsson 1969; Hirst 1994; Offe 1997a; Hicks 2001.
23 See the contrast drawn in M. G. Schmidt 2000: 389ff; on the United States, see Hutton 2002.
24 Croissant 2002.
25 See chapter 8.
26 See the evidence and rationale offered in previous chapters drawn from the outcomes of a twenty-nation study.
27 O'Donnell 1994.
28 Vester et al. 1993.
29 Dryzek 1996.
30 Classical libertarians concur that the social components of democracy should be excluded from its theory and practice in order to insure that it remains stable and free. See, for example, Hayek 1952: 143–4; Friedman 1962. Hayek depicts justice as a dangerous illusion that may destroy liberty (1952: 137).

Conclusion

1 Rasmussen 2003.
2 Giddens 1984; Scharpf 2000.
3 Merkel 1993.

References and Bibliography

Ackerman, Bruce, and Alstott, Anne (1999): *The Stakeholder Society*. New Haven, CT: Yale University Press.

Adler-Karlsson, Gunnar (1969): *Functional Socialism: A Swedish Theory for Democratic Socialism*. Stockholm: Prisma.

Adonis, Ali Ahmad (1998): "Kultur und Demokratie in der arabischen Gesellschaft," in Heller, Erdmute, and Hassouna, Mosbahi (eds), *Islam, Demokratie, Moderne*. Munich: Beck.

Albert, Michel (1993): *Capitalism against Capitalism*, trans. Paul Haviland. London: Whurr.

Alemann, Ulrich von (2003): *Das Parteiensystem der Bundesrepublik Deutschland*. 3rd rev. edn, Opladen: Leske & Budrich.

Allmendinger, Jutta, and Leibfried, Stephan (2002): "Bildungsarmut im Sozialstaat," in Burkart, Günter, and Wolf, Jürgen (eds), *Lebenszeiten, Erkundungen zur Soziologie der Generationen (Martin Kohli zum 60. Geburtstag)*. Opladen: Leske & Budrich, 287–315.

Almond, Gabriel A., and Verba, Sidney (1963): *The Civic Culture: Political Attitudes and Democracy in Five Nations*. Princeton, NJ: Princeton University Press.

Alston, Philip, and Quinn, Gerard (1987): "The Nature and Scope of State Parties' Obligations under the International Convenant on Economic, Social and Cultural Rights," *Human Rights Quarterly* 9: 156–229.

Altvater, Elmar, and Mahnkopf, Birgit (2002a): *Globalisierung der Unsicherheit: Arbeit im Schatten, schmutziges Geld und informelle Politik*. Münster: Westfälisches Dampfboot.

Altvater, Elmar, and Mahnkopf, Birgit (2002b): *Grenzen der Globalisierung: Ökonomie, Ökologie und Politik in der Weltgesellschaft*. Münster: Westfälisches Dampfboot.

Anheiner, Helmut K., Priller, Eckhard, and Zimmer, Annette (2000): "Zur zivilgesellschaftlichen Dimension des dritten Sektors," in Klingemann,

Hans-Dieter, and Neidhardt, Friedhelm (eds), *Zur Zukunft der Demokratie: Herausforderungen im Zeitalter der Globalisierung*. Berlin: Sigma, 71–98.

Anwar, Muhammad (1998): *Between Cultures: Continuity and Change in the Lives of Young Asians*. London: Routledge.

Archibugi, Daniele, Held, David, and Köhler, Martin (eds) (1998): *Re-imagining Political Community: Studies in Cosmopolitan Democracy*. Cambridge: Polity.

Arendt, Hannah (1993): *Was ist Politik?*, ed. Ursula Ludz. Munich: Piper.

Arkoun, Mohammed (1998): "Religion und Demokratie: Das Beispiel Islam," in Heller, Erdmute, and Hassouna, Mosbahi (eds), *Islam, Demokratie, Moderne*. Munich: Beck.

Ashraf, Ali (ed.) (1995): *The Emerging Political Culture in India*. New Delhi: Hira Publications.

Athanasiou, Tom (1996): *Divided Planet: The Ecology of Rich and Poor*. Boston: Little, Brown.

Aydin, Mustafa (ed.) (1998): *Turkey at the Threshold of the 21st Century: Global Encounters and/vs. Regional Alternatives*. Ankara: International Relations Foundation.

Baldwin, Robert, and Cave, Martin (1999): *Understanding Regulation: Theory, Strategy, and Practice*. Oxford: Oxford University Press.

Barbalet, Jack M. (1988): *Citizenship: Rights, Struggle, and Class Inequality*. Milton Keynes: Open University Press.

Barber, Benjamin (1984): *Strong Democracy: Participatory Politics for a New Age*. Berkeley: University of California Press.

Barber, Benjamin (1995): *Jihad versus McWorld*. New York: Random House.

Barbier, Edward B. (1994): "Natural Capital and the Economics of Environment and Development," in Jansson, Annmarie, et al. (eds), *Investing in Natural Capital: The Ecological Economics Approach to Sustainability*. Washington, DC: Island Press, 291–322.

Barry, Brian (2001): *Culture and Equality: An Egalitarian Critique of Multiculturalism*. Cambridge, MA: Harvard University Press.

Bator, Francis M. (1958): "The Anatomy of Market Failure," *Quarterly Journal of Economics* 72 (3): 351–79.

Beck, Ulrich (1992): *Risk Society: Towards a New Modernity*. London: Sage.

Beck, Ulrich (1997): *Kinder der Freiheit*. Frankfurt am Main: Suhrkamp.

Beck, Ulrich (1998): *Politik der Globalisierung*. Frankfurt am Main: Suhrkamp.

Beck, Ulrich (2000a): *What is Globalization?*, trans. Patrick Camiller. Cambridge: Polity.

Beck, Ulrich (2000b): *The Brave New World of Work*, trans. Patrick Camiller. Cambridge: Polity.

Beck, Ulrich (2005): *Power in the Global Age*, trans. Kathleen Cross. Cambridge: Polity.

Bello, Walden F. (1999): "The Asian Financial Crisis: Causes, Dynamics, Prospects," *Journal of the Asia Economy* 4 (1): 33–55.

Bello, Walden F. (2002): *Deglobalization: Ideas for a New World Economy.* Dhaka: Dhaka University Press; London: Zed Books.

Benhabib, Seyla (2002): *The Claims of Culture: Equality and Diversity in the Global Era.* Princeton, NJ: Princeton University Press.

Benhabib, Seyla, Butler, Judith, Cornell, Drucilla, and Fraser, Nancy (eds) (1995): *Feminist Contentions: A Philosophical Exchange.* London and New York: Routledge.

Benner, Mats, and Bundgaard Vad, Torben (2000): "Sweden and Denmark: Defending the Welfare State," in Scharpf, Fritz W., and Schmidt, Vivian A. (eds), *Welfare and Work in the Open Economy,* Vol. 2: *Diverse Responses to Common Challenges.* Oxford: Oxford University Press, 399–466.

Berger, Peter L., Berger, Brigitte, and Kellner, Hansfried (1973): *The Homeless Mind: Modernization and Consciousness.* New York: Random House.

Berkes, Fikret, and Folke, Carl (1994): "Investing in Cultural Capital for Sustainable Use of Natural Capital," in Jansson, Annmarie, et al. (eds), *Investing in Natural Capital: The Ecological Economics Approach to Sustainability.* Washington, DC: Island Press.

Berlin, Isaiah (1958): *Two Concepts of Liberty.* Oxford: Clarendon Press.

Berlin, Isaiah (1969): *Four Essays on Liberty.* Oxford: Oxford University Press.

Bernstein, Eduard ([1899] 1993): *The Preconditions of Socialism,* trans. Henry Tudor. Cambridge: Cambridge University Press.

Bernstein, Eduard (1999): *Zur Theorie und Geschichte des Socialismus: Gesammelte Abhandlungen.* Berlin: Dümmler.

Bertelsmann Stiftung (ed.) (2004): *Bertelsmann Transformation Index 2003: Auf dem Weg zur marktwirtschaftlichen Demokratie.* Gütersloh: Bertelsmann Stiftung.

Birnbacher, Dieter (1996): "Risiko und Sicherheit: Philosophische Aspekte," in Banse, Gerhard (ed.), *Risikoforschung, Disziplinarität und Interdisziplinarität: Von der Illusion der Sicherheit zum Umgang mit Unsicherheit.* Berlin: Sigma.

Blair, Tony (1998): *The Third Way: New Politics for the New Century.* London: Fabian Society.

Blanke, Thomas (1998): "Paradoxien und Zukunft des deutschen Sozialstaates," in Blasche, Siegfried, and Döring, Diether (eds), *Sozialpolitik und Gerechtigkeit.* Frankfurt am Main: Campus, 172–213.

Bobbio, Norberto (1987): *The Future of Democracy.* Cambridge: Polity.

Bosch, Gerhard (1998): *Zukunft der Erwerbsarbeit.* Frankfurt am Main: Campus.

Brandt, Willy (1986): "Demokratischer Sozialismus," in Meyer, Thomas (ed.), *Lexikon des Sozialismus.* Cologne: Bund, 120–3.

Brandt, Willy, with Wolther von Kieseritzky (2001): *Mehr Demokratie Wagen: Innen- und Gesellschaftspolitik 1966–1974*. Bonn: Dietz.

Briggs, Asa (1961): "The Welfare State in Historical Perspective," *Archives Européenes de Sociologie* 2 (2): 221–58.

Brunner, Georg (ed.) (1997): *Politische und ökonomische Transformation in Osteuropa*. Berlin: Berlin-Verlag.

Buchanan, James M., and Tullock, Gordon (1962): *The Calculus of Consent: Logical Foundations of Constitutional Democracy*. Ann Arbor: University of Michigan Press.

Burnell, Peter, and Calvert, Peter (eds) (1999): *The Resilience of Democracy: Persistent Practice, Durable Idea*. London: Frank Cass.

Butler, Judith P. (1990): *Gender Trouble: Feminism and the Subversion of Identity*. London and New York: Routledge.

Calleo, David (2002): *Musings on the World Political Economy of the Future: A Plural Global System*. Cheltenham: Edward Elgar.

Castles, Stephen, and Davidson, Alastair (2000): *Citizenship and Migration: Globalization and the Politics of Belonging*. Basingstoke: Macmillan.

Cohen, Gerald A. (1989): "On the Currency of Egalitarian Justice," *Ethics* 99: 906–44.

Cohen, Joshua (1989): "Deliberation and Democratic Legitimacy," in Hamlin, Alan, and Pettit, Philip (eds), *The Good Polity: Normative Analysis of the State*. Oxford: Blackwell, 18–34.

Cohen, Joshua, and Rogers, Joel (1983): *On Democracy*. Harmondsworth: Penguin.

Cover, Robert (1983): "The Supreme Court 1982 Term: Foreword: Nomos and Narrative," *Harvard Law Review* 97 (4): 4–25.

Croissant, Aurel (2002): *Demokratische Entwicklung in Asien: Eine vergleichende Analyse defekter Demokratien in den Philippinen, Südkorea und Thailand*. Wiesbaden: Westdeutscher Verlag.

Crouch, Colin (1993): *Industrial Relations and European State Traditions*. Oxford: Clarendon Press.

Crouch, Colin (1999): *Social Change in Western Europe*. Oxford: Oxford University Press.

Czada, Roland, Lütz, Susanne, and Mette, Stefan (2003): *Regulative Politik: Zähmungen von Markt und Technik*. Opladen: Leske & Budrich.

Czech, Brian (2000): *Shoveling Fuel for a Runaway Train: Errant Economists, Shameful Spenders, and a Plan to Stop Them All*. Berkeley: University of California Press.

Czempiel, Ernst-Otto (1990): "Konturen einer Gesellschaftswelt: Die neue Architektur der internationalen Politik," *Merkur* 500 (10–11): 835–51.

Czempiel, Ernst-Otto (2002): *Weltpolitik im Umbruch: Die Pax Americana, der Terrorismus und die Zukunft der internationalen Beziehungen*. Munich: Beck.

Dahl, Robert A. (1989): *Democracy and its Critics*. New Haven, CT: Yale University Press.

Dahl, Robert A. (1994): "A Democratic Dilemma: System Effectiveness versus Citizen Participation," *Political Science Quarterly* 109: 23–34.

Dahl, Robert A. (1998): *On Democracy*. New Haven, CT: Yale University Press.

Dahl, Robert A. (2000): *Polyarchy: Participation and Opposition*. New Haven, CT: Yale University Press.

Daly, Herman (1994): "Operationalizing Sustainable Development by Investing in Natural Capital," in Jansson, Annmarie, et al. (eds), *Investing in Natural Capital: The Ecological Economics Approach to Sustainability*. Washington, DC: Island Press.

Daly, Herman (1996): *Beyond Growth: The Economics of Sustainable Development*. Boston: Beacon Press.

De Swaan, Abram (1993): *Der sorgende Staat: Wohlfahrt, Gesundheit und Bildung in Europa und den USA der Neuzeit*. Frankfurt am Main: Campus.

Dettling, Warnfried (1980): *Die Zähmung des Leviathan: Neue Wege der Ordnungspolitik*. Baden-Baden: Nomos.

Deutscher Bundestag (ed.) (2002a): *Schlussbericht der Enquete-Kommission "Globalisierung der Weltwirtschaft."* Opladen: Leske & Budrich.

Deutscher Bundestag (ed.) (2002b): *Schlussbericht der Enquete-Kommission "Zukunft des Bürgerschaftlichen Engagements": "Auf dem Weg in eine Zukunftsfähige Bürgergesellschaft?"* Opladen: Leske & Budrich.

Deutsches PISA-Konsortium (ed.) (2001): *PISA 2000: Basiskompetenzen von Schülerinnen und Schülern im internationalen Vergleich*. Opladen: Leske & Budrich.

Deutsches PISA-Konsortium (ed.) (2003): *PISA 2000: Ein differenzierter Blick auf die Länder der Bundesrepublik Deutschland*. Opladen: Leske & Budrich.

DiZerega, Gus (2002): "Unexpected Connections: The Socialist Calculation Debate and the Control of Nature," paper presented at the annual convention of the Southwestern Political Science Association, New Orleans.

Dower, Nigel, and Williams, John (eds) (2002): *Global Citizenship: A Critical Introduction*. New York: Routledge.

Dryzek, John S. (1987): *Rational Ecology: Environment and Political Economy*. Oxford: Blackwell.

Dryzek, John S. (1996): *Democracy in Capitalist Times: Ideals, Limits and Struggles*. Oxford: Oxford University Press.

Dubiel, Helmut (1994): *Ungewissheit und Politik*. Frankfurt am Main: Suhrkamp.

Dworkin, Ronald (1990): "Foundations of Liberal Equality," in *The Tanner Lectures on Human Values*, vol. 11. Salt Lake City: University of Utah Press.

Dworkin, Ronald (2000): *Sovereign Virtue: The Theory and Practice of Equality*. Cambridge, MA: Harvard University Press.

Ehrlich, Paul R. (1994): "Ecological Economics and the Carrying Capacity of the Earth," in Jansson, Annmarie, et al. (eds), *Investing in Natural Capital: The Ecological Economics Approach to Sustainability*. Washington, DC: Island Press.

Eichler, Willi (1973): *Zur Einführung in den demokratischen Sozialismus*. Bonn: Verlag Neue Gesellschaft.

Eide, Asbjørn (1989): "Realization of Social and Economic Rights and the Minimum Threshold Approach," *Human Rights Law Journal* 10 (1–2): 35–51.

Eliot, Jennifer A. (1999): *An Introduction to Sustainable Development*. New York: Routledge

Elsenhans, Hartmut (1995): "Die Rolle internationaler Entwicklungszusammenarbeit unter veränderten wirtschaftlichen und gesellschaftsstrukturellen Rahmenbedingungen," in Barsch, Dietrich, and Karrasch, Heinz (eds), *Die Dritte Welt im Rahmen weltpolitischer und weltwirtschaftlicher Neuordnung*. Stuttgart: Franz Steiner, 140–57.

Elster, Jon (1986): "The Market and the Forum," in Elster, Jon, and Hylland, Aanund (eds), *Foundations of Social Choice Theory*. Cambridge: Cambridge University Press.

Ende, Werner (1996): *Der Islam in der Gegenwart*. 4th edn, Munich: Beck.

Engels, Markus (2000): "Verbesserter Menschenrechtsschutz durch Individualbeschwerdeverfahren? Zur Frage der Einführung eines Fakultativprotokolls für den internationalen Pakt über wirtschaftliche, soziale und kulturelle Rechte," dissertation, University of Munich.

Esping-Andersen, Gøsta (1990): *The Three Worlds of Welfare Capitalism*. Cambridge: Polity.

Esping-Andersen, Gøsta (1999): *Social Foundations of Postindustrial Economies*. Oxford: Oxford University Press.

Esping-Andersen, Gøsta (2002): *Why We Need a New Welfare State*. New York: Oxford University Press.

Esping-Andersen, Gøsta (2003): "Herkunft und Lebenschancen: Warum wir eine neue Politik gegen soziale Vererbung brauchen," *Berliner Republik* 6: 42–57.

Etzioni, Amitai (1997): *The New Golden Rule: Community and Morality in a Democratic Society*. New York: Basic Books; London: Profile Books.

Evers, Adalbert, Rauch, Ulrich, and Stitz, Uta (2002): "Ist Engagement erwünscht? Sein Stellenwert im Kontext eines Umbaus von öffentlichen Dienst und Einrichtungen," in Meyer, Thomas, and Weil, Reinhard (eds), *Die Bürgergesellschaft: Perspektiven für Bürgerbeteiligung und Bürgerkommunikation*. Bonn: Dietz, 139–62.

Falk, Richard A. (2002): *Predatory Globalization: A Critique*. Cambridge: Polity.

Faulks, Keith (2000): *Citizenship*. London: Routledge.

Ferrara, Maurizio, and Rhodes, Martin (2002): *Recasting European Welfare States*. London: Frank Cass.

Fishkin, James (1991): *Democracy and Deliberation: New Directions for Democratic Reform*. New Haven, CT: Yale University Press.

Fraser, Nancy (1997): *Justus Interruptus: Critical Reflections on the "Postsocialist" Condition*. New York: Routledge.

Frenzel, Martin (2002): *Neue Wege der Sozialdemokratie: Dänemark und Deutschland im Vergleich (1982–2002)*. Wiesbaden: Deutscher Universitäts-Verlag.

Friedman, Milton (1962): *Capitalism and Freedom: A Leading Economist's View of the Proper Role of Competitive Capitalism*. Chicago: University of Chicago Press.

Fritsch, Michael, Wein, Thomas, and Ewers, Hans-Jürgen (2003): *Marktversagen und Wirtschaftspolitik: Mikroökonomische Grundlagen staatlichen Handelns*. 5th edn, Munich: Vahlen.

Fukuyama, Francis (1992): *The End of History and the Last Man*. London: Hamish Hamilton.

Gabriel, Oscar W., Niedermayer, Oskar, and Stöss, Richard (eds) (1997): *Parteiendemokratie in Deutschland*. Wiesbaden: Westdeutscher Verlag.

Gamillscheg, Hannes (2004): "Grund für Entlassung ist in Dänemark leicht zu finden," *Frankfurter Rundschau* online, http://www.fr.aktuell.de/ressorts/nachrichten_und_politik/wirtschaft_und_politik/?cnt=366813.

Giddens, Anthony (1984): *The Constitution of Society: Outline of the Theory of Structuration*. Cambridge: Polity.

Giddens, Anthony (1987): *Social Theory and Modern Sociology*. Cambridge: Polity.

Giddens, Anthony (1994): *Beyond Left and Right: The Future of Radical Politics*. Cambridge: Polity.

Giddens, Anthony (1998): *The Third Way: The Renewal of Social Democracy*. Cambridge: Polity.

Giddens, Anthony (ed.) (2001): *The Global Third Way Debate*. Cambridge: Polity.

Granados, Gilberto, and Gurgsdies, Erik (1999): *Lern- und Arbeitsbuch Ökonomie*. Bonn: Dietz.

Gray, John (1989): *Liberalisms: Essays in Political Philosophy*. London: Routledge.

Gray, John (1993): *Post-Liberalism: Studies in Political Thought*. London: Routledge.

Gray, John (1995): *Liberalism*. 2nd edn, Buckingham: Open University Press.

Greven, Michael T. (1998): *Einführungsvortrag: Demokratie – eine Kultur des Westens?* Opladen: Leske & Budrich.

Guéhenno, Jean-Marie (1995): *The End of the Nation-State*, trans. Victoria Elliott. Minneapolis and London: University of Minnesota Press.

Habermas, Jürgen (1984): *Theory of Communicative Action*, trans. Thomas McCarthy. 2 vols, Boston: Beacon Press.

Habermas, Jürgen (1987): *Philosophical Discourse of Modernity: 12 Lectures*, trans. Frederick Lawrence. Cambridge, MA: MIT Press.

Habermas, Jürgen (1990): *Kleine politische Schriften, 7: Die nachholende Revolution*. Frankfurt am Main: Suhrkamp.

Habermas, Jürgen (1992): "Drei normative Modelle der Demokratie: zum Begriff deliberativer Politik," in Münkler, Herfried (ed.), *Die Chancen der Freiheit: Grundprobleme der Demokratie*. Munich: Piper.

Habermas, Jürgen (1996): *Between Facts and Norms: Contributions to a Discourse Theory of Law and Democracy*, trans. William Rehg. Cambridge, MA: MIT Press.

Habermas, Jürgen (1997): "Dialog der Kulturen: Der interkulturelle Diskurs über Menschenrechte," *Entwicklung und Zusammenarbeit* 38 (July).

Habermas, Jürgen (1998): *The Inclusion of the Other: Studies in Political Theory*, ed. Ciaran Cronin and Pablo De Greiff. Cambridge, MA: MIT Press.

Hall, Peter, and Gingerich, Daniel W. (2001): "Varieties of Capitalism and Institutional Complementarities in the Macroeconomy: An Empirical Analysis," paper presented at the annual meeting of the American Political Science Association, San Francisco, 30 August.

Hall, Peter, and Soskice, David (2001): *Varieties of Capitalism: The Institutional Foundations of Comparative Advantage*. Oxford: Oxford University Press.

Haller, Gret (2002): *Die Grenzen der Solidarität: Europa und die USA im Umgang mit Staat, Nation und Religion*. Berlin: Aufbau.

Hammar, Tomas (1990): *Democracy and the Nation State: Aliens, Denizens and Citizens in a World of International Migration*. Aldershot: Avebury.

Harrington, Michael (1989): *Socialism: Past and Future*. New York: Arcade.

Hauchler, Ingomar, Nuscheler, Franz, and Messner, Dirk (eds) (2003): *Global Trends 2004/2005: Fakten, Analysen, Prognosen*. Bonn: Stiftung Entwicklung und Frieden.

Hawken, Paul, Lovins, Amory, and Lovins, Hunter L. (1999): *Natural Capitalism: Creating the Next Industrial Revolution*. Boston: Little, Brown.

Hayek, Friedrich August von (1952): *Der Weg zur Knechtschaft*. 3rd edn, ed. Wilhelm Röpke. Erlenbach: Eugen Rentsch.

Hayek, Friedrich August von (1977): *Drei Vorlesungen über Demokratie, Gerechtigkeit und Sozialismus*. Tübingen: Mohr.

Hayek, Friedrich August von (1979): *Liberalismus*. Tübingen: Mohr.

Hayek, Friedrich August von (1981): *Recht, Gesetzgebung und Freiheit*, Vol. 2: *Die Illusion der sozialen Gerechtigkeit: Eine neue Darstellung der liberalen Prinzipien der Gerechtigkeit und der politischen Ökonomie*. Landsberg am Lech: Verlag Moderne Industrie.

Heberer, Thomas (2000): "Henan – the Model: From Hegemonism to Fragmentism: Portrait of the Political Culture of China's most Populated Province," *Duisburger Arbeitspapiere Ostasienwissenschaften* 31. Duisburg: Institut für Ostasienwissenschaften.

Heberer, Thomas, and Derichs, Claudia (2000): "Politische Reform- und Demokratisierungsdiskurse im Lichte neuer Prozesse regionaler Gemeinschaftsbildung," *Duisburger Arbeitspapiere Ostasienwissenschaften* 31. Duisburg: Institut für Ostasienwissenschaften.

Heidelmeyer, Wolfgang (1972): *Die Menschenrechte*. Paderborn: Schöningh.

Heimann, Eduard (1929): *Soziale Theorie des Kapitialismus: Theorie der Sozialpolitik*. Tübingen: Mohr.

Heimann, Eduard (1954): *Wirtschaftssysteme und Gesellschaftssysteme*. Tübingen: Mohr.

Heimann, Eduard (1963): *Soziale Theorie der Wirtschaftssysteme*. Tübingen: Mohr.

Heimann, Horst, and Meyer, Thomas (eds) (1982): *Reformsozialismus und Sozialdemokratie: Zur Theoriediskussion des demokratischen Sozialismus in der Weimarer Republik*. Berlin: Dietz.

Held, David (1995): *Democracy and the Global Order: From the Modern State to Cosmopolitan Governance*. Cambridge: Polity.

Held, David (1996): *Models of Democracy*. Cambridge: Polity.

Held, David (2000): *A Globalizing World? Culture, Economics, Politics*. London: Routledge.

Held, David, and McGrew, Anthony (2000): *The Global Transformations Reader: An Introduction to the Globalization Debate*. Cambridge: Polity.

Heller, Hermann (1934): *Staatslehre*, ed. Gerhart Niemeyer. Leiden: Sijthoff.

Hemerijck, Anton (2002): "The Self-Transformation of the European Social Model(s)," in Esping-Andersen, Gøsta (ed.), *Why We Need a New Welfare State*. Oxford: Oxford University Press.

Hennis, Wilhelm (1977): *Organisierter Sozialismus: Zum "strategischen" Staats- und Politikverständnis der Sozialdemokratie*. Stuttgart: Klett.

Herder, Johann Gottfried (1968): *Johann Gottfried Herder: Schriften*, ed. Otto Conrady. Reinbek: Rowohlt.

Hicks, Alexander (2001): *Social Democracy and Welfare Capitalism: A Century of Income Security Politics*. Ithaca, NY: Cornell University Press.

Hinchman, Lewis (2006): "USA: Residual Welfare Society and Libertarian Democracy" in Meyer, Thomas (ed.), *Praxis der sozialen Demokratie*. Wiesbaden: Verlag für Sozialwissenschaften, 327–73.

Hinchman, Lewis, and Hinchman, Sandra (1996): "Nature Preservation in the Global South: A Survey and Assessment," in Wells, Robert N. (ed.), *Law, Values, and the Environment*. London: Scarecrow Press, 357–93.

Hinsch, Wilfried (ed.) (1997): *Zur Idee des politischen Liberalismus: John Rawls in der Diskussion*. Frankfurt am Main: Suhrkamp.

Hinsch, Wilfried (2002): *Gerechtfertigte Ungleichheiten: Grundsätze sozialer Gerechtigkeit*. Berlin: De Gruyter.

Hinsch, Wilfried (2004): "Menschenrechte und Pflichtenallokation," in Meyer, Thomas, and Vorholt, Udo (eds), *Zivilgesellschaft und Gerechtigkeit*. Bochum: Projektverlag.

Hirst, Paul (1994): *Associative Democracy: New Forms of Economic and Social Governance*. Amherst: University of Massachusetts Press.

Höffe, Otfried (1999): *Demokratie im Zeitalter der Globalisierung*. Munich: Beck.

Höffe, Otfried (2001): *Gerechtigkeit: Eine philosophische Einführung*. Munich: Beck.

Holland-Cruz, Barbara (1999): "Die Vergeschlechtlichung des Politischen: Etappen, Dimensionen und Perspektiven einer Theorieinnovation," in Greven, Michael T., and Schmalz-Bruns, Rainer (eds), *Politische Theorie – Heute: Ansätze und Perspektiven*. Baden-Baden: Nomos, 121–46.

Holz, Klaus (ed.) (2000): *Staatsbürgerschaft: Soziale Differenzierung und politische Inklusion*. Wiesbaden: Westdeutscher Verlag.

Honneth, Axel (1995): *The Struggle for Recognition: The Moral Grammar of Social Conflicts*, trans. Joel Anderson. Cambridge: Polity.

Horn, Manfred, Knieps, Günter, and Müller, Jürgen (1988): *Deregulierungsmaßnahmen in den USA: Schlussfolgerungen für die Bundesrepublik Deutschland*. Baden-Baden: Nomos.

Huntington, Samuel P. (1996): *Clash of Civilizations and the Remaking of World Order*. New York: Simon & Schuster.

Hutton, Will (2002): *The World We're In*. London: Little, Brown.

Independent Commission on International Development Issues (1980): *North–South: A Programme for Survival*. Cambridge, MA: MIT Press [Brandt Report].

Inter Action Council (1997): *A Universal Declaration of Human Responsibilities*, www.interactioncouncil.org/udhr/declaration/udhr.pdf.

International Labour Organization (ILO) 2004: *A Fair Globalization: The Role of the ILO: Report of the Director-General on the World Commission on the Social Dimension of Globalization*. Geneva: International Labour Office.

Iversen, Torben, and Pontusson, Jonas (2000): "Comparative Political Economy: A Northern European Perspective," in Iversen, Torben, Pontusson, Jonas, and Soskice, David (eds), *Unions, Employers, and Central Banks: Macroeconomic Coordination and Institutional Change in Social Market Economies*. Cambridge: Cambridge University Press, 1–38.

Jahoda, Marie, Lazarsfeld, Paul Felix, and Zeisel, Hans (2002): *The Sociology of an Unemployed Community*. New Brunswick, NJ: Transaction Books.

Jänicke, Martin, Kung, Philip, and Stitzel, Michael (1999): *Umweltpolitik.* Cologne: Dietz.

Jann, Werner (2003): "Evaluating Best Practice in Central Government Modernization," in Wollmann, Hellmut, and Reichhard, Christoph (eds), *Evaluating Public Sector Reforms.* Cheltenham: Edward Elgar.

Jann, Werner, and Reichhard, Christoph (2001): "Best Practices in Central Government Modernization," in Wollman, Helmut (ed.), *Evaluating Public Sector Reforms: An International and Comparative Perspective.* Special issue of *Revista International de Estudos Politicos.*

Jann, Werner, and Wegrich, Kai (2004): "Governance and Verwaltungspolitik," in Benz, Arthur (ed.), *Governance – Regieren in komplexen Regelsystemen.* Wiesbaden: VS Verlag.

Jansson, Annmarie, Hammer, Monica, Folke, Carl, and Costanza, Robert (eds) (1994): *Investing in Natural Capital: The Ecological Economics Approach to Sustainability.* Washington, DC: Island Press.

Johnson, Paul (1996): "Risk, Redistribution and Social Welfare in Britain from the Poor Law to Beveridge," in Dauton, Martin (ed.), *Charity, Self-Interest and Welfare in the English Past.* London: UCL Press.

Johnson, Paul (1999): "Inequality, Redistribution, and Living Standards in Britain since 1945," in Fawcett, Helen, and Lowe, Rodney (eds), *Welfare Policy in Britain: The Road from 1945.* Basingstoke: Macmillan.

Kaul, Inge, Grunberg, Isabelle, and Stern, Marc A. (eds) (2002): *Providing Global Public Goods: Managing Globalization.* New York: Oxford University Press.

Kay, John, and Vickers, John (1988): "Regulatory Reform in Britain," *Economic Policy* 8: 286–343.

Keohane, Robert O., and Nye, Joseph S. (2001): *Power and Independence: World Politics in Transition.* Boston: Little, Brown.

Kersting, Wolfgang (2000): *Theorien der sozialen Gerechtigkeit.* Stuttgart: Metzler.

Kim, Dae-Jung (1994): "Is Culture Destiny? The Myth of Asia's Anti-Democratic Values," *Foreign Affairs* (Nov.–Dec.): 189–94.

Kimminich, Otto, and Hobe, Stephan (2000): *Einführung in das Völkerrecht.* 7th edn, Tübingen: A. Francke.

Kitschelt, Herbert, Lange, Peter, Marks, Gary, and Stephans, John D. (eds) (1999): *Continuity and Change in Contemporary Capitalism.* Cambridge: Cambridge University Press.

Kittel, Bernhard (2003): "Politische Ökonomie der Arbeitsbeziehungen: Akteure, Institutionen und wirtschaftliche Effekte," in Obinger, Herbert, Wagschal, Uwe, and Kittel, Bernhard (eds), *Politische Ökonomie: Demokratie und wirtschaftliche Leistungsfähigkeit.* Opladen: Leske & Budrich, 81–111.

Klein, Ansgar (ed.) (2001): *Globalisierung, Partizipation, Protest.* Opladen: Leske & Budrich.

Klingemann, Hans-Dieter, Hofferbert, Richard I., and Budge, Ian (1994): *Parties, Policies, and Democracy*. Oxford: Westview Press.

Knetter, Michael M. (1989): "Price Discrimination by US and German Exporters," *American Economic Review* 79 (1): 198–210.

Koch, Susanne, and Walwei, Ulrich (2003): "Und der Arbeitsmarkt bewegt sich doch," *Frankfurter Rundschau* online, http://www.fraktuell.de/uebersicht/alle_dossiers/politik_inland/wie_viel_staat_braucht_der_mensch/der_sozialstaat/die_alternative/woche_der_arbeit/?cnt=357481.

Kohlberg, Lawrence (1981): *Essays on Moral Development*. San Francisco: Harper & Row.

Kohlberg, Lawrence (1984): *The Psychology of Moral Development: The Nature and Validity of Moral Stages*. San Francisco: Harper & Row.

Kokott, Juliane, Doehring, Karl, and Buergenthal, Thomas (2003): *Grundzüge des Völkerrechts*. 3rd edn, Heidelberg: C. F. Müller.

Krakowski, Michael (1988): "Die theoretischen Grundlagen der Regulierung," in Krakowski, Michael (ed.), *Regulierung in der Bundesrepublik Deutschland*. Hamburg: Weltarchiv, 19–116.

Kremendahl, Hans (1983): *Pluralismus, Strukturprinzip einer demokratischen Gesellschaft*. Berlin: Landeszentrale für politische Bildungsarbeit.

Kulke, Hermann, and Rothermund, Dietmar (1998): *Geschichte Indiens: Von der Induskultur bis heute*. Munich: Beck.

Küng, Hans (ed.) (2002): *Dokumentation zum Weltethos*. Munich: Piper.

Kymlicka, Will (1995): *Multicultural Citizenship*. Oxford: Clarendon Press.

Kymlicka, Will (1997): *States, Nations and Cultures*. Assen: Van Gorcum.

Kymlicka, Will (1999): "Citizenship in an Era of Globalization: Commentary on Held," in Shapiro, Ian, and Hacker-Cordòn, Casiano (eds), *Democracy's Edges*. Cambridge: Cambridge University Press.

Kymlicka, Will (2001): *Politics in the Vernacular: Nationalism, Multiculturalism, and Citizenship*. Oxford: Oxford University Press.

Kymlicka, Will, and Wayne, Norman (2000): *Citizenship in Diverse Societies*. Oxford: Oxford University Press.

Lassalle, Ferdinand (1970): *Reden und Schriften: Aus der Arbeiteragitation 1862–1864*. Munich: Deutscher Taschenbuch Verlag.

Leibfried, Stephan (ed.) (2001): *Welfare State Futures*. Cambridge: Cambridge University Press.

Lemân, Gudrun (1969): *Ungelöste Fragen im jugoslawischen System der Arbeiterselbstverwaltung*. Cologne: Bundesinstitut für Ostwissenschaftliche und Internationale Studien.

Lijphart, Arend (1999): *Patterns of Democracy*. New Haven, CT: Yale University Press.

Link, Werner (2001): *Die Neuordnung der Weltpolitik: Grundprobleme globaler Politik an der Schwelle zum 21. Jahrhundert*. Munich: Beck.

Lipset, Seymour M. (1959): "Some Social Requisites of Democracy: Economic Development and Political Legitimacy," *American Political Science Review* 53 (1): 69–105.

Lipset, Seymour M. (1960): *Political Man*. Garden City, NY: Doubleday.

Lipset, Seymour M. (1992): "Conditions of the Democratic Order and Social Change: A Comparative Discussion," in Eisenstadt, Samuel (ed.), *Democracy and Modernity*. Leiden: Brill.

Lipset, Seymour M. (1993): "Reflections on Capitalism, Socialism and Democracy," *Journal of Democracy* 4 (2): 43–55.

Lipset, Seymour M. (1994): "The Social Requisites of Democracy Revisited," *American Sociological Review* 59: 1–22.

Lipset, Seymour M. (ed.) (1998): *Democracy in Asia and Africa*. Washington, DC: Congressional Quarterly.

Lipset, Seymour M., and Marks, Gary (2000): *It Didn't Happen Here! Why Socialism Failed in the United States*. New York: Norton.

Locke, John (1970): *Two Treatises of Government*. Cambridge: Cambridge University Press.

Luhmann, Niklas (1989): *Die Wirtschaft der Gesellschaft*. Opladen: Leske & Budrich.

Luhmann, Niklas (1993): *Das Recht der Gesellschaft*. Frankfurt am Main: Suhrkamp.

Lütz, Susanne (2003): "Governance in der Politischen Ökonomie," *Max-Planck-Institute für Gesellschaftsforschung Arbeitspapiere* 3.

McDaniel, Carl N., and Gowdy, John M. (2000): *Paradise for Sale: A Parable of Nature*. Berkeley: University of California Press.

Macpherson, Crawford B. (1962): *The Political Theory of Possessive Individualism: Hobbes to Locke*. Oxford: Clarendon Press.

Macpherson, Crawford B. (1977): *The Life and Times of Liberal Democracy*. Oxford: Oxford University Press.

Mahathir, Mohamad (1998): *The Way Forward*. London: Orion.

Majone, Giandomenico (1997): "From the Positive to the Regulatory State: Causes and Consequences of Changes in the Mode of Governance," *Journal of Public Policy* 17 (2): 139–68.

Margalit, Avishai (1996): *The Decent Society*. Cambridge, MA: Harvard University Press.

Marshall, Thomas H. (1964): *Class, Citizenship and Social Development*. Garden City, NY: Doubleday.

Marty, Martin E., and Appleby, Scott R. (1996): *The Glory and the Power: The Fundamentalist Challenge to the Modern World*. Boston: Beacon Press.

Marx, Karl (1988): *The Communist Manifesto*. New York: Norton.

Matzner, Egon (1982): *Der Wohlfahrtsstaat von morgen: Entwurf eines zeitgemäßen Musters staatlicher Interventionen*. Frankfurt am Main: Campus.

Mayntz, Renate, Roseweitz, Bernd, Schimank, Uwe, and Stichweh, Rudolf (1988): *Differenzierung und Verselbständigung: Zur Entwicklung gesellschaftlicher Teilsysteme*. Frankfurt am Main: Campus.

Meier, Christian, Pleines, Heiko, and Schröder, Hans-Henning (2003): *Ökonomie – Kultur – Politik: Transformationsprozesse in Osteuropa: Festschrift für Hans-Hermann Höhmann*. Bremen: Temmen.

Merkel, Wolfgang (1993): *Ende der Sozialdemokratie? Machtressourcen und Regierungspolitik im internationalen Vergleich*. Frankfurt am Main: Campus.

Merkel, Wolfgang (1999): "Defekte Demokratien," in Merkel, Wolfgang, and Busch, Andreas (eds), *Demokratie in Ost und West: Für Klaus von Beyme*. Frankfurt am Main: Suhrkamp.

Merkel, Wolfgang (2002): *Social Justice and Social Democracy at the Beginning of the 21st Century*. Tel Aviv: Friedrich-Ebert Stiftung and Beit Berl College.

Merkel, Wolfgang (2003): "Institutionen und Reformpolitik: Drei Fallstudien zur Vetospieler-Theorie," *Berliner Journal für Soziologie* 2: 255–74.

Merkel, Wolfgang, and Croissant, Aurel (2000): "Formale Institutionen und informale Regeln in illiberalen Demokratien," *Politische Vierteljahresschrift* 41 (1): 3–33.

Merkel, Wolfgang, Puhle, Hans-Juergen, Croissant, Aurel, Eicher, Claudia, and Thiery, Peter (2003): *Defekte Demokratie*, vol. 1. Opladen: Leske & Budrich.

Merkel, Wolfgang, Egle, Christoph, Henkes, Christian, Ostheim, Tobias, and Petring, Alexander (2005): *Die Reformfähigkeit der Sozialdemokratie: Regierungspolitik in Westeuropa*. Wiesbaden: Verlag VS.

Meyer, Thomas (1977): *Bernsteins konstruktiver Sozialismus: Eduard Bernsteins Beitrag zur Theorie des Sozialismus*. Berlin: Dietz.

Meyer, Thomas (1980): *Demokratischer Sozialismus: Geistige Grundlagen und Wege in die Zukunft*. Munich: Olzog.

Meyer, Thomas (ed.) (1986): *Lexikon des Sozialismus*. Cologne: Bund.

Meyer, Thomas (1991): *Demokratischer Sozialismus – soziale Demokratie: Eine Einführung*. Bonn: Dietz.

Meyer, Thomas (1994): *Die Transformation des Politischen*. Frankfurt am Main: Suhrkamp.

Meyer, Thomas (2001a): *Die humane Revolution: Plädoyer für eine zivile Lebenskultur*. Berlin: Aufbau.

Meyer, Thomas (2001b): "Grundwerte im Wandel," in Müntefering, Franz, and Machnig, Matthias (eds), *Sicherheit im Wandel: Neue Solidarität im 21. Jahrhundert*. Berlin: Vorwärts, 13–30.

Meyer, Thomas (2002a): *Was ist Politik?* Opladen: Leske & Budrich.

Meyer, Thomas (2002b): *Soziale Demokratie und Globalisierung: Eine Europäische Perspektive*. Bonn: Dietz.

Meyer, Thomas (2002c): *Identitätspolitik: Vom Missbrauch kultureller Unterschiede*. Frankfurt am Main: Suhrkamp.

Meyer, Thomas (ed.) (2006): *Praxis der sozialen Demokratie*: Wiesbaden: Verlag für Sozialwissenschaften.

Meyer, Thomas, and Weil, Reinhard (ed.) (2002): *Die Bürgergesellschaft: Perspektiven für Bürgerbeteiligung und Bürgerkommunikation.* Bonn: Dietz.

Michels, Robert ([1911] 1970): *Zur Soziologie des Parteiwesens in der modernen Demokratie: Untersuchungen über die oligarchischen Tendenzen des Gruppenlebens.* Stuttgart: Kröner.

Milner, Henry (1989): *Sweden: Social Democracy in Practice.* Oxford: Oxford University Press.

Mommsen, Wolfgang, J. (ed.) (1978): *Liberalismus im aufsteigenden Industriestaat.* Göttingen: Vandenhoek & Ruprecht.

Münch, Richard (1986): *Die Kultur der Moderne.* Frankfurt am Main: Suhrkamp.

Murphy, Liam, and Nagel, Thomas (2002): *The Myth of Ownership: Taxes and Justice.* Oxford: Oxford University Press.

Nagel, Thomas (2002): *Concealment and Exposure.* Oxford: Oxford University Press.

Naphtali, Fritz (1977): *Wirtschaftsdemokratie: Ihr Wesen, Weg, und Ziel.* 4th edn, Frankfurt am Main: Europäische Verlagsanstalt.

National Research Council (Board on Sustainable Development, Policy Division) (1999): *Our Common Journey: A Transition Toward Sustainability.* Washington, DC: National Academy Press.

Neumann, Franz (ed.) (2000): *Handbuch politischer Theorien und Ideologien,* vol. 2. 2nd rev. edn, Opladen: Leske & Budrich.

Nida-Rümelin, Julian (1993): *Kritik des Konsequentialismus.* Munich: Oldenbourg.

Nida-Rümelin, Julian (1996): "Ethik des Risikos," in Nida-Rümelin, Julian (ed.), *Angewandte Ethik: Die Bereichsethiken und ihre theoretische Fundierung: Ein Handbuch.* Stuttgart: Kröner.

Norgaard, Richard B. (1994): *Development Betrayed.* New York: Routledge.

Novy, Klaus (1978): *Strategien der Sozialisierung: Die Diskussion der Wirtschaftsreform in der Weimarer Republik.* Frankfurt am Main: Campus.

Nozick, Robert (1974): *Anarchy, State and Utopia.* New York: Basic Books.

Nussbaum, Martha (1999): *Gerechtigkeit, oder Das gute Leben,* ed. Herlinde Pauer-Studer. Frankfurt am Main: Suhrkamp.

Nussbaum, Martha, and Sen, Amartya (1993): *The Quality of Life.* Oxford: Oxford University Press.

O'Connor, James (1998): *Natural Causes: Essays in Ecological Marxism.* New York: Guilford Press.

O'Donnell, Guillermo (1979): *Modernization and Bureaucratic-Authoritarianism.* Berkeley: University of California Press.

O'Donnell, Guillermo (1994): "Delegative Democracy," *Journal of Democracy* 5 (1): 55–69.

OECD (Organization for Economic Cooperation and Development) (2001): *Sustainable Development: Critical Issues.* Paris: OECD.

Offe, Claus (1996): " 'Homogenität' im demokratischen Verfassungsstaat:

Sind politische Gruppenrechte eine adäquate Antwort auf Identitätskonflikte?" *Peripherie* 16 (64): 26–45.

Offe, Claus (1997a): "Microaspects of Democratic Theory: What Makes for the Deliberative Competence of Citizens?" in Hadenius, Axel (ed.), *Democracy's Victory and Crisis*. Cambridge: Cambridge University Press, 81–104.

Offe, Claus (1997b): "Towards a New Equilibrium of Citizens' Rights and Economic Resources," in OECD: *Societal Cohesion and the Globalizing Economy: What Does the Future Hold?* Paris: OECD, 81–108.

Offe, Claus (2000): "Staat, Markt und Gemeinschaft: Gestaltungsoptionen im Spannungsfeld dreier politischer Ordnungsprinzipien," in Ulrich, Peter, and Maak, Thomas (eds), *Die Wirtschaft in der Gesellschaft*. Bern: Haupt, 105–29.

Offe, Claus (2003): "The European Model of 'Social' Capitalism: Can it Survive European Integration?" *Journal of Political Philosophy* 11 (4): 437–69.

Ostheim, Tobias (2003): *Praxis und Rhetorik deutscher Europapolitik: Arbeitspapier für das DFG-Forschungsprojekt "Sozialdemokratische Antworten auf integrierte Märkte – Dritte Wege im internationalen Vergleich."* Heidelberg: Ruprecht-Karls-Universität.

Panebianco, Angelo (1988): *Political Parties: Organization and Power*. Cambridge: Cambridge University Press.

Pesthoff, Victor (1997): "Empowering Citizens as Co-Producers of Social Services: The Case of Day Care in Sweden," paper presented at the international research conference of the ICA, Bertinoro, 2–5 October.

Pierson, Paul (2000): "The Three Worlds of Welfare Capitalism Research," *Comparative Political Studies* 33: 791–821.

Polanyi, Karl ([1957] 2001): *The Great Transformation*. Boston: Beacon Press.

Pontusson, Jonas (1992): "At the End of the Third Road: Swedish Social Democracy in Crisis," *Politics and Society* 20: 305–32.

Pontusson, Jonas, and Yong Kwon, Hyeok (2004): "Welfare Spending, Government Partisanship, and Varieties of Capitalism," paper presented at the Conference of Europeanists, Chicago, 11–13 March.

Powell, G. Bingham, Jr. (1982): *Contemporary Democracies: Participation, Stability and Violence*. Cambridge, MA: Harvard University Press.

Powell, Martin, and Hewitt, Martin (2002): *Welfare State and Welfare Change*. Buckingham: Open University Press.

Prisching, Manfred (ed.) (2003): *Modelle der Gegenwartsgesellschaft*. Vienna: Passagen.

Prugh, Thomas, Costanza, Robert R., and Daly, Herman E. (2000): *The Local Politics of Global Sustainability*. Washington, DC: Island Press.

Przeworski, Adam (1985): *Capitalism and Social Democracy*. Cambridge: Cambridge University Press.

Przeworski, Adam (1996): *Sustainable Democracy*. Cambridge: Cambridge University Press.

Przeworski, Adam, and Sprague, John (1986): *Paper Stones: A History of Electoral Socialism*. Chicago: University of Chicago Press.

Putnam, Robert (1996): *The Decline of Civil Society: How Come? So What?* Ottawa: Canadian Centre for Management Development.

Putnam, Robert (2000): *Bowling Alone: The Collapse and Revival of American Community*. New York: Simon & Schuster.

Randzio-Plath, Christa (1983): *Lasst uns endlich mitregieren: Wege von Frauen in die Politik*. Freiburg: Herder.

Randzio-Plath, Christa (1999): "Frauen und Gleichberechtigung," *Globale Trends 2000*. Frankfurt am Main: Fischer.

Rasmussen, Poul Nyrup (2003): *Europe and a New Global Order: Bridging the Global Divide: A Report for the Party of European Socialists*. May.

Rawls, John (1958): "Justice as Fairness," *Philosophical Review* 67 (2): 164–94.

Rawls, John (1971): *A Theory of Justice*. Cambridge, MA: Belknap Press.

Rawls, John (1993): *Political Liberalism*. New York: Columbia University Press.

Rawls, John (1994): *Die Idee des politischen Liberalismus: Aufsätze 1978–1989*, ed. Wilfried Hinsch. Frankfurt am Main: Suhrkamp.

Redclift, Michael (1987): *Sustainable Development: Exploring the Contradictions*. New York: Methuen.

Rein, Martin (1996): "Is America Exceptional? The Role of Occupational Welfare in the United States and the European Community," in Shaley, Michael (ed.), *The Privatization of Social Policy? Occupational Welfare and the Welfare State in America, Scandinavia and Japan*. London: Macmillan.

Rein, Martin (2000): "The Third Way in the United States," paper presented at the international symposium on "The Challenges of the 21st Century and the Third Way," Institute of European Studies/Chinese Academy of Social Sciences, Beijing.

Rein, Martin (2004): *Rethinking the Welfare State: The Political Economy of Pension Reform*. Cheltenham: Edward Elgar.

Rhodes, Martin (1997): "Globalisation, Labour Markets and Welfare States: A Future of 'Competitive Corporatism'?" in Rhodes, Martin, and Meny, Yves (eds), *The Future of European Welfare*. London: Macmillan.

Rieger, Elmar, and Leibfried, Stephan (2001): *Grundlagen der Globalisierung: Perspektiven des Wohlfahrtsstaats*. Frankfurt am Main: Suhrkamp.

Rodriguez, Maria João (ed.) (2002): *The New Knowledge Economy in Europe: A New Strategy for International Competitiveness and Social Cohesion*. Cheltenham: Edward Elgar.

Roth, Roland (2001): "Auf dem Weg zur Bürgerkommune? Bürgerschaftliches Engagement und Kommunalpolitik in Deutschland zu Beginn des 21. Jahrhunderts," in Schröter, Eckhard (ed.), *Empirische Policy- und Verwaltungsforschung*. Opladen: Leske & Budrich.

Roth, Roland (2004): "Die dunklen Seiten der Zivilgesellschaft: Grenzen einer zivilgesellschaftlichen Fundierung von Demokratie," in Klein, Ansgar, Kern, Kristine, Geißel, Brigitte, and Berger, Maria (eds), *Zivilgesellschaft und Sozialkapital: Herausforderungen politischer und sozialer Integration*. Wiesbaden: Verlag VS, 41–64.

Rothstein, Bo (1996): *The Social Democratic State: The Swedish Model and the Bureaucratic Problem of Social Reforms*. Pittsburgh: University of Pittsburgh Press.

Rothstein, Bo (2002): "The Universal Welfare State as a Social Dilemma," in Rothstein, Bo, and Steinmo, Sven (eds), *Restructuring the Welfare State: Political Institutions and Policy Change*. New York: Palgrave.

Rueschemeyer, Dietrich, Huber, Evelyne, and Stephens, John D. (1992): *Capitalist Development and Democracy*. Cambridge: Polity.

Ruggie, John Gerard (1999): *Constructing the World Polity: Essays on International Institutionalization*. London: Routledge.

Sachverständigenrat Bildung bei der Hans Böckler Stiftung (2002): *Reformempfehlungen für das Bildungswesen*. Weinheim: Juventa.

Salanié, Bernard (2000): *The Microeconomics of Market Failures*. Cambridge, MA: MIT Press.

Samuelson, Paul A. (1954): "The Pure Theory of Public Expenditure," *Review of Economics and Statistics* 36: 387–9.

Sandel, Michael (1996): *Democracy's Discontent: America in Search of a New Public Philosophy*. Cambridge, MA: Belknap Press.

Sartori, Giovanni (1997): *Demokratietheorie*. Darmstadt: Primus.

Sassoon, Donald (1999): *The New European Left*. London: Fabian Society.

Scharpf, Fritz W. (1970): *Demokratietheorie zwischen Utopie und Anpassung*. Konstanz: Konstanz Universitäts Verlag.

Scharpf, Fritz (1989): "Politische Steuerung und politische Institutionen," *Politische Vierteljahresschrift* 30 (1): 10–21.

Scharpf, Fritz W. (1992): "Versuch über Demokratie in Verhandlungssystemen," *Max-Planck-Institut für Gesellschaftsforschung Diskussionspapiere* 92 (9).

Scharpf, Fritz W. (1997): *Games Real Actors Play: Actor-Centered Institutionalism in Policy Research*. Boulder, CO: Westview Press.

Scharpf, Fritz (1998): "Demokratie in der transnationalen Politik," in Beck, Ulrich (ed.): *Politik der Globalisierung*. Frankfurt am Main: Suhrkamp.

Scharpf, Fritz W. (1999a): "The Viability of Advanced Welfare States in the International Economy: Vulnerabilities and Options," *Max-Planck-Institut für Gesellschaftsforschung Arbeitspapiere* 99 (9).

Scharpf, Fritz W. (1999b): *Governing in Europe: Effective and Democratic?* Oxford: Oxford University Press.

Scharpf, Fritz W. (2000): *The Future of Work, Employment and Social*

Protection: New Challenges and Political Responses. Cologne: Max Planck Institute for the Study of Societies.

Scharpf, Fritz W., and Schmidt, Vivian A. (2000): *Welfare and Work in the Open Economy*, vols 1–2. Oxford: Oxford University Press.

Schiller, Theo (1978): *Liberalismus in Europa*. Baden-Baden: Nomos.

Schimank, Uwe (1988): "Gesellschaftliche Teilsysteme als Akteurfiktion," *Kölner Zeitschrift für Soziologie und Sozialpsychologie* 40 (3): 619–39.

Schimank, Uwe (1992): "Determinanten politischer Steuerung – akteurtheoretisch betrachtet: Ein Themenkatalog," in Bußhoff, Heinrich (ed.), *Politische Steuerung: Steuerbarkeit und Steuerungsfähigkeit: Ein Beitrag zur Grundlagendiskussion*. Baden-Baden: Nomos, 165–91.

Schimank, Uwe (1996): *Theorien gesellschaftlicher Differenzierung*. Opladen: Leske & Budrich.

Schimank, Uwe (2000): *Handeln und Strukturen: Einführung in die akteurtheoretische Soziologie*. Weinheim: Juventa.

Schleicher, Andreas (2003): *Bildung auf einen Blick 2003*. Paris: OECD.

Schmalz-Bruns, Rainer (1994): "Zivile Gesellschaft und reflexive Demokratie," *Forschungsjournal NSB* 7 (1): 18–33.

Schmidt, Manfred G. (2000): *Demokratietheorien*. 3rd rev. edn, Opladen: Leske & Budrich.

Schmidt, Vivien A. (2000): "Values and Discourse in the Politics of Adjustment," in Scharpf, Fritz W., and Schmidt, Vivian A. (eds): *Welfare and Work in the Open Economy*. Oxford: Oxford University Press, Vol. 1, 229–309.

Schwan, Gesine (1982): *Sozialismus in der Demokratie? Theorie einer konsequent sozialdemokratischen Politik*. Stuttgart: Kohlhammer.

Schweizer, Urs (1999): *Vertragstheorie*. Tübingen: Mohr Siebeck.

Seidelmann, Reimund (1998): "Kants 'Ewiger Friede' und die Neuordnung des Europäischen Sicherheitssystems," in Dicke, Klaus, and Kodalle, Klaus-Michael (eds), *Republik und Weltbürgerrecht*. Weimar: Böhlau, 133–80.

Seldon, Arthur (1996): *Re-privatising Welfare: After the Lost Century*. London: Institute of Economic Affairs.

Seliger, Martin (1985): "John Locke," in Fetscher, Iring, and Münkler, Herfried (eds), *Pipers Handbuch der politischen Ideen*, vol. 3. Munich: Piper.

Sen, Amartya (1999): "Human Rights and Economic Achievements," in Bauer, Joanne R. (ed.), *The East Asian Challenge for Human Rights*. Cambridge: Cambridge University Press, 88–99.

Sen, Amartya (2000): *Ökonomie für den Menschen, Wege zu Gerechtigkeit und Solidarität in der Marktwirtschaft*. Munich: Carl Hanser.

Sen, Amartya (2002): "Global Justice: Beyond International Equity," in Kaul, Inge, et al. (eds), *Providing Global Public Goods: Managing Globalization*. New York: Oxford University Press, 116–25.

Sen, Faruk, Sauer, Martina, and Halm, Dirk (2001): *Intergeneratives*

Verhalten und (Selbst)Ethnisierung von türkischen Zuwanderer. Zentrum für Türkeistudien, im Auftrag des Bundesministeriums des Inneren.

Shaw, George Bernard, et al. (1962): *Fabian Essays.* London: Allen & Unwin.

Sik, Ota (1973): *Argumente für den dritten Weg.* Hamburg: Hoffmann & Campe.

Sik, Ota (1979): *Humane Wirtschaftsdemokratie: Ein dritter Weg.* Hamburg: Albrecht Knaus.

Simma, Bruno (ed.) (1995): *The Charter of the United Nations.* Oxford: Oxford University Press.

Soskice, David (1999): "Divergent Production Regimes: Coordinated and Uncoordinated Market Economies in the 1980s and 1990s," in Kitschelt, Herbert, et al. (eds), *Continuity and Change in Contemporary Capitalism.* Cambridge: Cambridge University Press, 101–34.

Stieglitz, Joseph (2002): *Die Schatten der Globalisierung.* Berlin: Siedler.

Strasser, Johano (1999): *Wenn der Arbeitsgesellschaft die Arbeit ausgeht.* Zurich: Pendo.

Strasser, Johano (2003): *Leben oder Überleben: Wider die Zurichtung des Menschen zu einem Element des Marktes.* Zurich: Pendo.

Strasser, Johano, and Traube, Klaus (1984): *Die Zukunft des Fortschritts: Der Sozialismus und die Krise des Industrialismus.* Bonn: Dietz.

Streeck, Wolfgang (1991): "On the Institutional Conditions of Diversified Quality Production," in Matzner, Egon, and Streeck, Wolfgang (eds), *Beyond Keynesianism: The Socio-Economics of Production and Full Employment.* Aldershot: Edward Elgar, 1–20.

Streeck, Wolfgang (1992): *Social Institutions and Economic Performance: Studies of Industrial Relations in Advanced Capitalist Economies.* London: Sage.

Streeck, Wolfgang (1997): "German Capitalism: Does it Exist? Can it Survive?" in Crouch, Colin, and Streeck, Wolfgang (eds), *Political Economy of Modern Capitalism.* London: Sage, 33–54.

Streeck, Wolfgang (1999): *Korporatismus in Deutschland: Zwischen Nationalstaat und Europäischer Union.* Frankfurt am Main: Campus.

Taylor, Charles (1992): *Multiculturalism and the Politics of Recognition.* Princeton, NJ: Princeton University Press.

Telò, Mario (ed.) (2001): *European Union and New Regionalism: Regional Actors and Global Governance in a Post-Hegemonic Era.* Aldershot: Ashgate.

Telò, Mario (2003): *Die USA und die Rolle der EU als zivile Macht.* Bonn: Friedrich-Ebert-Stiftung.

Telò, Mario (2006): *A Civilian Power? European Union, Global Governance, World Order.* Basingstoke: Palgrave Macmillan.

Tibi, Bassam (1993): *Islamischer Fundamentalismus, moderne Wissenschaft und Technologie.* Frankfurt am Main: Suhrkamp.

Tibi, Bassam (2003): *Im Schatten Allahs: Der Islam und die Menschenrechte.* Munich: Ullstein.

Tinbergen, Jan (1965): *International Economic Integration.* 2nd edn, Amsterdam: Elsevier.

Tocqueville, Alexis de (2000): *Democracy in America.* Chicago: University of Chicago Press.

Trainer, Ted (1995): *The Conserver Society: Alternatives for Sustainability.* Atlantic Highlands, NJ, and London: Zed Books.

Traxler, Franz (1995): "From Demand-Side to Supply-Side Corporatism," in Traxler, Franz, and Crouch, Colin (eds), *Organized Industrial Relations in Europe.* Aldershot: Avebury, 271–86.

Turner, Bryan S. (1986): *Citizenship and Capitalism.* London: Allen & Unwin.

Turner, R. K., Doktor, P., and Adger, N. (1994): "Sea-Level Rise and Coastal Wetlands in the UK: Mitigation Strategies for Sustainable Management," in Jansson, Annmarie, et al. (eds), *Investing in Natural Capital: The Ecological Economics Approach to Sustainability.* Washington, DC: Island Press.

United Nations (2000): *UN Millennium Development Goals,* www.un. org/milleniumgoals/.

Van den Anker, Christien (2002): "Global Justice, Global Institutions and Global Citizenship," in Dower, Nigel, and Williams, John (eds), *Global Citizenship: A Critical Introduction.* New York: Routledge, 158–68.

Van Parijs, Philippe (1992): "Basic Income Capitalism," *Ethics* 102 (3): 465–84.

Van Parijs, Philippe (1995): *Real Freedom for All: What (if Anything) Can Justify Capitalism?* Oxford: Oxford University Press.

Varshney, Ashutosh (2002): *Ethnic Conflict and Civic Life: Hindus and Muslims in India.* New Haven, CT: Yale University Press.

Vester, Michael, Oertzen, Peter von, Geiling, Heiko, Hermann, Thomas, and Müller, Dagmar (1993): *Soziale Milieus im gesellschaftlichen Strukturwandel.* Cologne: Bund.

Vilmar, Fritz (1973): *Strategien der Demokratisierung,* 2 vols. Darmstadt: Luchterhand.

Vilmar, Fritz, and Runge, Brigitte (1986): *Auf dem Weg zur Selbsthilfegesellschaft? 40,000 Selbsthilfegruppen: Gesamtüberblick, politische Theorie und Handlungsvorschläge.* Essen: Klartext.

Visser, Jelle, and Hemerijck, Anton (1998): *Ein holländisches Wunder? Reform des Sozialstaates und Beschäftigungswachstum in den Niederlanden.* Frankfurt am Main: Campus.

Visser, Jelle, and Hemerijck, Anton (2000): "Die pragmatische Anpassung des niederländischen Sozialstaates – ein Lehrstück?" in Leibfried, Stephan, and Wagschal, Uwe (eds), *Der deutsche Sozialstaat: Bilanzen – Reformen – Perspektiven.* Frankfurt am Main: Campus, 452–73.

Vivekanandan, Bhagavathi P. (1997): *International Concerns of European Social Democrats*. Basingstoke: Macmillan.

Vivekanandan, Bhagavathi P. (2000): *Building on Solidarity: Social Democracy and the New Millennium*. New Delhi: Lancer's Books.

Vorländer, Hans (ed.) (1987): *Verfall oder Renaissance des Liberalismus*. Munich: Olzog.

Wallerstein, Michael, and Golden, Miriam (2000): "Postwar Wage Setting in the Nordic Countries," in Iversen, Torben, Pontusson, Jonas, and Soskice, David (eds), *Unions, Employers, and Central Banks: Macroeconomic Coordination and Institutional Change in Social Market Economies*. Cambridge: Cambridge University Press, 107–38.

Walzer, Michael (1983): *Spheres of Justice: A Defense of Pluralism and Equality*. New York: Basic Books.

Weber, Max (1979): *Economy and Society*. Berkeley and London: University of California Press.

Weizsäcker, Carl-Christian von (2000): *Logik der Globalisierung*. Göttingen: Vandenhoeck & Ruprecht.

Wellmer, Albrecht (1993): *Endspiele: Die unversöhnliche Moderne: Essays und Vorträge*. Frankfurt am Main: Suhrkamp.

Western, Bruce, and Beckett, Katherine (1999): "How Unregulated is the US Labor Market? The Penal System as a Labor Market Institution," *American Journal of Sociology* 104 (4): 1030–60.

White, Julie A. (2000): *Democracy, Justice and the Welfare State*. University Park: Pennsylvania State University Press.

Whyman, Philip (2003): *Sweden and the "Third Way": A Macroeconomic Evaluation*. Aldershot: Ashgate.

Willke, Helmut (1993): *Systemtheorie entwickelter Gesellschaften*. Weinheim: Juventa.

Willke, Helmut (2003): *Heterotopia: Studien zur Krise der Ordnung moderner Gesellschaften*. Frankfurt am Main: Suhrkamp.

WCED (World Commission on Environment and Development) (1987): *Our Common Future*. Oxford: Oxford University Press [Brundtland Report].

Zakaria, Fareed (1997): "The Rise of Illiberal Democracy," *Foreign Affairs* 76 (6): 22–43.

Zürn, Michael (1998): *Regieren jenseits des Naionalstaates*. Frankfurt am Main: Suhrkamp.

Index